Gary L. Harmon
Ruth F. Dickinson

write now!
substance, strategy, style

Holt, Rinehart and Winston, Inc.

New York Chicago San Francisco Atlanta
Dallas Montreal Toronto London Sydney

For The Magnificent Eight

Sue	Joel
Tom	Kristin
Jamie	Erica
	Joey
	Alison

Library of Congress Catalog Card Number: 73-183250
ISBN: 0-03-085303-6
Printed in the United States of America
2345   090   9 8 7 6 5 4 3 2 1

NOTES FOR THE INSTRUCTOR

Naturally, we think *Write Now!* is a good book. But here are several features that might make its advantages more apparent.

We view writing as one of the best ways for an individual to expand and complicate his own personality and public identity. Moreover, it seems to us that writing is a way of encouraging our responsibility as sensitive human beings to sympathize and identify with those toward whom we aim our writing.

We designed this book as a compact introduction to inform and interest students who have some basic understanding and accomplishment in their writing skills, though any section of the book can be expanded and refined in discussions with advanced students as well. In other words, the book is flexible enough to accommodate students at various degrees of sophistication in writing, to be used by students without constant direction, and to allow a course to develop without the book's interference.

Most, if not all, of the chapters are brief, but they are lavish with explanations, illustrations, exercises, and basic pointers about the vast majority of writing skills. Moreover, we have tried to present the writing basics with topical and occasionally timeless allusions.

The two-part Index should help you find the illustrative quotations and the discussions of writing techniques, conventions, style, and mechanics.

The grammar and punctuation conventions are compressed into what may seem a slim section (Chapter VI). It is organized to be easily consulted, with coordinated marking symbols in the margin that match the list of symbols inside the back cover. But the slimness may be misleading. In that brief space, we identify the sorts of difficulties that account for the student writer's major problems and offer numerous examples with self-helps besides.

Four complete exemplary essays are included in the book, just after Chapter VIII, "Essay Forms." If an instructor wishes examples of ways to expand or to organize writing, he will find such matters (as analysis, comparison and contrast, defining by restatement, etc.) amply illustrated in Chapter IV, "Paragraphs." But the four complete essay examples should offer a full-length demonstration of principles discussed in the text and interest the reader in their timely content. For a research article, for instance, Marshall Fishwick's contribution has to be read to be appreciated.

A few particularly useful places in the book should also be pointed out:

Inside the front cover are some helpful guides to note-taking, both in class and while reading.

Outside the back cover is a brief schema for evaluating quality level on six major facets of a piece of writing—useful to the student who wishes to review his writing before final copy and to the instructor who wishes to identify a student's main difficulties. It deserves repeated consultation.

The last chapter, "Evaluating Your Own Essay," covers in more detail the matters sketched on the back cover.

The Learning Aids at the end of each chapter or at the end of some sections, extend a practical involvement and review of the material.

The last part of Chapter XI, "Library Investigation," includes the names and helpful descriptions of nearly all the major library references that one should consult to seek particular kinds of material.

The typed-out footnote and bibliographical illustrations in Chapter X, "The Research Process," provide examples of what the undergraduate writer needs for almost all of his documented writing.

A self-help explanation of plagiarism, that nemesis of the inexperienced writer, deserves the dog-eared marker, our students have informed us, to check for the necessity of a footnote in a paper.

Our attempt has been, in an age of experimentation, to include some of the fruits of that experimentation and yet not lose sight of the fundamental features of our language and the process of learning easily and with enjoyment.

Finally, we have found four tactics especially helpful in the use of this book. First, we recommend that, before a student writes for the first time in the course, he should read at least the first chapter. Second, no matter what sort of writing the student does—narratives, critical reviews, news reports, satires, sketches, journal entries, researched papers, formal essays—he should identify the readers toward whom he aims his writing. Such identification not only helps the student choose his language, style, and substance to better effect, but it also helps him appraise the choices more effectively.

Third, although this book "teaches by itself" in many sections, our colleagues have found great advantage in expanding on certain sections in class. For instance, the section in Chapter II called "The Test of Originality" is not as easy to assimilate as one might hope. In class, therefore, students might be asked, one by one, to accumulate for the group a set of commonly-held ideas about some subject of interest and value—and then to think up several uncommon notions about that subject. After some trial runs, the rewards of original thinking often trickle in through the next writing experiences. And fourth, we recommend referring individual students to specific sections of the book to focus on individual problems, for such a personalized tactic is appropriate for this book.

Finally, we hope instructors have as much enjoyment in using it as we have had in writing it.

GARY L. HARMON
University of North Florida

RUTH F. DICKINSON

ACKNOWLEDGMENTS

In a creative effort as complicated and precarious as this book has been, we have proven once again that no one—not even two—can go it alone. We thank our colleagues, particularly Richard Caram and Judith Clark, in the English Department at Stephens College and the hundreds of students from two successive classes who tried our book as it developed.

To our editor, Jane Ross, we are indebted for her spirited calm and her genius for nurturing our own peace of mind and creativity. Thanks to Sally Arbuthnot, the care and feeding of manuscript details did not lapse. And, Susanna M. Harmon, whose constant interest and deft counsel improved the manuscript as it developed, deserves unending thanks. We especially thank her for the useful index and the section, "Main Library References To Consult."

CONTENTS

an introduction for students

Perhaps it is the nature of things that all our experiences—the world, its people, its events—kindle confusions in us. Our notions of who we are, what truth is, what we believe, and what we think important in life—these basic matters often disappear under the relentless deluge of events in our lives. We latch onto newspapers, television, books, lectures, or films—whatever we think might provide us with more information that will lead us to our own beliefs, our own undiscovered attitudes, our own selves. And we talk a lot, too. It should be no surprise, therefore, that we often think we *know* what we think.

Talking and thinking, by themselves, can give us the illusion that we know our own ideas, but we rarely apply the brakes to give our thoughts a close examination. Writing forces us, first, to discover exactly how we think and what we think. Then, writing forces us to scan our thinking processes and to *order,* to *substantiate,* to *illustrate,* and to *review* our thoughts. Further, we want to tell others these thoughts. Thus, there may be two motives to compel us to write: To find out—and check—what we think as individuals. And to communicate our thoughts to someone else accurately, interestingly, and convincingly.

Whatever experience, whatever words and images, whatever powers you have, you can use for these purposes. Finding your own way of expressing your own ideas to a particular reader or group of readers is a complicated challenge for writing is the creation as well as the expression of your own personality.

You will find that this book is full of strategies, patterns, option-plays for writing to a reader. What the book contains is actually quite simple—so familiar that you will swear that you have seen it (and perhaps known it) all before. For instance, you will read about paragraphs, sentences, words, logical fallacies, the research process, using the library. And you will find a brief section on common punctuation and grammar problems that often mar the surface of your writing, whomever you might write for. All these matters are surely familiar. But they are also what polished, professional writers of all styles struggle with, no matter how old they are or how much experience they have. Further, the patterns and strategies we discuss are the elements that readers focus on to read swiftly and with comprehension.

Adapting these various options and strategies for any readers you might aim to reach is a long-term project. But focusing on the simple basic matters should increase your freedom to use and develop your own writing strategies and style. These "basic matters" are the writer's means of shaping his thinking so that someone else can read and appreciate his ideas. He uses words, sentences, paragraphs, illustrations, substantiated information, and all the rest with care.

Our hope is that you will see the possibilities of discovering your own mind and then choosing strategies to fit the situation, whether you are writing a class assignment or a statement for the Associated Press. *Ideally, your purpose should be to improve the accuracy of your writing's focus and thrust.* Such a direction should involve you in polishing and honing your organization, your choice of examples, your words, sentences, and paragraphs until *you* taste new awareness delightedly . . . and your readers understand and enjoy your thinking as you want it understood.

thinking about writing

Writing is good for us because it brings our thoughts out into the open, as a boy turns his pockets inside out to see what is in them.

Oliver Wendell Holmes

Writing can be, like the practice of any other art, a way of life. It is what we all want, to find a way to live.

Sherwood Anderson

SOME EARLY CONSIDERATIONS FOR WRITING

Every writer faces the lonely task of deciding what to write about before he actually begins. And popular folklore spreads the lies that "writers are born, not made," or, "either you have ability or you don't." These myths too often impair the writer's strength to get started. But the rewards of stepping into an uncharted domain of yet undiscovered feelings are too great to be trapped by inhibiting notions.

The earliest consideration is therefore to develop a positive outlook of searching, questioning, testing—and the effect will surely be an alert and responsive mind in which new ideas beget still other ways of thinking about people, politics, social conditions, religion, sexual relationships, work, ideals, or whatever becomes important to you. Such an outlook helps us make the best use of our associates and our environment for writing . . . and our very selves. Passivity, hopelessness, frustration, or dullness should vanish from our consciousness.

The Search for Fresh Ideas

What sparks a new idea? You can take any subject—authority, for instance, or joining clubs, or lipstick, or fat—and examine it for an unusual aspect or an unnoticed significance. *What can you see that others have not, but should have seen?* Some say authority is good. Others say it is bad. Can it be, however, that others have missed seeing *why* authority is good or bad? Apply the idea of authority—assuming that you define and describe it carefully first—to a "new" setting, one that people do not ordinarily associate with your definition. Does the nature of authority change in a playground setting, in a dining hall, at a swimming pool, at a political demonstration, in a traffic jam? Authority as a subject might not be your pet interest, but there is the rest of the world to choose from.

Five considerations can help you choose your subject:

Your curiosity. What are you curious about? What are you interested in? What *might* you be interested in if you investigated the subject for a while? *How about these*: chemical discoveries, fashion design, poverty programs, water pollution, traffic congestion, poets, rock music, economics, the nature of women, your family tree?

Your competence. What are you good at? What special skills can you improve by exploring the subject in writing? *How about these*: radio hamming, wood carving, etching, weaving, interior decorating, house design, social action, tutoring the underprivileged, computer programming, repairing motors, singing, giving talks?

Your readers' potential interest. What will appeal to and stimulate your readers? If you don't know, how might you find out? *How about these*: losing weight, being noticed, cleaning up our air, enjoying freedom, changing a life style, making money, understanding a painting, avoiding unknown dangers to health, pleasing others, guessing what will happen in the future?

The subject's significance. What is worth learning? What will help you and possibly help your readers? *How about these*: learning what is really important in life, seeing one's social or occupational life from a new perspective, learning about the nature of certain kinds of people or groups, avoiding pollution of the ocean, learning about another religion or a minority group, feeling the joy of creation, helping others?

Your access to information on the subject. Where can you obtain reliable information about the subject? How much is available? How easy is it to obtain? *How about these places?*

place	how much available	the difficulty
your memory	countless incidents	requires patient pondering
listening to others	innumerable comments	requires alert ability to "record" while participating
your environment	limitless details	requires perception of usefulness and ability to adapt into writing context
magazines, films, newspapers, television, signs, letters, etc.	perhaps overabundant	requires selective and critical receptivity, as well as ability to adapt to writing needs

place	how much available	the difficulty
library reference sections or book stacks	most likely more than adequate	requires ability to find the specific kinds of information needed (see "Library Investigation," Chapter XI)

As you grope for the subjects you are curious about and competent at, you will necessarily be doing many other things—such as attending classes, seeing a film, hearing a lecture, dating, reading, working, walking, and a hundred other activities—while you think. But at least four activities teem with sources for generating new ideas or fresh angles on old ones:

Reading. Reading magazines, newspapers, dictionaries, brochures, advertisements, and other sources helps to develop a sense of words that others use. Reading is like a magnet, a suction cup for the language, for thinking about one subject and applying those ideas to another subject is a common method of generating ideas.

Furthermore, reading provides any number of leads for details like quotations, facts, allusions, opinions, illustrations, or events—which might be used to amplify and clarify a subject you might choose. Reading is thus a way of checking out a subject for convincing support—as well as fresh angles. For example, if your subject is authority, and you have read *Soul on Ice* or *The Godfather*, you might discuss authority in terms of Eldridge Cleaver or organized crime, if it suits your purpose.

Observing. Look around you, but not just with your eyes. Ask questions of your environment, describe in terms of other things, or compare the worth of events and scenes. Television, protest marches, the lobby of a downtown hotel at midnight, a children's playground, a vacant lot, a stray cat, an art exhibition, a drive-in movie, a drugstore counter, five o'clock traffic, a concert, a play—any chance sources of inspiration or association might be the clue to seeing fresh possibilities for a subject. The movements of laborers on strike might provide an illustration or even a central idea for writing about authority; or, incidents or details at a drugstore counter, in a children's playground, and in a movie might provide illustrations or ideas for writing on some aspect of prejudice.

Listening. You are living in a civilization that is essentially sound deaf, so listening is a particularly difficult task. We are generally not used to thinking about what we hear because we hear so much. If you really listen, what do you hear? What recurring words, expressions, ideas, or nonverbal sounds do you hear? What patterns do you detect? What significance is there that seems at first to be mundane? Can you find some significance to mundane life itself? What is behind what people say? And what does this reveal about them or the society that produced them? If you listen for the words in some popular songs, could you use them sometime in your writing? Could you, for instance, make a point by associating or comparing the song "The Impossible Dream" with certain strains of American political ideals?

Relating and Questioning. If you are using your senses to the utmost, involving yourself in the world you meet every day, you will have developed some ideas, some conclusions about a subject you can continue to embellish as you proceed. Furthermore, as you store away your observations and feelings with the purpose of asking "Why?" or "What is this comparable to?" you could scan this storage supply later for possible use while you write.

You might, for instance, describe the shattering of a suburbanite's middle-class success ethic during an economic recession as resembling "a string of double-bogeys that extended through the years." You are, here, depending on your readers to know how bad golfers (golf being a middle-class game) feel when they take two more strokes to play a hole than is desired. To reach a broader spectrum of readers, you might explain the recession's effect on the middle class by citing several details you could have noticed: "Patches appeared on the children's clothes, Mother fixed fewer steak dinners with fancy desserts, and Dad took to riding a bicycle to the employment agency." By relating events you may have lived through to a complex social phenomenon, you sense the overtones of precisely what happened to many affluent Americans.

Thinking of your subject in this way *while choosing it* should help you decide whether it is also a subject that you can explain.

A Few Pointers Before You Write in a Course

Quite often, students write for a course before the opportunity arises for the instructor to explain much about writing. The reason for this is that the instructor needs to see "a diagnostic writing" to discover at what level his students are functioning before he begins specific instruction. It is a getting-acquainted process, but most students can probably profit from a few reminders.

Here are five last-minute pointers that may help you:

First, once you have chosen a subject, you will no doubt have several ideas about it. *Choose one good idea* that you subject to the five considerations mentioned earlier.

Many a young writer wants to write as if he were Plato trying to advance a new idea about life in every sentence. Just recall that neither you nor your readers can absorb or retain many ideas tossed out in quick succession. *Remember: ONE good idea.*

Second, support or amplify each part of the explanation of that idea with information, facts, examples, illustrations, or other such material. Most likely every paragraph needs to contain supporting information or images that clarify and substantiate the point of the paragraph. *Remember: Provide support or amplification* for each important generalization.

Third, so that your ideas will be easier to follow and remember, decide upon an order in which you present them. Each observation you have to make about your central, single idea is probably worthy of a paragraph. Decide what observations you plan to make and then arrange them in the best order you can for your reader's interest and understanding. *Remember: Decide on an organization for your observations* (or events or scenes if you are writing a narrative).

Fourth, while you might first explain your observations or experiences or scenes as *you* perceive them, in your language, examples, or information, you will eventually need to think how your reader might interpret your language. No one can write so that everyone understands his intended meaning, but we recommend that you scan your writing as if you were someone else.

This matter, to be sure, is a difficult one. We mention it at this early stage because we believe it is one of the few fundamental "musts" in writing; later, we shall devote an entire chapter to the subject.

Fifth, try to decide what your attitude, your point of view is toward the subject. Are you critical, amused, angry, indifferent, dejected, cynical, ironic, hopeful, or what?

Many a young writer begins to write without knowing just how he has come to regard that subject. How you feel will influence your choice of words, examples, information, and emotional pitch. If you fail to discover how you really feel about the subject, you may simply be filling the page with words, images, or examples and information that do not match each other in tone. *Remember:* After you have chosen your subject, *identify your attitude toward that subject and what your central observation is.*

Finally, we recommend that before you submit a paper for the first time or even begin to think about it, you should sit down for an hour and write about a subject you have chosen. Use pen and good paper. And find a quiet place in which to write. You will probably write between 200 and 300 words, unless you are unusually swift or unless you have thought out your subject quite well. Have some scratch paper nearby to jot down some of your ideas and some supporting, illustrative material to go with them.

Three Trial Subjects

To prepare for requested writing and before you get involved in the course and this book, attempt some trial writing to sharpen your focus on the process of defining your point of view, selecting words, and ordering your thoughts. Find your own interesting subject to write about, or, try one or more of these three subjects. We pose these as questions, and we urge you to seek out increasingly detailed answers:

> What event, or series of events, has strongly influenced the course of your life?
>
> What is most worth living for? (Or, what might you be willing to die for?)
>
> What value is there in a recent book or film that you have read or seen?

As soon as you begin to take a point of view, try to imagine your readers saying, "What makes you think that?" "What do you mean by that?" "What is enjoyable or worthwhile in this writing for *me*?" We have posed, we hope, some worthwhile, thought-provoking problems that deserve your efforts to work out your own beliefs and communicate them to others.

writing
in
college

PREPARING TO WRITE THE ESSAY

So far, we have talked about a writer's outlook, a few ways to select a subject, and some pointers to try out in some practice writing before writing to be marked and diagnosed. Assume that you now have a subject. How do you prepare to write? While there are perhaps as many patterns as writers, nearly everyone moves through phases similar to the ones described here. In these early stages, you will be doing several things, sometimes simultaneously:

Finding Your Purpose Why do you write? To fulfill an assignment? That is surely true most of the time, but what other possible purpose might you have? Generally, you will want to inform or convince a particular reader or group of readers of some belief that you have come to feel worthwhile. You have "something to say."

Narrowing the Subject Obviously, a 500-word paper about "animal habits" or "humanism" is much too short to contain such rangy topics. You will not only need to name the specific topic itself—heroism—but you will have to select a facet, a subdivision, an angle of the topic that is interesting to readers and within your own competence, with available examples and supporting information. You might even narrow your subject and find your purpose at the same time.

Try this procedure of narrowing on the list of subjects below. Note that they range from broad to narrow, significant to possibly inane.

animal habits	rebellion	football in the schools
club women	Jews	heroism
walking races	humanism	plastics
war	morality	instant coffee
nudity	modern painting	the Dixie Cup

As you scan these topics, you may feel that "morality" is an appealing subject. Then, to narrow that broad topic, you might wish to discuss "lying." But, though people are always interested generally in lying, you might recall your own earlier discovery that lying can actually be a moral act—and that other people seldom think about lying in this way. You then have your purpose: to change people's automatic attitudes and increase their awareness of the ambiguous nature of lying in certain situations. If you happen to think of Huckleberry Finn as a moral liar, you could then, with one stroke, decide another matter by selecting the tentative title for your paper, "Huck Finn, Moral Liar," and a purpose to discuss how an immoral act, lying, can be moral depending on the social situation.

Thinking About Titles It is no accident that you should think of a title here, for the title is a way of naming specifically the subject you wish to write about. In fact, titling can be fun, but somewhat difficult. Here are some hints on selecting a title: (1) It should, usually, imply the main idea of the essay. (2) It should be short, original, and noticeable—"different." (3) It should *not* be a title of a book, and it should not appear in quotation marks. (4) The reader should be able to describe the specific subject of the essay just by looking at the title.

Gathering Information   If you continue with the subject—under your working title, "Huck Finn, Moral Liar," you will obviously reread the primary source, Mark Twain's novel *The Adventures of Huckleberry Finn*. You will do well to take some notes on Huck's evaluation of the Duke and the King and the lies he tells to protect Jim. You will see patterns emerge, patterns that indicate the nature of his lies—their purpose, his motives for telling them, and the consequences. You could also consider the consequences of his telling the truth—any angle that leads you to tell your reader something significant, interesting, and, you hope, surprising.

If you choose to write on "Jewish Expressions in American Life" (a narrowing of the subject "Jews"), then you could collect specimens of the language from television (the Tonight Show, Jewish comedians), from magazines like *Commentary* or *The New Yorker*, from hearing your family, friends, or chance acquaintances use the language. And you might be Jewish, in which case your memory and experience might serve as strong resources. Such a collection should amount to enough instances that you could begin to draw some conclusions about how Jewish culture has been assimilated into American life, the adoption of the language being one indication.

Of course, both these subjects have attracted other writers, and, after you have gathered a few specimens of information and chosen a direction for your observations, you should check secondary sources—magazines, newspapers, or journals in the library—for essays by other writers on the subject. Such sources can indicate some directions for you, though principally they provide expressions and ideas to include (but remember to document properly). If you continue such inquiry and gather your information from such sources, you are actually writing a research paper and not writing a short essay on the subject. Thorough investigation of a topic through the library is also a research project, taken up later in Chapter X. But for a short essay with one main idea, gathering some information from library materials is often helpful.

Arriving at the Thesis   After you have seen the kinds of material that are available to you, selected a fresh angle on the subject that is worthwhile, you will need to decide just what your central idea, *your thesis,* should be.

What is the thesis? It is the statement which you wish to make about the subject, and which you must support by means of the evidence which you know to be available. The thesis is what guides you to reject some examples or facts and accept others for possible inclusion in the essay. **This thesis—called a central notion by some and the main idea by others—must be carefully worded** (and reworded when you discover weaknesses or ambiguity in it), **for it is the basis on**

which all the paragraphs and the evidence of the essay rest. And it is good advice to write it down in order to examine and review it. (Some instructors require this.)

What should it be? Commonly, it is:

1. An assertion, a hypothesis, a belief that needs defense and explanation. Example: "Huck's experience in two Missouri river towns reveals that civilization produces a condition of mental slavery." Another example: "Yakov Bok, in Bernard Malamud's *The Fixer*, is more Christian than his self-proclaimed Christian tormentors."

2. An assertion that gives direction to the rest of the paper. Notice in the two examples the "directional" phrases "two Missouri river towns" and the direction by contrast in "more Christian than. . . ."

3. An assertion that reveals your purpose and attitude. Notice how the two examples reveal the writer's intent and what he believes about his subject matter (his argument).

4. A sentence that makes a statement, even if it is the answer to some question you might have raised earlier in your thinking. A thesis statement must be declarative in order to be clear, to commit the writer to a direction so that he can proceed with a firm understanding of what he is about, even if he alters this direction after he discovers more about his subject.

This sounds so simple, how can anyone possibly go wrong? A thesis statement should NOT be:

1. A statement of fact which needs no proof or evidence, as "*The Adventures of Huckleberry Finn* is a novel about Huck's and Jim's travels on a raft down the Mississippi River." This might be informative to someone who has not read the book, but the resulting paper would be a book report, not an "essay," which is an *attempt* to support a point about one subject in an extended piece of writing.

2. A statement of threadbare platitudes, as "Prejudice against Negroes is bad," or "Freedom ends at the end of the other guy's nose," or "War is an inhuman social act that should be stopped." These are not the fresh stuff from which a reader might gain new perspectives, new information.

3. A question or a command. Note that the question "Who is the true Christian in *The Fixer*?" commits the writer to no idea. The writer could well have begun his thinking about the essay with this question, but before writing, he must clarify his own considered answer to the question in a thesis statement. The same is true of such questions or commands as:

"Abolish slavery!"

"Is marijuana addictive?"

"Should abortion be legalized?"

"Expel and jail student protestors who break the law in the process of their protests."

These could be titles, by the way, but not thesis statements.

4. A collection of two or more main clauses. One might say that an essay cannot contain two independent main ideas at the same time. Consider this faulty thesis statement: "Dixie Cups are symptomatic of a civilization that is in a rush and that has abandoned taste and refinement as a way of life, but they also symbolize the paper-thin values of a society that encourages instant obsolescence as opposed to permanence." The writer cannot have his essay both ways. Both ideas might prove to open the eyes or kindle the anger of some reader, but an essay can have only one. Subordinate clauses might improve this thesis somewhat: "Although Dixie Cups encourage attitudes of instant obsolescence as opposed to permanence, their real meaning is that they are symptomatic of a people in a rush and careless about retaining taste and refinement as a way of life." Now the thesis is *one* statement, with a qualification indicated in a subordinate clause.

Evaluating Ideas

While you have been inching through these early stages of preparing a paper, you might have been evaluating your ideas as you proceeded. You will surely have asked such questions of yourself as, "What is the significance of this topic for me and the reader?" Or, "Can I find enough information on this subject to make it worthwhile?" Even so, it is possible to arrive at a thesis and actually begin to write without probing the idea for its strengths and weaknesses. At this point, before you invest too much time, you should evaluate.

Two points about evaluation are important to remember. First, valid judgment depends on objectivity. You must do a nearly impossible thing—divorce your sense of self from what you have written. In fact, many writers use a very simple ploy to accomplish this; they leave their notes and their written thesis statement for a day or so, whatever they can afford, and return to the writing to view it with a new mind that may have resulted from the day's experiences. Second, evaluating ideas does not mean simply agreeing or disagreeing with them. A good writer considers approaches that will improve his ideas; he might reject *portions* of his thesis that, in retrospect, are impossible to define or to support, but more often he will modify, shape, and redirect in order to produce the clearest and most valuable piece of writing he can in the most orderly fashion.

He might apply four tests to his writing at this point:

1. the test of rationality
2. the test of maturity
3. the test of originality
4. the test of adequate support

The Test of Rationality   You apply the test of rationality when you ask whether an idea can be defined with facts and with well-reasoned concepts.

Conversely, if the idea is defensible only by emotional belief or mindless but heartfelt assent, then it lacks rationality. For instance, an essay on the imminent second coming of Jesus is defensible by emotional argument and, perhaps, by marshaling hundreds of coincidental events of our time that indicate the need for a new Messiah. The accumulation of such facts does not provide enough rational support for contending that Christ is coming soon to judge the world. The writer could, however, investigate a sample of the 800-odd references in the Bible to the Second Coming of Christ, note the similarities and differences, consider the various contexts, research the positions of Biblical scholars on the subject, or defend an interpretation of those Biblical passages. Then the subject is defensible, and it is simultaneously open to scrutiny by the critical reader. Essays containing "I feel" or "I believe" very often lapse into emotional arguments, though such expressions can be used in a personal essay. A good example is Dorothy Lee's essay "Suburbia Revisited: Diversity and the Creative Life," located after Chapter VIII on "Essay Forms." When a writer as important as Miss Lee writes an essay on what she thinks, she is allowed some latitude with emotion-based statements. But most writers do not write such essays except when they have a specific purpose for doing so. Billy Graham might attract readers to his essay about "What I Believe" even if the subject were the Second Coming, but such an essay would not be considered a type of rational inquiry in a college environment.

The rationality of ideas also depends on their inclusiveness, their magnitude. The writer must reject an all-inclusive idea—freedom is good, prejudice exists, American blacks are persecuted, middle-aged women are club joiners by nature—because such assertions, although possibly true, cannot be defended rationally. You can, however, narrow these gangling notions to defensible topics—for example, attitudes of selected middle-aged women in your town toward club joining, the right of individuals to be free from wiretapping, exclusion from membership in clubs as an instrument of prejudice against blacks in Chicago. Similarly, a statement such as "Everyone yearns for a house on Long Island, a yacht, large stock investments, and college for their children" is equally indefensible. Do you know "everyone"? How probable is the idea, after all? Are there many people to whom such a life would be a curse rather than a blessing? Try "Many middle-class white Americans yearn for . . ." and then support your statement with examples from your neighborhood, your Uncle Jack, or a fellow student or two. Such a defense is believable and rational, for it is limited in its use.

The Test of Maturity   Even in high school, you may have been praised for the maturity of your ideas; that is, although you may have been only sixteen or seventeen, you could have had insights that are normally associated with someone older, someone with more experience. But in college, you are often expected to have mature ideas all the time. And this expectation changes things. It is *expected* that your writing and your comments reflect age and experience as well as intelligence.

No idea by itself is mature. What makes it so is what you do with it. Consider some of the simple, seemingly homely subjects that poets deal with—paths, nights, walls, trees, to use some of Robert Frost's subjects—and recall how such seemingly trivial or insignificant subjects can contain maturity, universality, and significance in the hands of thoughtful people. Consider the subject "Dixie Cups," which appeared in the list of subjects you could consider. One might consider such a subject puerile, but in the section "Arriving at the Thesis," it is obvious that the puny Dixie Cup could be transformed into a powerful lever to expose some people's values today.

The Test of Originality   It is only too easy to think like others, speak like others, act like others. We are, however, all unique in some way; the trick is to expand this uniqueness, to take advantage of it. Thus, as you read earlier in the section on searching for fresh ideas, you can seek out some new angle, some unused aspect of a subject. An essay on a familiar subject becomes original when you look for new details and new examples. Try a common subject, such as "Football in the Schools." Try it for the typical associations that you—and most people—think of when you discuss it. You might come up with some ideas like this:

Football in the schools . . . teaches sportsmanship.
                         fosters cooperation.
                         encourages hard work to achieve a goal.
                         emphasizes precision.
                         improves memory.
                         helps a person think while acting fast.

Already, you recognize that these are time-worn. On the other hand, as you think, you envision the speed of a football player and the inevitable collision with the opposite team. So you follow this image along until you hit on a fresh approach.

Football in the schools . . . encourages a penchant for violence.
                         extols he-man traits as opposed to creativity and thoughtfulness.
                         inspires a false sense of values, since the fostered ideals are short-lived. (Most players cannot be so violent, ruthless, or visible after the season is over.)
                         fosters questionable values by creating a special language of violence and ruthlessness.

Now you stop a bit. You see that the last idea is one that few people have noticed. It is "fresh." You've never heard anyone talk about it, and you are quite sure that it is valuable, since it explores the values that people live by.

You then begin to think more about the possibilities of your notion as a thesis idea. Is there supporting evidence that you can find? Then you recall some expressions: "wipe out," "opened a hole so big a Mack truck could go through," "run over," "wear him down," "go for broke," "blast through the line," "clean up," "blitz," "ruin the opponents." Then you think of the language that the fans yell to spur their team on: "kill them," "smear the quarterback," "bloody their heads," or "kick them off the field." With this beginning, you are sure you have noticed something that others have not. In fact, you can be sure of this because many people often have great difficulty seeing the patterns and implications of their own "normal" behavior.

In general, you should thus try to avoid platitudes, maxims, or stock truisms not only because they are clichéd and obvious, but also because they are likely to bore your reader.

The Test of Adequate Support   Just as the writer looked quickly to see if he could find support for his thesis about football in schools, all writers must find enough support to cause the reader to question his own previous notions about the subject, to change his mind, or to help the reader understand a new concept clearly. While the problem of finding support will be discussed and illustrated more fully in Chapter IV on "Paragraphs," a few statements may clarify the importance of this test at this early point.

First, the processes of creating ideas, evaluating ideas, and supporting ideas are really simultaneous processes when a good writer handles them, even though we list them in a one-two-three order. Sometimes support comes first, sometimes the generality comes first, as in the football example. But another person may have attended a football game and, while listening to the crowd vent its violence, he may have thought of the violence of their language, then the violence of the sportscaster's language. He then might have asked what such an abundance of violent language about football might imply for teaching football in the schools. Thus, he arrived at his general idea *inductively*—moving from specific instances to generalization—rather than *deductively*—moving from generalization to specific instances.

Second, writers need more than one instance for support, and although you may not be able to weave all the instances you find into the space you are allowed, a good rule of thumb is to choose the best instances for support, mixing the familiar with the less familiar, and then to try to make it possible for the reader to gather other examples on his own.

Third, allusions and authority can be used as support for observations. References to other writers, to other historical events, to other contemporary instances, can add uniqueness, maturity, and wider significance to your discussion. In the discussion on football and violent language as a revelation of values, you might allude to the language of hockey, soccer, political demonstrations, or boxing for application of language which reinforces an inclination to violence and ruthlessness. Also, an authority, such as a psychologist, can add support to your essay. As you read, you will learn who the authorities on a subject are and what they have to say. An *occasional* reference to an authority on the subject can supply an implied set of "findings" that you don't have room for in the essay itself. Essays without quoted authorities *can* be equally convincing, but the authority's weight is sizable indeed. (If you simply borrow or paraphrase an authority, remember to provide a footnote for this.)

WRITING THE ESSAY

All that we have explained so far may take you a very short time—perhaps only an hour or less—or much longer—perhaps a week or so—if you have a long or difficult essay to write. Moreover, you may already have begun the actual writing of the essay itself in order to find your way into the topic. But to see your way to the end, it is best to take a pen and pad and think about arranging the material for easier writing. Assume that you have decided on modern painting for your subject and that you have decided to narrow the topic to Pop Art as an area you are interested in, one that you think others might be interested in, and one about which you have learned a few things by reading and attending a recent exhibition. *Your thesis is "Pop Art implies that the world we live in is materialistic, humanly degrading, and object-stressing."* Because your essay is to be only 500–600 words long, and you hope to gauge the space you may need to develop a number of topic ideas that support this observation, you begin by finding the order and the number of principal ideas to discuss.

So far, you have decided to use in your paper five or six works that you saw in the exhibition you visited and some notes you took when you returned. You might write such organizing notes as those below. (We do not use a formal sentence or topic outline here, since such an outline is *usually* the kind of outline that is developed after the paper is written. The point of this early arrangement is to arrange the pieces of your essay, the paragraphs, into a planned sequence.) Such loose outlining might begin this way:

> Intro.—Open with example of outsize tomato soup cans and green stamps. Explain a bit about definition of Pop Art. Then state main idea, that this kind of art comments on our society indirectly.

You are started at least, for you hope *to attract interest* and *inform the reader* in this first paragraph, as well as *focus on the central idea* of your essay. Note that you could decide not to restate the entire thesis as you had originally developed it, *even though it was first necessary for you to work it out in writing.* While you thought through the introduction and what was to follow, you concluded that it would be best to point direction in the first paragraph and let the full force of the thesis idea occur at the end, especially since you had arrived at that thesis after viewing a group of works yourself. Your theme then took the "natural" shape of a compact, written gallery tour, from picture to picture.

Your next step is to arrange a number of observations you have noted about the paintings and sculptures you saw. You jot them down in what appears to be a random fashion, with a few notes under each on the illustrations you plan to use under each. *Each one is to be the main idea of one paragraph, all subordinated to the main thesis.*

3. Pop Art exposes the commonplace *objects* of urban civilization.
    giant hamburger   soap box   Brillo pad   whiskey bottle

1. Pop Art painting uses comic strip characters as
    Superman flying with girl he has just saved
    Dick Tracy calling on his wrist radio
    beautiful girl refusing to yell for help as she is drowning

2. Pop Art obliterates details of landscape and signs of civilization (details in paintings).
    bathing-suited girl eating hot dog—beach not depicted
    portrait of two women on park bench, talking—park not shown

4. Pop Art exaggerates the repetition of familiar people and objects as a kind of echoed multiplication to absurdity.
    Marilyn Monroe poster
    Andy Warhol portrait
    Jackie Kennedy painting, including 64 identical reproduced images of her
    repeated image of the Golden Gate, in the cliché picture postcard view of it

Thesis for first paragraph: Pop Art selects and exaggerates our cultural trivia in order to sensitize us to some of our commonplace absurdities.

It is worthwhile to make a few observations here. First, if you examine all the ideas, you will notice that *they are parallel*; no one topic is much smaller or much larger than the others. Each can be discussed in a paragraph of illustration and explanation. Second, you might jot down more examples than you can discuss in each paragraph, but you thereby store them for the possibility that you might use them all, as well as others that might occur to you while you are writing. Third, you decide on the order of the paragraphs after you have jotted them down in this rough outline form so you can see them clearly. Furthermore, your decision to order them the way you have was based on your feeling that you can deal with the most obvious observations first and move to the more subtle and difficult observations later.

Fourth, you recall that your assignment was to write a 500-600 word long paper. If your introduction is about 75-100 words (surely not many fewer) and your conclusion is about 100 words, then you will have only about 300 to 400 words left to make these points. If you are the least bit thorough in advancing any one of the ideas, you will probably have no more than 125 words for each of *three* (not four) points. Thus, you may have to make a decision while you are writing that the least interesting or significant of these points, brilliant though it may be, will have to be jettisoned. In any case, you have imposed a workable, original order on the subject, and you are ready to write.

THE COLLEGE ESSAY: CENTRAL FEATURES OF THE DESIGN

Mastering the basic form of the college essay should serve your essay writing in any class, whether it be anthropology, political science, biology, philosophy, or literature. *Form* describes the structure of an essay, and close familiarity with a widely-used structure for college essay writing should lay a basis for trying variations. The basic form consists of three parts: the introduction, the body (developing paragraphs), and the conclusion. A drawing of this form resembles a column, the base and capital of which span outward from the middle part, the shaft.

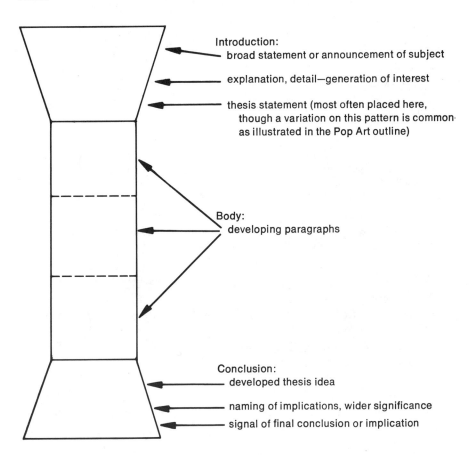

Introduction:
broad statement or announcement of subject

explanation, detail—generation of interest

thesis statement (most often placed here, though a variation on this pattern is common as illustrated in the Pop Art outline)

Body:
developing paragraphs

Conclusion:
developed thesis idea

naming of implications, wider significance

signal of final conclusion or implication

Once you can control the form, you can experiment endlessly within this form. But master the basic form first. The rewards are many: a sharpening of your critical powers, a focusing of your own perhaps vague and diffused thoughts, and even an increasing delight in writing.

The Introduction   The introduction provides your essay with direction and interest. The reader will want to know where he is going and what to expect. It can provide preliminary information or background observations about the subject under discussion. It sets the tone of the paper. But, generally, it should accomplish three functions: it should (1) announce the subject, (2) interest the reader (by using apt illustrations, facts, or examples—or by explaining the significance of the subject), and (3) state the thesis either completely or in such a way that you prepare the reader for the full statement of the thesis in your conclusion.

Introductions may extend to two or three paragraphs or even two or three pages, depending on the length of the essay. Most often, a paper under 1,000 words long contains one or, at the most, two paragraphs for an introduction. The main structure of the introduction, no matter how long, is to begin with a broad view of your subject and then to narrow down to the point of your essay: the thesis projection—or, simply, the statement itself. This is a time-honored and workable convention of the college essay.

Two other conventions are worth knowing and following:

1. Avoid referring indirectly to the title or any word in the title. For example, avoid such references as these:

   "This subject is ripe for reconsideration." (What subject?)

   "Few people know that, among all possible debilitating elements, these two are the primary pollutants that precipitate a sense of psychological insecurity, respiratory ailments, and early death." (What pollutants?)

   "These two women launched women's liberation groups through the latter part of the nineteenth century." (Which women?)

   "It was a time of political hell and social malaise." (What time?)

2. Avoid paraphrasing the title in the introduction. If you refer to the title, use the exact words of the title itself, as if the reader had not seen it.

These conventions aid the reader. You are, in effect, gently reminding him of the announced subject of the essay, keeping his focus on that topic as he proceeds.

Here is a sample introductory paragraph from an essay by Arthur M. Schlesinger, Jr., entitled "The Crisis of American Masculinity" from his book *The Politics of Hope*.

General
Statement
What has happened to the American male? For a long time, he seemed utterly confident in his manhood, sure of his masculine role in society, easy and definite in his sense of sexual identity. The frontiersmen of James Fenimore

Cooper, for example, never had any concern about masculinity; they were men, and it did not occur to them to think twice about it. Even well into the twentieth century, the

Examples—
Development
of Interest

heroes of Dreiser, of Fitzgerald, of Hemingway remain men. But one begins to detect a new theme emerging in some of these authors, especially in Hemingway: the theme of the male hero increasingly preoccupied with proving his virility to himself. And by mid-century, the male role had plainly lost its rugged clarity of outline. Today men are more and more conscious of maleness not as a fact but as a problem. The ways by which American men affirm their masculinity are uncertain and obscure. There are multiplying signs

Thesis
Statement

indeed, that something has gone badly wrong with the American male's conception of himself.

The Body (Developing Paragraphs)   The arrangement of materials for the Pop Art essay was a matter of naming the topic sentences of each paragraph, and this is the way short essays up to 1,000 to 1,200 words or so can best be thought out; a longer essay might move by sections rather than paragraphs. In any case, each paragraph or each section contains a topic sentence (most often at the beginning) that clearly supports or extends the thesis idea. And the development of each paragraph supports and extends the topic sentence—including examples, details, facts, proof of all sizes and shapes. The concluding sentence, moreover, contains a transition to lead to the next paragraph.

The **developing paragraph** is a group of related sentences designed to develop a single unit of thought. It should help the reader to understand some phase of an argument, to assimilate around one point a collection of particular details, examples, or illustrations. While it is an essay in miniature, it must also serve as an integral part of the essay idea which it supports. Briefly, the functions of the developing paragraph are: (1) to explain an idea or answer a question that is subordinate to the thesis, (2) to provide supporting evidence of some kind for the thesis, and (3) to extend the purpose of the essay, whether it be to inform, to convince, to define, to narrate, or to judge and evaluate. The developing paragraphs are the entrée, the meat and potatoes of the essay. Without them, the thesis must remain as an apéritif for a meal that never comes.

Although Chapter IV on "Paragraphs" illustrates variations on standard paragraph forms, it is important to notice here the kinds of supporting evidence the writer can use to advance his thesis or topic sentences:

examples	personal experiences	news events or stories
statistical facts	illustrations	allusions
specific incidents	anecdotes	authorities' statements
apt quotations	comparisons	logical reasoning

The accomplished writer never leaves a paragraph without providing such supporting material.

The Conclusion   The **concluding paragraph** focuses the reader's attention on the purpose, thesis, and subject once again. It explores the implications and general significance of the observations made in the developing paragraphs. In it, you should make certain that the reader is convinced or informed of the idea or purpose that you wish to achieve. Somehow, it should make the reader *feel* satisfied, better informed than when he began, convinced that he must reexamine his old assumptions, or at least be unsettled about them.

The structure of the conclusion for the college essay is usually a kind of inverted funnel. That is, the paragraph begins with an altered or extended statement of the thesis and then traces the implications or consequences of that idea outwardly to broader applications. Finally, the writer should signal the reader that the end of the essay has come. Such a structure appears in the concluding paragraph to Schlesinger's essay.

Refined Statement of Thesis	As the American male develops himself by developing his comic sense, his aesthetic sense and his moral and political sense, the lineaments of personality will at last begin to emerge. The achievement of identity, the conquest of a sense of self—these will do infinitely more to restore American masculinity than all the hormones in the test tubes of our scientists. "Who so would be a *man*," said Emerson, "must
Discussion of Wider Implications	be a misconformist" and, if it is the present writer who adds the italics, nonetheless one feels that no injustice is done to Emerson's intention. How can masculinity, femininity, or anything else survive in a homogenized society, which seeks steadily and benignly to eradicate all differences between the individuals who compose it? If we want to have men again in
Final Note— A Suggestion for Action	our theaters and our films and our novels—not to speak of in our classrooms, our business offices and our homes—we must first have a society which encourages each of its members to have a distinct identity.

A comparison with Schlesinger's introductory paragraph should reveal the close relationships of these two paragraphs to provide balance, unity, and coherence for the essay.

OUTLINING: A SPECIAL SECTION OF EXPLANATION

When we discussed arranging the material for writing the essay, our explanation included a loose system of organization—not a formal outline. That is because most writers use such loose outlining while they are in the process of writing and wait until they finish the essay to compose a formal outline, if they want one. Because papers over 2,000 words or so often include an outline to help the reader follow the organization of the paper and locate the discussion of particular subjects, we identify the main conventions and uses of the formal outline.

The following pattern of lettering and numbering is one recognized convention for outlining:

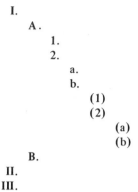

I.
  A.
    1.
    2.
      a.
      b.
        (1)
        (2)
          (a)
          (b)
  B.
II.
III.

Several observations are important to make here:

First, *an outline must have at least two sections at the roman numeral level.* Also, *any subdivision must contain at least two parts;* this is so because any division of a subject results in at least two parts. If you are outlining and find only one subtopic, you cannot list it; indeed, you should re-check to see whether the topic is not actually the main topic for the section.

Second, your indentation of each heading will indicate the relative importance of the material; you progress from the major concepts or topics to the minor ones.

Third, the length and complexity of your paper should determine the degree to which you continue your subheads. College essay or research paper outlines seldom subordinate beyond the first arabic numerals; in fact, many papers probably use only the first two layers of subordination, the roman numeral and the capital letter.

Fourth, outlines should not be too complex (consult ours), for they function to help the reader quickly assess the sequence of subjects within a paper.

You can compose an outline in topic, sentence, or paragraph form, *remembering, however, that you cannot alternate forms within any outline intended for others to read.* Shifting between forms is confusing to the reader, for each outline form communicates different purposes. Consider the examples of each of these three outline forms below.

The Topic Outline   This is the most common of the three types, probably because of its brevity, simplicity, and readability. The outline here is for an essay called "Great Comic Book Heroes and Their Love Ethics." The thesis is "Several comic book heroes extol particular value patterns for love relationships."

  I. Several comic book heroes
    A. Flash Gordon
    B. Prince Valiant
    C. Superman
    D. Jiggs

 II. "Flash Gordon" and his women
    A. His preoccupations
    B. Time spent with women
        1. His treatment of them
        2. Characteristics of the women
        3. Their functions in danger

III. Prince Valiant and his wife
    A. Apparent attitude toward her
    B. Expectations of her

 IV. Superman
    A. His identity as Clark Kent
    B. Superman as savior of Lois Lane
    C. Kent, wanting Lois to love his fake self
    D. Lois as chaser of he-man, Superman

  V. Jiggs
    A. His status with Maggie
    B. "Love" in subordination role
    C. The absence of love

 VI. Implications in portraits for American males
    A. "Thou shalt not love"
    B. The woman as object
    C. Women as companions for men
    D. Reflection of a desexed society

The Sentence Outline Most writers use this kind of outline to exhibit a particular, complex line of reasoning, or to help them remember the exact order of the details they wish to include in an essay. The value of a sentence outline lies in its complete sentence form: the complete sentences allow the writer to check his unity and coherence by using transitional words and phrases. (See Chapter IV on "Paragraphs," for a fuller explanation of transitional devices, unity, and coherence.)

The following outline is incomplete, since it is intended for illustration purposes only. The thesis is "Richard Wagner's ideal of the opera unified music, poetry, drama, scenery, and acting in order to achieve a 'synthesis of the arts,' culminating in the apotheosis of Romanticism."

  I. Wagner extended the historic German attempt to combine music and play into one single entity.
    A. Poetry, action, staging—all had to be related to musical drama, as in Wagner's opera *Tannhäuser*.

1. Wagner characterized his hero through narrative "song-speeches."
2. Wagner created atmosphere through scenic design and stage directions, as well as through a variety of musical instruments.

B. Wagner broke with the stultifying distinctions between recitative and melody.
1. His melodies are sometimes sensuously lyrical, as in *Tristan und Isolde.*
2. His melodies sometimes approximate actual speeches, as in *Die Meistersinger.*

C. Most important, Wagner gave the orchestra new symphonic techniques, especially in *The Ring of the Nibelungs.*
1. He composed the *leitmotif*, or leading motive, to identify characters or themes.
2. He enriched the harmonic and orchestral effects by weaving the themes polyphonically, creating a lush, rich texture for dramatic purposes.

II. Wagner brought Romanticism to its final flowering, leaving room only for imitators of or rebels against his conventions.

The Paragraph Outline   For purposes of comparison, the following outline, also incomplete, is simply a different outline form of the same essay on Wagner's art. Note that the function of this outline form is to provide several clusters of notes that the writer can follow as he writes.

I. Wagner and the musical drama
A. Wagner combined music and play into one entity by unifying poetry and action with "song-speeches" and scenic designs. He thus enriched the atmosphere dramatically and characterized his heroes more realistically.
B. Wagner broke with the stultifying distinctions between the traditional operatic recitative and melody by making some melodies sensuously lyrical and by approximating actual speech. These techniques are evident in *Tristan und Isolde* and in *Die Meistersinger.* His innovations severely taxed his singers' capabilities.
C. Finally, Wagner elevated the orchestra to new importance, primarily by creating the *leitmotif*, or leading motive, thus identifying characters by a particular musical phrase or brief melody. And he created a lush, rich texture by weaving the themes polyphonically, enriching the harmonic and orchestral effects. *The Ring of the Nibelungs* exemplifies these dramatic orchestral techniques.
II. Wagner, the last of the Romantics

You can see that outlining is a kind of shorthand and that each form of outlining meets a slightly different purpose. The main point to remember is that the outline exists to help see the relationships among and the sequence of different parts of the essay. Whatever represents this progression fairly and simply will help the writer as well as the reader immeasurably.

LEARNING AIDS

1. Most students find that the material in these first two chapters is easier read than remembered. Now that you have read them, note whether you have marked them. If not, consult the suggestions for taking notes inside the front cover and make use of some marking scheme as you proceed through the remainder of the book.

2. More important, take notes on these first chapters or outline them as a quick and thorough way to reread the material.

3. Choose any topic that interests you. Now jot down five commonly held ideas about that topic, ideas that you think many people hold. Next, jot down as many original ideas or attitudes as you can conceive about that topic. (This will be a strain if you are not used to doing it. Most writers improve their ability to be original—even if the "new idea" is only new to them—quite slowly at first and faster as it becomes a habit.)

4. Now that you have thought enough to find what seems to you to be an original idea on your chosen topic, jot down allusions, references, quotations, examples, or whatever supporting material is relevant to illustrate and enliven your chosen central point.

5. Jot down now what you regard as the significance of your topic and the point you wish to make in your essay.

6. List the main points you can advance in the body of the essay and insert supporting detail from the list you made in item three.

7. Write an introduction in which you (1) announce the main subject, (2) generate the reader's interest through example or detail or explained relevance, and (3) state the main point of the essay.

8. Write a three-paragraph body in which you further advance the point and refine its parts by covering each in a separate paragraph with appropriate supporting material.

9. Write a conclusion of about 100 words in which you point to the wider significance of the central point. Create a final sentence that signals to the reader that he has finished the essay and that he has reason for further thoughts or for thoughtful pleasure.

10. Create a title that indicates the main idea, that catches the reader's attention, and that is specific enough in its references that the reader might guess rather accurately what the essay concerns.

the writer and his readers

No writer writes in a vacuum. He writes to communicate, to establish a relationship with his readers. He has many audiences to which he will eventually write, and he needs to judge the needs and tasks of his readers.

A good writer develops strategies, especially if he wants to "win" his reader's attention and approval. A good writer cannot write unfeelingly, blindly, or blandly, as if the reader has to listen to him. No reader need spend his hours with any writing that does not engage his interest. Perhaps all readers have a right to ask, "What's in it for me if I read this person's writing?" The writer's first task is to interest the reader and to write so that the reader will be interested and will understand. He is to make the reader more aware, more sensitive to a particular part of life.

Indeed, the writer might think *he* knows what he is talking about and that this knowledge alone is enough. But he will be successful in communicating insofar as he can tell "what he knows" in the language of the reader—by appropriate word choice, by appealing example, by attitude. He must anticipate the reader's needs and satisfy them. The writer is thus much like the lawyer who pleads his case before the jury. He must size up his reader and then adopt an appealing writing voice that stirs the hoped-for response.

SIZING UP THE READER

In order to accomplish his purpose, the writer needs essentially to anticipate the reader, to look at the subject as the reader might. In this way, the smart writer anticipates as much as he can the problems and objections that the potential reader might raise. If, for instance, you are writing to a manufacturer whose plant is polluting the air and creek water of an area, and your purpose is to convince him to divert some of his profits to anti-pollution devices, you will surely not begin your request by stating that "Industries like yours make this country unfit for human living." A successful manufacturer has had years of experience learning that people want and benefit from his product.

The trick will be to acknowledge what the manufacturer already holds to be true and yet lead him to the point where you spring the conclusion that he might benefit himself and humanity even more by controlling the wastes from his industry. You should not be surprised to learn that he may require mountainous evidence to reverse the direction of his thinking.

This strenuous effort may involve other modes than argument to achieve the purpose. You ordinarily use one of four main strategies in writing: explanation, description, narration, or argumentation. These strategies are well known, but the most used one for the college writer is that of argumentation. For this reason, we discuss sizing up the reader in terms of changing his mind.

TO ARGUE or TO PERSUADE	AIMS AT	convincing the reader, changing his mind, and/or moving the reader to *action*

To argue a point, to persuade a person to change his mind, or to influence his actions requires a keen knowledge of both the reader and yourself, the writer.

Why not begin with some likely assumptions we can make about *any* reader of an essay? You will probably discover some of these assumptions by asking yourself, "What do I usually look forward to in the essays I read?" You can ask this same question whether the essay you read is your roommate's reading assignment in a college class, a *Time, Saturday Review*, or *Playboy* essay, an article from *The Journal of Clinical Psychology*, or a newspaper editorial. Your response might be something like this:

I look for and appreciate writing that—

- catches my interest with unusual examples and surprising information
- gives me ideas and information that I can use later myself
- indicates that the author is competent
- uses precise language with color and artistry
- displays occasional humor if the subject allows
- discusses a subject that is significant to me
- takes a fresh angle on an interesting subject

Conversely, you probably do *not* want to find such bogglers as the following:

- hard-to-follow sentences
- dry language, lacking originality
- clouds of abstract assertions
- lack of interesting details or examples
- an apologetic tone
- no clear indication of the subject or the intention in the first paragraph
- a sketchily explained conclusion, lacking significance
- a wandering organization
- poor use of punctuation signals (so rereading is necessary)
- "talking down" to me

If you have thought about these matters at all, you are a more successful writer for it. You have thought about yourself as part of that vast group called "the *general* reader."

But, not all readers are general. Other readers often define themselves automatically; they are *special* readers, an audience with a special interest or set of experiences, and you then have a specific purpose to accomplish in your piece of writing. Such readers and plausible purposes could be these:

Reader   an insurance company agent
Purpose   to demonstrate that the accident was not your fault

Reader   your English professor
Purpose   to convince him that you should be allowed to research anti-pollution strategies by interviewing industrial chemists, selected businessmen, and environmental activists

Reader   the college film society
Purpose   to interpret a film your group saw

Reader   a faculty committee and the college dean
Purpose   to persuade them to create a course in Black American culture

Reader   a hometown women's club group that gave you a $500 scholarship to attend college
Purpose   to evaluate your accomplishments since you have arrived on campus, assuring the group that their faith in you was well founded

Reader   a local Parent-Teacher Association group
Purpose   to convince the group that the main reason for youth discontent is parental pampering, not a breaking down of law and order

You need to consider carefully a number of possible characteristics of the specific reader. If you miscalculate—even though you write a grammatically correct, well-organized paper—you run the risk of paying for the accident yourself (in the insurance company example) or displeasing the hometown club (and thus not receiving a second $500 scholarship for next year). Such losses can be avoided.

Sample Audience Types

How do you size up such specific audiences as these? You should ask the following questions about any specific audience:

Who are your readers? One reader is surely easier to size up than a group. But into whose hands will the proposal for a course in Black American culture fall? The dean and the faculty committee will read it carefully, but who else might? Will you also send a copy to the college newspaper editor? Will the dean and his committee use your written proposal as supporting material when they speak to, say, the history or English or social science department chairman, the president, the entire faculty? Anticipating such readers helps you choose supporting details and arguments. Simply demanding such a course, without reasons and documented facts, may slow the consideration of the proposal or, worse, may defeat it when the faculty votes on it. Then, the proposers might be frustrated because the writers of the proposal did not anticipate the readership.

What is the educational level and range of experience of the reader(s)? Such a question should serve as a stimulus for you to scan the language of your essay. If you are writing to a college professor, you might use the most precise and formal vocabulary you know as long as you do not create a verbal logjam of long, difficult words. Use long words when they are necessary to express a complicated idea, but avoid showing off your hours of dictionary or thesaurus study.

On the other hand, if you are writing to a not-yet-educated audience of high school students who want to know what college life is like from one of their own graduates, you will seem pretentious if you use a string of polysyllabic words to tell of the glories and headaches of your English class. They will, moreover, think nothing is happening to you if you say: "College. It's just great! There's something happening all the time, and lots of people here are smart." What, in fact, is "great"? What, specifically, happens? Which people? What do you mean by "smart"? And if you speak of "matriculating," "credit hours," or "tutorials," you had better explain these terms, since they are not within the experience of your readers.

In what situation will the reader(s) most likely read the essay? Such a consideration might seem like small potatoes, but you will run risks by not thinking about it. A magazine article writer is naive if he does not realize that his potential reader will generally pick up the magazine in the evening after a hard day at work. The reader will have only a short time—perhaps an hour or two if he is lucky—to give to reading. The writing should therefore be designed to lure him on and snare his interest.

Likewise, the college writer will probably be writing an application for a summer job at a time when many more applicants apply than there are jobs available. The harried employer's attitude is that "time is money" and that he will consider seriously only those applications that are intelligent and concise but revealing. For instance, he will notice whether the writing reveals a person who is thorough and practical and who foresees an employer's needs.

What are the likely attitudes of the reader(s)? This is perhaps the most difficult consideration in assessing your reader, for you will know the least about what people think—of you, of the subject you wish to discuss, of your expertise in the subject. The trick to this question is to raise it but not to press it so far that you try to answer all objections you can think of. The best bet is to assume confidence (which is probably justified if you have done your homework) and forge ahead.

Nevertheless, what *could* you anticipate if you were writing to those club women back home about your college experience so far? As you consider the subject, you might recall that you learned that a Mrs. Meddle had nominated another worthy scholar and had argued not only *for* that person but also *against* you! So, if your letter—which will be read aloud at the next club meeting—betrays the weaknesses of character and intelligence that Mrs. Meddle had used in her argument, then she might pave the way for awarding next year's scholarship to another candidate.

Thus, you have considered your readership for identity, level of education and range of experience, reading situation, and attitude toward you and your subject. Now, let us take on the most challenging readers of all, the college professor and your classmates.

The College Writer's Readers: The Professor and Classmates

You can assume, first of all, that the professor and your classmates resemble both you and the general audience in what they hope to find in your essay. They are thus a splendid trial reading audience for sizing up a specific reader.

Your professor and classmates are representatives of literate, college-level standards of thought, reasoning, and style as well. Your professor is a kind of stand-in for other college-educated, informed, and literate readers to whom you might eventually write or speak on the subject of your essay. What is interesting, convincing, or understandable to him should also be interesting, convincing, and understandable to many others. He is the many-in-one kind of audience who is always asking: "Would my colleagues, my friends, and my students understand this?" In short, the writer should be wise to think of some of the apparent special interests of the professor but also a wider, unseen group which he represents. Likewise, if your paper is used in class for whatever purpose, as sometimes happens, your classmates will want to be interested in your observations as well as to understand them. This means that clear language, an engaging point of view, and ample illustration or evidence are necessary to effect good communication with them.

Further, what kind of situation is typical when a professor reads a paper? Because the physical situation cannot always be predicted, it may be wise to prepare the paper so that it can be read in his college office, at home in his study, on an airplane or train or bus, in a motel room, or even in the living room of his own home where other sounds and people are circulating. But more than the physical environs, the college writer takes uncalculated risks if he does not consider that his professor must divide his time among teaching, preparing lectures, reading, committees, meetings, writing, some travel, appointments for consultation, and his family. Furthermore, after he has read fifty other papers—and thousands of pages during the semester—he is looking forward to that paper which is a fresh breeze, full of information that is well-organized and thought out, original in its approach, and significant in the conclusions the writer draws.

Classmates, like most readers, won't want to labor over the ideas, no matter how brilliant they might be, if the language is dull, trite, or extravagant; if the ideas are too abstruse or underdeveloped and unexplained; if the supporting material for the assertions is incomplete; or if the punctuation signals are confusing and the language imprecise or ungrammatical. Any of these matters provokes impatience if it appears that the writer has not given sufficient attention to writing clear, easy-to-read prose.

Moreover, the writer who submits his paper typed rather than handwritten, organized for easy reading, spaced so that advice and assuring remarks can easily be entered in the margins or between the lines, and clipped together so the pages do not wander is most likely to receive the closest attention of the professor and students. Writing for reading ease and pleasure involves not only the arrangement of words and paragraphs but also the physical arrangement of the paper as well.

If you ask yourself, "What would I like to read if I were the professor—or my classmates?," you stand a much better chance of being read sympathetically and thoroughly.

PROJECTING A WRITING VOICE

Think of yourself for a bit. How many people are you? Most people are able to "try on" different personalities without much conscious deliberation about the process, and that is what a writer does. Unless the writer tries to neutralize the tone of his writing so that no particular variations of tone can be perceived, he generally uses a variety of tones for his *voice*—a term often used to mean the tonal effect of writing on a reader. Furthermore, he will most likely change his tone according to the writing context, just as a person changes his speaking voice to match the mood of the moment. If, for instance, the writer begins to discuss a point that will arouse antagonisms, damaging the effect of his argument or explanation, he will subtly change his voice to achieve his purpose—perhaps to arouse latent antagonisms or, more likely, to allay such objections as might exist in the potential reader's attitude.

Very often, anticipating the effect of the essayist's voice on a reader is difficult, for learning how to write rationally, correctly, and in an orderly manner—common objectives of a writing course—sometimes deafens the writer to considerations of the effect his tone may have on his readers. In fact, the common misconceptions about writing, discussed earlier, most often lead to an unconscious adoption of voices that do not achieve the desired effect on the reader. What voices can the writer have? The list is surely limitless. And some voices drive the reader elsewhere. Consider some of the following miscalculated exaggerations in voice and their more persuasive possibilities:

Miscalculated Voices	Attractive Voices
the chronic complainer	the responsible critic
the emotional pleader	the calm, rational persuader
the smart-aleck	the energetic, inventive thinker
the apologetic man-on-the-street	society's informed spokesman
the rebel	the responsible analyst of the *status quo*
the rager	the forceful, but fair explainer
the know-it-all "brain"	the intelligent but modest observer
the cynic	the optimistic skeptic
the oracle/the sage	the cautious and documenting speculator

Such a listing should not suggest that the tone of one's written voice will fall into either one or the other list of categories, for there are variations in tone control in writing. Neither should such a listing indicate that assuming the voice of the rager or the cynic is *always* a miscalculation. Chances are that these voices are less likely to be accepted willingly, but occasionally, to rage or to be cynical is appropriate to a writer's purpose. The writer might not want sympathy or agreement; his purpose might be to curb the overconfidence of his readers in some ideal. Nevertheless, appealing to emotions and shattering beliefs by such tones are not generally condoned in an environment where rationality, restraint, and responsibility are most admired and expected. In a situation where reasonable, intelligent people might read what you have to say, your written ideas will receive more sympathetic attention if they are voiced with calm reason and thoroughness.

Miscalculations in Choosing a Voice

Often, a student comes to believe that he will receive the best recognition and attention if he can convey that he is honest, true, and selflessly dedicated to ideas that his professor seems to respect. Thus, when he is asked to analyze an issue in racial prejudice, he grabs the opportunity to "write liberal," as he thinks his professor thinks. The miscalculated interpretation: trying to agree with what you think your readers think. The resulting voice appears in this excerpt from the student's essay entitled "Racial Robbery: The Mexican-American as Victim":

> When it is clear that Mexican-Americans have constantly been in low-income brackets and when it is clear that so few knowledgeable people have taken pains to help them, what else should each of us do but correct such injustice immediately? I favor a picketing of businesses that do not pay Mexican-Americans adequately and government enforcement of laws that prohibit job and wage discrimination. All of us should help in whatever way we can to stop this outrage of wholesale robbery of Mexicans who have come to the United States. Such liberalizing attitudes can only affect liberty and justice for all of the Mexican-Americans all of the time.

Such articulate one-sidedness is almost convincing, except that, in his concentrated effort to demonstrate his own purity of devotion, the student forgot that he was to analyze the issue—which means to consider the issue in its parts and to appraise it rationally. The voice the student tried for is there, but he overlooks the possibility that causes other than job and wage discrimination could cause the Mexican-Americans to be in low-income brackets and that, even if such "robbery" was a fact, other possible interpretations might serve better.

Another typical miscalculation of the reader occurs when the student assumes that readers will think highly of a writer who can stuff his sentences with complications and long words. This student chose to write about the effects of the mass media on American life; his "brainy" voice emerged in passages like this one:

> Horrendous monstrosities of banal, vapid images exercise our helpless nerve synapses with messages of anthropomorphic significance until the result is a refraction of sensibility, concentration ability, logicality, and creative imagination; moreover, there is an implausible correlation of similarly barbaric bombardments of imbecilic commercial ballyhoo emanating from radio stations and publishing concerns that, for all their touted wit and social responsibility, coarsens the human intellect.

Not only is this passage difficult to follow, but the reader thinks the writer is a thesaurus bug, hunting up synonyms for every other word and hoping to overwhelm with his verbal thunder. The result is redundancy and incomprehensibility. The better practice is to mix the appropriate short words, image words, and polysyllabic words so that the sentences read smoothly, but not monotonously.

Still another kind of miscalculation occurs when a writer assumes that his reader wants wit and wisdom cleverly expressed. One student sage voices his ideas this way in a passage from a paper called "Status and Money as Middle-class American Dream":

> The sight of Jehovah and the angels is surely less impressive to the average middle-class American status-seeker. Unprecedented affluence is the holy grail and the golden calf to millions of self-satisfying Americans whose anxiety neuroses about failing to drag home enough bacon to keep up with the Joneses are symptomatic of the dream that ails them. No one loves the beggar—at least no one who has the respect of "the forgotten Americans"— for the beggar has not managed to accumulate the necessary wealth to achieve status, even though he works as hard as a middle-class businessman and is possibly even more virtuous. Virtue is not its own reward; it is the reward of those who are affluent and "successful" enough to have earned the respect of their own middle-class friends. To have money is success; not to have it is failure.

It is evident that this student has done some tall thinking, though he never once supports his wise and witty assertions with information or fact. No proof has been offered; each statement is a separate but equal assertion that needs individual support. The result is merely a series of broad generalizations.

Thus, these writers by concentrating single-mindedly on one notion about their reading audience, blundered into some common difficulties of inexperienced writers. That they indirectly reveal their ability to become accomplished writers makes their blunders disappointing. Another example should indicate by contrast what a controlled, accurately calculated voice can accomplish. The following excerpt came from a student's essay on "Student Power in American Colleges Today":

Since a university administration has a fundamental responsibility to protect free speech and free inquiry for all members of the university, it cannot permit the use of force to abridge these rights. I can see no objection, in principle, therefore, to the use of police to defend a free and pluralistic community, if that becomes necessary. Obviously, because the use of police leads to consequences that greatly damage the cohesiveness of the university community, such a course of action is always regrettable, and I sympathize with those who try to avoid it. But it is not "repression" to prevent people from infringing on other people's rights, and the consequences are even worse if a university, through vacillation, tolerates intolerance.

Here, the student has made his assertion and has given reasons for it; he has not resorted to complaints, rage, emotional appeals, or exaggerations. Instead, he has carefully tried to state his ideas in an honest, open manner and yet has taken into account possible objections. Agree with him or not, he has stated his idea in a tone of voice that sounds rational, critical-minded, and yet forceful.

Four Voices on One Subject

Perhaps the most obvious conclusion we can draw so far about the use of a writing voice is that it is an important factor in effectiveness. Furthermore, it should also be clear that, like the speaker, the writer should be able to change his voice throughout a piece of writing when doing so becomes appropriate. The changes cannot be radical, for the writer's purpose must be kept in mind—resulting in a harmony of voices, sometimes forceful, sometimes witty, sometimes energetic.

In this final section, we shall see how authors have, upon occasion, written about a subject that has received increasing attention in recent years. Each writes on some aspect of today's students. Each writer's voice is distinct because of the differences in the situations, the purposes, and the readerships.

Voice 1: Emotionally charged.   The following excerpt is from a widely-circulated underground essay, "The Student as Nigger," by Professor Jerry Farber, who taught at California State College in Los Angeles. The piece was first given as a speech in November, 1967. His audience and eventual readership are students, faculty, and administrators of American colleges; his purpose becomes apparent in his use of language and detail.

A student at Cal State is expected to know his place. He calls a faculty member "Sir" or "Doctor" or "Professor"—and he smiles and shuffles some as he stands outside the professor's office waiting for permission to enter. The faculty tell him what courses to take (in my department, English, even electives have to be approved by a faculty member): they tell him what to read, what to write, and frequently, where to set the margins on his typewriter. They tell him what's true and what isn't . . . . What school amounts to, for white and black kids alike, is a twelve-year course in how to be slaves. What else could explain what I see in a freshman class?
They've got that slave mentality: obliging and ingratiating on the surface but hostile and resistant underneath.

This is effective writing, in the sense that its voice is accurately calculated to disturb the readers' complacency and to expose possible weaknesses in traditional education. Farber's voice is one of outrage and pity for his "underdog"—students. He has pitched his voice well; he is aware that his audience is sympathetic to underdogs, that his audience will pay attention when he explodes the word "nigger" beyond its usual meaning, and that he will avoid rational explanation for his central argument, for that would blunt his purpose of transmitting a sense of urgency and outrage to a whole college population. Farber forces recognition of his assumption that nearly everything in the contemporary academic environment serves to promote unnecessary and arbitrary restraints on individual freedom.

No one can deny that, for its purpose, Professor Farber's point was effectively written. Even so, as readers of such essays become more alert to the implications, the alternative explanations, the faulty premises, or the part-truths of such statements, such emotionally charged voices should be received more skeptically. One need only think of every student he has met and ask the question, as a start, "Are these students I know 'ingratiating on the surface' and 'hostile and resistant underneath'?" The answer should be obviously no—to the experienced critic. Also, could there be a sound reason why a student might reasonably expect to await an invitation to enter a professor's office? Such probing questions can dispel some emotional heat that Farber generates.

Voice 2: Dispassionately assertive. Other voices have been used on the same subject in other places. Consider, for example, this passage from an abridged version of a research report on students. The paragraph comes from a chapter in a book called *College and Character* edited by Professor Nevitt Sanford, a psychologist at Stanford University, who also wrote the chapter "Freshman Personality: A Stage in Human Development."

> To understand the freshman's development stage is to know how he might be changed and what the college might do to bring about desirable development. Effective teaching does not deliberately call a student's attention to his private motives or mechanisms; instead it undertakes to show the student something of the variety and complexity of the social world of which he is a part; it tries to show him the inner feelings and motives and mechanisms of people in general; it seeks to broaden self-awareness by inducing empathy with many kinds of people—real and fictional—and by confronting the student with some of the deficiencies of his old, automatically adopted values, so that he experiences conflict and has to make decisions.

Again, Professor Sanford's voice is quite effective for his purpose, which is to summarize, without emotional arguments or explanations, the results of his research on the freshman personality. His readers are college counselors, psychologists, and interested professors in other disciplines.

The voice is so devoid of passion, so intent on using words that lug around no heavy connotations, that the reader might wonder if Sanford's students are the same kinds of beings that Farber describes. They are, of course, but then why does Sanford deliberately use such a bland, innocuous tone? One obvious reason is that Sanford does not intend to be inflammatory, stirring up his readers emotionally as Farber does. A second reason should be apparent when we consider his purpose. Sanford does not intend to talk about individual students, or even individual groups of students, not those living, smelling, cavorting, loving, demonstrating freshmen. Rather he wants to theorize, to examine the group as a whole, and, in this paragraph, not to direct attention to the students themselves, but to discuss "effective teaching," to suggest what "the college might do to bring about desirable development."

Because his audience is composed of interested academic colleagues, Sanford maintains objectivity by dispassionate assertions in order to focus on the possibilities for changing the college situation. That is his purpose; he knows how to appeal to his readers. Thus, his voice and language derive from his precise estimate of his audience.

Voice 3: Sympathetically explaining. Still another variety of voice on the subject of today's student commonly appears in some of the more popular magazines. The excerpt below is from an article published in 1966 in *The Nation*; the title is "Why the Students Revolt"; the author is Bill Ward, a journalism professor at Syracuse University when a small student revolt broke out over the issue of extending the Christmas vacation. Professor Ward tries to explain several causes for campus demonstrations in the United States in the essay. He identifies five groups of students who might have cause to demonstrate and who find their brotherhood in demonstrating: the self-justifying academic failures, the student leaders without followers, the students who "struggle from vacation to vacation," the students who feel the "notoriously strait-laced" and the "lean and dry" quality of academia, and, finally, those who fear being "buried alive" in "a materialistic city of research, of grinding out profit and interest. . . . " Such verbal tidbits as these indicate that Ward's voice, colorful and passionate, is sympathetic to the students. Since his audience is a politically interested and intelligent readership of a national magazine, he chooses his tone effectively to explain some of their reasons for revolting. Consider this passage in which he explains a technique of those student leaders who desire power:

> When the student support is not satisfactory, the leader may draw upon emotional words. One is "apathetic." If a student were to get an honor point every time he is called "apathetic" today, he would easily be graduated *cum laude*. Leaders know that the word bites, so if few undergraduates show up at a rally, the campus is "apathetic." Students are never thought of as being in their rooms, trying to study for examinations; they are "apathetic" to the cause. They are never conceded to be out of sympathy with a nifty maneuver designed to aggrandize student government; they are "apathetic." They are never called self-reliant or self-thinking, never sensible about controversy; they are instead always "apathetic." To defend themselves against the charge, students must rally behind their young leaders and besiege the administration building.

Professor Ward's writing contains a tone of slight disgust at the cheap emotional trick that the student leaders he sees are playing on their peers, but he nevertheless attempts to be fair by following the leaders' ploy to its logical conclusion, student demonstrations. He might deplore the tactic, but he must try to communicate an understanding of the "logicality" of the result. He even plumps for the alternative vision of today's student as "self-reliant or self-thinking," but he cannot deny that masses of students demonstrate anyway—in spite of the possibility that a large number of them are "self-reliant." His voice is also, by the way, an "interesting" one; he risks distracting from the idea by slipping in surprising expressions, such as "the word bites," "a nifty maneuver," or "he would easily be graduated *cum laude*." This writer is no plodding, overly critical, lifeless adult who is an outsider to the spirit of youth. His voice manifests his liveliness and his respect for his readers' intelligence. He uses crisp language and sprinkles his serious explanation with just enough humor to tease the reader into paying attention to the end.

If you compare Ward's voice to the first two examples, it should be clear that his is a rational, yet critical and forceful attitude. Moreover, he is sympathetic throughout to the student, is not an anthropologist's remove from his specimen tribal culture as Sanford is, nor is he interested in moving a mob of readers emotionally, as Farber is.

Voice 4: Orderly rationality. Close to the voice that appeals to a mass, educated readership is that of Lewis Mayhew, a professor of education at Stanford University and, at the time of this essay, president of the American Association of Higher Education, an organization of deans, professors, and college presidents, for whom his essay was written. His voice is also an effective one in this excerpt from "A Rendering of Accounts." His voice betrays considerable erudition as well as distance from his subject, the students, but his anthropological objectivity is commingled with sympathy as he describes some causes of the current restlessness:

> There are, of course, a number of other explanations or hypotheses as to why students, especially the restless or militant ones, seek confrontations. One is that the permissiveness of liberal parents has resulted in children who, wanting immediate gratification of desires and not gaining their ends, protest violently, give up, or descend into despair. Related is the theory that students have been so led to underlying psychological bases for behavior that they are unwilling to assume responsibility for their own conduct. If blame for problems can be placed on parental conduct as recalled in an analytic session, the student is thereby relieved of responsibility or guilt over lack of responsibility. Then, too, there is the belief that affluence has taken from the young the need to earn things for themselves. Boredom and restlessness come when the spirit of service goes. Some have thought, but without much clinical evidence, that restless students are merely reflecting family pathology and disorganization. . . . Then, a series of other explanations are advanced. The fact of impersonality of life in a complex society is seen as a stimulus to

protest. The despair that comes when students see the difficulty of acting in the political sphere is suggested as the reason radicals prefer direct action. And feelings of powerlessness in the face of the inexorable advance of technology are said to be involved in feelings of determinism tending toward nihilism. Then, there is the opposite force. College youth have been bred on lessons of the power of science and the perfectibility of man. When they experience the spotted reality, they are shattered.

Professor Mayhew's purpose was to identify for his audience of professors and administrators the number of reasonable, but relatively "hidden" sources of pressures which feed demonstrations. It is true that nearly every one of his assertions could be followed by an essay of accumulated argument and evidence, but he is aware that many of his audience have realized the truth of what he observes. He puts the reasons for student demonstrations in quick successive nutshells so he can move on to his larger purpose—to suggest ways in which the colleges and universities might change to accommodate today's students.

His voice is forceful. He conveys a commanding tone, and he is orderly, naming one idea at a time. His voice conveys a sense of respect for his audience at the same time that he is about to ask them to change what they have been doing. He does not try to "entertain" with humor; he is never guilty of emotionalizing the assertions he makes. His voice conveys his authority; he is aware that others acknowledge his reputation (a foremost scholar and interpreter of higher education in America); thus, he does not use a cautious voice, qualifying his assertions.

He so convinces the reader with a list of articulately expressed observations that he can, a bit later, step back somewhat. Thus, he remarks that if there is "even limited validity" in his analysis, then that is cause enough for a change of direction in higher education. This further reduces the reader's will to challenge each assertion as it appears. We do not ask, for instance, whether the "spirit of service" has really deserted the college student because of affluence. We accept the assertion because of the confident, intelligent voice of one who knows, if anyone does.

Afterword

What makes a piece of writing interesting? That depends on who is reading it and the skill of the person who is writing it. While the essay samples in this chapter have mostly been on subjects that students are as capable of researching and writing about as their professors, we suggest that the subject itself and the purpose contribute less to interest than the writer's approach, that is, his skill in understanding how to reach his reader and then doing it. What is uninteresting? Nothing. Not how to peel a grape, not a classroom chair, not a broken ruler, not a tube of toothpaste. Any of these seemingly dull subjects can be made significant and relevant to the reader. But stimulating his interest depends on what associations, what examples, and what voice or attitude the writer projects if he correctly sizes up his readers.

LEARNING AIDS

1. Scan the Exemplary Essays that follow Chapter VIII. Identify the voice the author assumes; in each essay analyze and evaluate the effectiveness of the voice.

2. Write a paragraph to each of three readerships in a calm, sincere, but forthright voice on the subject of the need for a teen center in your home town.

   Audience a: the town council—in multiple copies to be sent to each member

   Audience b: a group of twenty-five seniors from your high school at an after-school meeting

   Audience c: the local Rotary Club—at their weekly luncheon

3. Identify the main features of the following audiences if they were to read an essay (by you) on the subject of learning in the high schools today:

   Audience a: your high school principal and/or superintendent

   Audience b: the parents of all your friends

   Audience c: all the teachers in your high school

4. What is the nature of the voice in each of the following excerpts from essays and books? Judge whether each voice conveys an exaggerated, acceptable, or repugnant feeling. Try to estimate the audience; for what kinds of people do you think these authors were writing? How does the vocabulary choice help indicate the kind of audience?

   a. Isn't it tiring to have to play the stereotype role, usually in terms of what society—men AND women—regard as "normal"? A girl approaching dating or marriage is faced with some real image problems of who she is: often, she must be Miss America in daytime courtship, Playmate of the Month on a picnic, the Innocent Virgin at the altar, Betty Crocker in the daytime when she is married—but a fine hostess in the evening and a tigress at night. Women can be many things, but in such a scheme, the roles are too much defined in terms of the male in their lives. To many people these days, such patterning amounts to a game of charades, and their attitude is that it is time to pitch out the whole mess and get some new ideas about what a woman can be. Where will they look? At other women doing things that are not the "expected" or "proper" things, at cartoons, films, television. And many will look to literature that depicts women in a heroic light . . . humanizing women by pointing up alternatives, by raising new standards of dignity, courage, and justice where a woman sluffs off the dogmas, the tired stereotypes of the past, and, in her own way, copes with heroine-sized problems. (Gary L. Harmon, "The Hero as Humanist")

   b. We live increasingly, then, in a system in which little direct attention is paid to the object, the function, the program, the task, the need; but immense attention to the role, procedure, prestige, and profit. We don't get the shelter and education because not enough mind is paid to *those* things. (Paul Goodman, *Growing Up Absurd*)

c.   Don't worry too much about figuring out what the instructor thinks about the subject so that you can cuddle up to him. If he does have convictions and you oppose them, his problem is to keep from grading you higher than you deserve in order to show he is not biased. And if the subject assigned is "My Pet Peeve," do not begin, "My pet peeve is the English instructor who assigns papers on 'my pet peeve.' " This was still funny during the War of 1812, but it has sort of lost its edge since then. (Paul Roberts, "How to Say Nothing in 500 Words")

d.   A procedure was devised which seems useful as a tool for studying obedience. It consists of ordering a naive subject to administer electric shock to a victim. A simulated shock generator is used, with thirty clearly marked voltage levels that range from 15 to 450 volts. The instrument bears verbal designations that range from Slight Shock to Danger: Severe Shock. The responses of the victim, who is a trained confederate of the experimenter, are standardized. The orders to administer shocks are given to the naive subject in the context of a "learning experiment" ostensibly set up to study the effects of punishment on memory. (Stanley Milgram, "A Behavioral Study of Obedience")

e.   Man, for centuries a random hunter of the sea, is developing ways to farm it. Confronted by the increasingly acute food shortage on land and visualizing much richer harvests than conventional agriculture can produce, pioneers in the new science of aquiculture, or mariculture, have plans to raise fish, shellfish and even plants by plowing the sea, warming areas by atomic energy, fertilizing and weeding the ocean, fencing off underwater farms electronically. Only a few years ago such ideas seemed mere "raptures of the deep" but today they are taken seriously. (Lawrence Galton, "Aquiculture is More Than a Dream")

f.   Women do have real difficulties combining a demanding job with a family. But how many businesses consider a flexibility in hours to make this adjustment of an otherwise highly useful employee possible? As for "emotional" women, consider some of the male executives you may know—including, even, your own husband. Who has not seen them at times moody, irritable, resentful, or even explosive? (Marya Mannes, "Women are Equal, But—")

paragraphs

Writers who know what writing is all about still have the joys of discovery, the struggle of creation to experience. The basic writing skill is the composing of paragraphs and sentences. The sentences are to the paragraph what the paragraph is to the entire essay, for paragraphs are the components, the integral parts, of the well-constructed essay. A paragraph can be defined in several ways: Visually, it is a series of typed lines, with the first line indented. Logically, it is a series of closely related statements. Effectively, it is a group of sentences so arranged as to achieve a single or unified purpose of importance.

As a distinct type, the journalistic paragraph bears little resemblance to the usual expository paragraph beyond the visual appearance. Whereas the journalistic paragraph is short and choppy, usually one or two sentences long, the expository paragraph is longer and more developed, *but emphasizing and stressing one point*. The journalistic paragraph is short because of the narrow newspaper columns (designed for speedy reading) and because editors need to be able to *cut* a piece of reporting at any point; the expository paragraph is longer because of the width of the page. More important, the purposes of the two types of paragraphs differ. The journalistic paragraph is designed to offer factual but brief information. The expository paragraph offers lengthy proof for an assertion, or expanded explanation for a generalization.

The beginning writer seldom thinks about ordering, arranging, or calculating the development of a paragraph; professional writers do not always do so the first time through an essay either. But they do recognize that such arrangement is a necessary part of the strategy if the paragraphs and essay are to be effective. Revision and rewriting, of course, can always strengthen flawed paragraphs, but a writer can conserve energy if he attempts order and expansion in the original process.

Skeptical readers demand proof for each assertion; thus, you will want to provide supporting evidence and detail, arranged and expanded to suit your purpose. *Unity* (the single intent or the one point to be made), *coherence* (the sticking-together of parts), and *emphasis* (the stressing of importance) are the three rhetorical terms frequently used to describe a good paragraph. This chapter therefore describes some strategies you might employ to develop your paragraphs:

Introductions, Middles, Conclusions
The Ordering of Paragraphs: Common Paragraph Patterns
The Expanding of Paragraphs: Varieties of Idea Support and Amplification
Coherence: Between and Within Paragraphs

INTRODUCTIONS, MIDDLES, CONCLUSIONS

Introductions

The introductory paragraph prepares and conditions the reader for what is to follow in the main body of the essay. *You need to set the stage, to entice the reader, to dangle the bait, to titillate the imagination so that he will want to read on.* A good beginning accomplishes these tasks:

- Names or implies the subject
- Interests the reader
- Indicates the subject's significance
- Prepares the reader for what is to follow

The most common way of introducing an essay has been described in Chapter II, "The College Essay." Other ways to begin can be equally effective, however. For instance, you may want to consider the possibilities of starting with these:

- A personal experience or concern
- A striking incident, event, or quotation
- Some background information

The personal experience or concern helps establish the tone and attitude you assume for the whole essay, highlighting *your* link to the subject. For instance, you may be writing a paper on epilepsy because your youngest sister has this nervous disorder. Thus, your introductory paragraph might briefly explain the difficulty your sister encountered because others did not know the nature of epilepsy. Or, if you are writing a paper on the harmful effects of smoking, you might begin by recounting your experience as a chain smoker.

A striking incident or event or quotation does not have the personal immediacy of a writer's experience, but the brief narrative of a tornado, of a woman's attempt to rear children in a slum, of a drug user's bad trip engages the reader's emotional compliance almost instantly. Likewise, an unusually effective quotation, linked to your purpose, can also tease the reader into a willing attentiveness.

Background material of a historical nature, or a general account of the broad subject, serves also to help your reader into your subject. Some essay ideas need such legitimate preparation as surveying the history or summarizing the preliminary information. A paper, for instance, on the need for restructuring the operations of the post office, a paper on the value of liberal education, or a paper on the responsibilities of dissent requires background information.

An introduction that begins "In this paper, I will try to discuss Toqueville's views on . . . " seems to hold a sign that reads "This way to the real sign." Since you want to convince your reader that you are neither apologetic nor sophomoric, it is best to get right to the point: "Toqueville's views on. . . . " (And even if the title of your paper is "Toqueville's Views on . . . ," you will want to repeat the name Toqueville in your opening statement rather than saying "His views . . . "–since repetition of the name is effective transition.)

Furthermore, establishing the tone of your entire essay in the introduction is vital. Sarcastic, highly argumentative, or overly cute beginnings give the wrong impression; a bitterly cutting tone at the beginning followed by a serious and sincere tone confuses your reader. Likewise, superficiality or sensationalism in an introduction leads a reader to expect superficial or sensational treatment of the subject within the essay, countering your more serious intent.

Finally, many writers find that a blank piece of paper duplicates itself instantly in their minds. Blank meets blank. Try then to get started; get something down. Try beginning with the thesis and writing the middle paragraphs. With luck, your adrenalin will surprise you, and your thoughts will come crowding one on another, almost faster than you can get them down. Later, you might return to the introduction without the earlier mental deepfreeze.

Consider these beginning paragraphs by writing students. What do they accomplish? How does the writer set the stage for what is to follow?

1. Maria Rodriquez, aged 24, mother of six small children, woke up in the damp fog on a hillside in Puerto Rico. The smallest children were beginning to whimper, stuffing their fists into their mouths, sucking on the corners of tattered blankets, while Maria's husband shuffled about trying to stuff a few sticks of kindling into a decrepit stove. Maria rummaged around in the cooking area of her hut, hunting for a few dried beans, the remnants of previously smoked fish, and some crusts of stale bread.

    Maria's activities were duplicated in the hundreds of shacks near hers, while downtown the social welfare workers began their day, as they had countless other days, with a committee meeting on the difficulty of solving the problems of the indigent slum dwellers.

2. Contemporary man in an age of abundance and astounding technological advances seems to have lost perspective on his situation and relationship to his fellow man. He is plagued by a solely materialistic society, finding that he therefore cannot relate to human beings, but merely to goods. James Baldwin, a contemporary novelist, cries out against such dehumanization, begging men to love one another. In his novel *Another Country*, Baldwin demonstrates a way of cultivating meaningful relationships by revealing some destructive and some constructive associations between Cass and Richard, Cass and Eric, and Ida and Vivaldo.

3. "You ache with the need to convince yourself that you do exist in the real world, that you're part of all the sound and anguish, and you strike out with your fists, you curse and you swear to make them recognize you. And, alas, it's seldom successful." So Ralph Ellison writes in the opening chapter of *Invisible Man*. But Ellison is not merely exploring the identity problem of one man; rather, he is exploring the identity problem of a whole race since slavery—a race of people who have been seen, yet not heard, categorized, yet not individualized.

4. Marya Mannes, a columnist for *McCall's* magazine, has noted that "in the past decade four of the most powerful exposures of ills in our society were written or initiated by women." Miss Mannes names Rachel Carson,

author of *The Silent Spring*, who alerted the nation to the accumulative effects of pesticides; Jessica Mitford, author of *The American Way of Death*, who exposed the funeral racketeers' exploitation of bereaved relatives; Dr. Frances Kelsey, Food and Drug administrator in Washington, who banned the use of thalidomide in the U.S.; and Senator Maurine Neuberger, who persistently warned us about the links between cancer and cigarettes. Yet three of these women were attacked, impugned, vilified, on the grounds that they were women. The debunking of their findings because of their sex is all part of a hidden discrimination which few men will admit but which most women know only too well.

Middles

Middle paragraphs comprise the largest part of your essay. *In the middle paragraphs you define, prove, argue, persuade, narrate, describe; whatever the purpose of the essay is, your middle paragraphs accomplish it.* In this way, they are obedient to your thesis, for the thesis sentence of the essay controls the paragraphs. If the thesis sentence classifies or divides the subject into parts, each middle paragraph is devoted to an explanation of one of those parts. If the thesis sentence indicates cause and effect, the paragraphs inform the reader about the causes and depict the effects. For instance, if the thesis is the one above about "hidden discrimination," you might divide the subject into areas of discrimination against women, as (1) in the home, (2) in social affairs, and (3) in jobs. And, since those areas are quite large, you might further subdivide, devoting each paragraph to one area. Or, if your thesis indicates cause and effect about hidden discrimination, you might develop a paragraph by beginning with hidden discrimination in the home and then showing its effect upon women's attitudes and values.

The point, of course, is that you succeed or fail in your purpose, depending on the substance of your middle paragraphs. Most beginning writers tend to write in a chain-link fashion, that is, elongating their essays by adding one idea to another, to another, to another, without really enlarging. The chain-link fashion is a valid way of developing a thesis of a sequential subject, such as a narrative, a process, or an abstract argument *if it also enlarges*. Consider these subjects for expanding by chain-links:

Narrative—My experience in a senator's office
> *Expansion*—application and acceptance for the summer program, arrival in Washington, assignment to Senator Kennedy's office, acquaintance with Kennedy's staff, my routine duties, my meeting the Senator.

Process—Assembling a swing set for the neighborhood park
> *Expansion*—unpacking the crated parts; sorting the nuts, bolts, screws; attaching the shafts and vertical bars; erecting the supports; hanging the swings.

Abstract argument—Scientists need liberal arts education
> *Expansion*—scientists as molders of lives; scientists without knowledge of

art, literature, philosophy, or religion fail to understand what makes men human; scientists need to link technological advances with deep concerns for man's individuality.

Each of these examples accumulates ideas in sequence, yet to be an effective essay each example needs in-depth explanation. For this reason, the chain-link fashion *without enlarging* tends to produce short paragraphs and loosely related ideas that resemble a tot's Tinker Toy structure, a conglomerate of sticks and knobs of ideas that lacks control and form. To avoid this effect, a writer must carefully explore the significance of his ideas.

The kinds of middle paragraphs that college students are called upon to write, though, are usually informative, analytical, or argumentative paragraphs. Such paragraphs accomplish these tasks:

- Make assertions (topic sentences)
- Explain the assertions (define, clarify)
- Provide evidence (details, examples, illustrations, or other types of proof)
- Comment on the significance of the evidence

The *assertion* or *topic sentence* is derived directly from the thesis sentence. And the topic sentence can appear at the beginning of each paragraph, or in the middle, or at the end—or it may be implied. Wherever it is written, or however it is implied, the rest of the paragraph is devoted to explaining what that assertion means, such as defining the terms or clarifying the situation, and then proving the truth of the assertion. Further, the writer will want to explain the significance of the proof to his reader, to be sure that the reader understands why these particular kinds of proof were chosen, and to allow him to judge the validity of the assertion.

An assertion, most often, either begins or ends a paragraph. If the paragraph starts with the assertion and proves it by offering examples, or details, or other types of evidence, the paragraph is said to be *deductive*. If the list of examples or details appears first, followed by a general statement, the paragraph is said to be *inductive*. Within these inductive and deductive orders, the writer can arrange and display his wares for the most emphatic effect.

Both of the following paragraphs discuss Hitchcock's film *Psycho*, but their approaches differ. The first illustrates the *deductive* order; the second, the *inductive* order:

Deductive

Topic idea directly stated	What seems "natural," common, and harmless in the film *Psycho* actually becomes horrid and dangerous. That is, the central features of the story—the innocent-looking young man, the quiet country setting, the
Explanation	opening detective story plot—all mislead the viewer to expect a tale about two bandit-lovers on the run. Instead, the countryside becomes a burial plot and the

Examples	film records the twisted logic of a psychologically disturbed lonesome young man. The money, for example, would ordinarily constitute the object of a vast search, but in *Psycho*, this money becomes unimportant to the examination of the labyrinthine ways of a psychotic mind. And the common act of taking a shower becomes a horror and a disaster for the young woman as well as for the robbery caper in which she is involved.
Explain meaning of the point of the paragraph	One of Hitchcock's purposes is thus to bring the audience to sense the unexpected possibilities of disaster in our everyday routines.

Inductive

Quotation, detail, example, data, facts, etc.	A wide-eyed Tony Perkins, a young lady on the run with a stolen bankroll, a quiet motel, and a rustic setting unfold into one of the most gruesome film murders of our time. In the film *Psycho*, the audience witnesses two
Explanation	rural murders and a most insignificant robbery where the robber (Janet Leigh) is not captured but is instead recovered from a lake bottom. Alfred Hitchcock, the *Psycho* director, twists the familiar cops-and-robbers film into a frightening murder story with a mentally deranged clean-cut American boy at its center. Such a
Topic idea	preoccupation with turning the commonplace into the terror-ridden and dangerous is Hitchcock's way of
Possible summary statement—an extension of the topic ideas	unsettling the predispositions of his viewers. After the film, everyday existence will contain potential horrors for those who dared to stay through the entire film— with their eyes open.

The following are examples of paragraphs by well-known authors. Russel B. Nye writes *deductively* about mid-nineteenth century popular songs in this excerpt from *The Unembarrassed Muse*. He supports his main thought with memorable events and examples:

Deductive

Topic idea	Most popular of all were topical songs that dealt with current events and reflected the tastes of the times. The public seemed to want songs about everything that happened, about the stock market, city life, politics, country life, elections, scandals, deaths, fads and fashions, anything of interest. Musicologist Paul Glass has
Statistical support	calculated that between 350,000 and 400,000 such songs probably appeared between 1830 and 1910. Major
Background	events like the antislavery crusade, the California gold rush, or presidential elections naturally called forth dozens of songs, but so did matters of passing and lesser
Example	interest. Mrs. Frances Trollope's book, *Domestic Man-*

<table>
<tr><td>Example
Example

Example

Example</td><td>ners of the Americans (1832), an attack on American culture, elicited "The Mrs. Trollope Quick Step." Darwin's Origin of Species brought "Darwin's Little Joke." Edward Payson Weston's record-breaking walk from Maine to Chicago in 1867 was immortalized in "March to Chicago." "The Bloomer's Complaint" satirized Mrs. Bloomer's attempt at dress reform; "Velocipediana" celebrated the bicycle craze of 1869.</td></tr>
</table>

In his autobiography, *Making It*, Norman Podhoretz describes his struggles to rise in the literary world. This paragraph from the chapter "Becoming a Boss" is another example of the *deductive* pattern:

Deductive

<table>
<tr><td>Topic statement

Narrows topic to the privileges accompanying new position
Examples

Example

Example
Concluding example</td><td>There was a third kind of power the editorship of *Commentary* automatically brought with it: a new position in the world, and to this I responded with mixed feelings. *Commentary* was an institution, and as its head I was now entitled to certain of the perquisites of rank. Invitations: to banquets, to parties, to join the boards of directors of committees, to appear on television, to lecture, to consult. *Time* magazine, until it decided that I was moving dangerously far to the Left, regularly asked for my opinion on a variety of subjects and printed my picture as one of a group of "distinguished intellectuals"; reporters often interviewed me and quoted my statements in the press; and people in general treated me with a degree of deference greater than anything I had experienced before.</td></tr>
</table>

Now notice how two other authors design their paragraphs *inductively*. The first paragraph is an excerpt from Robert Warshow's *The Immediate Experience* in his chapter "Movie Chronicle: The Westerner":

Inductive

<table>
<tr><td>Question

Detail

Detail</td><td>What does the Westerner fight for? We know he is on the side of justice and order, and of course it can be said he fights for these things. But such broad aims never correspond exactly to his real motives; they only offer him his opportunity. The Westerner himself, when an explanation is asked of him (usually by a woman), is likely to say that he does what he "has to do." If justice and order did</td></tr>
</table>

Detail	not continually demand his protection, he would be without a calling. Indeed, we come upon him often in just that situation, as the reign of law settles over the West and he is forced to see that his day is over; those are the pictures which end with his death or with his departure for some more remote frontier.
Beginning of answer; specific support for "honor" and "gentleman" image	What he defends, at bottom, is the purity of his own image—in fact his honor. This is what makes him invulnerable. When the gangster is killed, his whole life is shown to have been a mistake, but the image the Westerner seeks to maintain can be presented clearly in defeat as
Answer; further support for "honor" and "gentleman" image	in victory: he fights not for advantage and not for the right, but to state what he is, and he must live in a world which permits that
Topic statement	statement. The Westerner is the last gentle-
Explanation	man, and the movies which over and over again tell his story are probably the last art form in which the concept of honor retains its strength.

Next, educator A. S. Neill discusses sportsmanship in an unusual school in Suffolk, England. This *inductive* paragraph is an excerpt from *Summerhill: A Radical Approach to Child Rearing*:

Inductive

Example about sports	Sports in Summerhill are in their proper place. A boy who never plays a game is never looked down upon and never considered an inferior. "Live and let live" is a motto that finds its ideal
Detail about attitude of freedom to choose	expression when children are free to be them- selves. I, myself, have little interest in sports, but
Focus on sportsmanship	I am keenly interested in good sportsmanship. If
Hypothetical example	Summerhill teachers had urged, "Come on, lads, get on the field!" sports in Summerhill would have become a perverted thing. Only under
Topic statement	freedom to play or not to play can one develop true sportsmanship.

Conclusions

The concluding paragraph simply ends the essay: that is, it conveys the idea that the writer has finished his task. It is the dominant-tonic harmony, giving a sense of completion and rest. Generally, it accomplishes these tasks:

- Reminds reader of main subject and purpose
- Explores greater implications and general significance of the subject

- Satisfies the reader's desire for a new, informed outlook
- Convinces him of the subject's value

Just as several ways of beginning an essay suggest different purposes, several ways of ending an essay convey a sense of finality:

- Summary of ideas with suggestions for further study
- Personal evaluation of the presented ideas
- Appropriate quotation and a comment about its significance
- Extension of thesis into larger truth or universal consideration

Sometimes a brief summary of the substance of the essay is all that is necessary. Thus, you might restate or rephrase your thesis, reviewing briefly the emphatic parts of the middle of the essay. Consider this thesis example:

D. H. Lawrence's explicit views of the place of women contrast with his characterizations of Mrs. Morel and Lady Chatterly.

Extending this thesis into some larger truth or universal consideration works especially well in an essay that began with some background material or some universal problem. Consider this ending:

Thesis statement	The characterizations of Mrs. Morel and Lady Chatterly, therefore, seem to contrast with Lawrence's directly stated opinions about the relationship between
Extension of particular idea	men and women. Perhaps Lawrence unwittingly is revealing the strange dichotomy most men hold subconsciously about their women, believing rationally that
to	women have a right to individuality but preferring them to maintain a subordinate and inferior position. If so,
General comment	this unconscious desire could help explain the widely evident discrimination against women in jobs, in salaries, in status.

In addition to summarizing the thesis or extending it into a larger context, writers sometimes reinforce the idea with an anecdote or incident. Such an ending performs well in a personal essay, or in a light or entertaining essay. Whichever method you choose, you will want to restate the subject in order to remind the reader of the intent of the essay. And you will need to proportion the concluding paragraph to fit the length of the entire essay. If the essay is short, around 500 words, a brief restatement will close the paper simply and naturally. If the paper is longer, five or six pages, an extended ending may be necessary to recapitulate the significance and to explore the larger implications. Here are two examples of endings by professional writers. The first one is from Cindy Nemser's essay "The Alchemist and the Phenomenologist" in *Art in America*:

Thesis restatement	In the final analysis, Matta and Sonfist, the alchemist and the phenomenologist, the internal

Restating the
comparison

Details of artists'
differences in
technique

Reinforcement of thesis

and the external, the mystical and the scientific, are more closely related than one would initially suspect. Both artists focus on nature and by incorporating it into their works are attempting to shield man from the dangerous onslaughts of the technological world in which he has entrapped himself. Matta transmutes nature into art with the aid of mythology and magic, while Sonfist works his transformations with the help of science and phenomenology. Yet both artists would agree that ultimately art is the only means through which man will rediscover his own origins and once more become part of the natural world.

This second illustration of a vivid conclusion reinforces the significant points in Gore Vidal's essay "Tarzan Revisited":

Thesis restatement

Comparison

Expansion

Detail

Explanation

Personal Reaction

There is something basic in the appeal of the 1914 Tarzan which makes me think that he can still hold his own as a daydream figure, despite the sophisticated challenge of his two young competitors, James Bond and Mike Hammer. For most adults, Tarzan (and John Carter of Mars) can hardly compete with the conspicuous consumer consumption of James Bond or the sickly violence of Mike Hammer, but for children and adolescents the old appeal continues. All of us need the idea of a world alternative to this one. From Plato's Republic to Opar to Bondland, at every level, the human imagination has tried to imagine something better for itself than the existing society. Man left Eden when he got up off all fours, endowing his descendants with nostalgia as well as chronic backache. In its naïve way, the Tarzan legend returns us to that Eden where, free of clothes and the inhibitions of an oppressive society, a man is able, as William Faulkner put it in his high Confederate style, to prevail as well as endure. The current fascination with L.S.D. and non-addictive drugs—not to mention alcohol—is all a result of a general sense of boredom. Since the individual's desire to dominate his environment is not a desirable trait in a society that every day grows more and more confining, the average man must take to daydreaming. James Bond, Mike Hammer, and Tarzan are all dream selves, and the aim of each is to establish personal primacy in a world that, more and more, diminishes the individual. Among adults, the current popularity of these lively fictions strikes me as a most significant and unbearably sad phenomenon.

THE ORDERING OF PARAGRAPHS:
COMMON PARAGRAPH PATTERNS

Planning, working out strategies, and calculating the placement of parts of the essay are processes similar to those in arranging material within paragraphs. What works for an entire essay frequently works also for a single paragraph. Thus, the manner and method of ordering and arranging can be applied to the development of one paragraph. In effect, a paragraph is a small essay: it introduces a subject, develops it, and closes it. Writers need to learn to think of paragraphs as outlined blocks to be filled in logically.

The inductive and deductive orders, as the examples on pages 50–53 illustrate, arrange information from particular to general and from general to particular respectively. The other common orders or patterns of paragraphs are these:

Restatement: defining and explaining

Classification: dividing into groups

Comparison and Contrast: likening one to another, showing differences, creating analogies

Cause and Effect: showing results of attitudes, situations

Emphasis: details, examples, illustrations arranged from least important to most important

Each of the above patterns assists analysis—the major intent of most expository writing.

Two other types of orders or patterns also occur frequently:

Chronological: processes or historical order

Spatial: direction, size, and distance patterns

Since these two types are natural orders—that is, the order is inherent within the material a writer wishes to develop—most writers do not need to impose order upon them. For instance, a paragraph dealing with beliefs in witchcraft from the twelfth century through the fourteenth century lends itself well to time order. A process—how to do something—also follows *chronological order*. Informing someone of the steps in constructing a brick fireplace or in making a soufflé offers a natural one-two-three organization. *Spatial* ordering is perhaps a result of our linear print culture; when we look at a building, a stage setting, a costume, a printed page, or even a street scene, our eyes tend to move from left to right, up to down, or front to back. Since descriptions of visual experiences frequently order themselves in this "natural" way, the writer can take advantage of the space order.

Restatement

Explaining the meaning of a term encourages a writer to restate, to define, to expand upon the concept in order to clarify and lend that concept meaning.

Here is an example:

Topic idea Definition of term Restatement of definition Restatement by expanding the concept Example Further definition	Primitivism crops up again and again in literature, in art, in society. Essentially, primitivism is a belief in the innate goodness of man. That is, man is not by nature selfish, cruel, or evil. Civilization is the corruptor of man's goodness; thus, society and men living in complex societies organized by law and order are inferior to men living simply close to nature. Primitivism involves the idea that instinct, reason, imagination, and sensuous pleasures in the "noble savage," as Rousseau called him, are joyous, unfettered, and pure. Primitivism can refer to chronological primitivism, the belief that men of an earlier age are thought to be superior to a later age, that men in feudal times were happier than men in modern times, or that men in rural life were happier than men in urban, industrialized life. It can also mean cultural primitivism, in which men in some cultures are more naturally good than others. The life of a contemporary shepherd or hippie in a commune is thus regarded as superior to the lives of engineers, businessmen, or suburban housewives. Central to primitivism is the hope that man can move to a state that is free, similar to regaining a lost and probably imagined idyllic childhood.

Professor Susanne K. Langer's paragraph from *Mind: An Essay on Human Feeling* also illustrates restatement as she explains the abstraction "quality" in art:

Topic idea about "quality" Explanation of how "quality" inter- twines with "feeling" Further explanation	It is quality, above all, that pervades a work of art, and is the resultant of all its virtual tensions and resolutions, its motion or stillness, its format, its palette, or in music, its pace, and every other created element. This quality is the projected feeling; artists refer to it as the "feeling" of the work as often as they call it "quality." The image of feeling is inseparable from its import; therefore, in contemplating how the image is constructed, we should gain at least a first insight into the life of feeling it projects.

Another illustration of defining by restatement is Robert Ardrey's paragraph from *The Territorial Imperative*:

Definition Another definition Restatement	A territory is an area of space, whether of water or earth or air, which an animal or group of animals defends as an exclusive preserve. The word is also used to describe the inward compulsion in animate beings to possess and defend such a space. A territorial species of animals, therefore, is one in which all males, and

> sometimes females too, bear an inherent drive to gain and defend an exclusive property.

The restatement paragraph pattern, therefore, enhances the discussions of such broad concepts as primitivism, quality, and territory. Rather than literal repetition, restatement is an explanation of an idea, term, or abstraction in different words, through different examples or details that lend color and emphasis.

Classification

Classification is the act of dividing a topic into significant parts or of listing categories, sometimes with description of the parts. Classification is a common experience to each of us. People classify us according to political affiliation, religion, family size, accent, level of education, and even the section of town we live in. Such everyday categories as introvert and extrovert and carnivore, vegetarian, or natural food "purist" are endless.

A writer analyzes by grouping similarities or differences of events, people, inanimate objects, abstract ideas, or whatever topic he selects. To assist his reader, the writer can list the topic parts or give the number of units, usually in the first sentence. This paragraph, for instance, indicates three classes:

Topic idea divided	Three types of frontiersmen pushed quickly into the west: genuine adventurers, frustrated and dissatis-
First type described	fied farmers, and fugitives from the law. The genuine adventurers were attracted by the wild and colorful talks of other mountain men. They were eager to engage their wits with raw nature, to scan a new river, to sense a primeval stillness from a mountain top. The
Second type described	second type of frontiersmen were those who were too individualistic to be fettered by common society. They failed in crop farming in the east, they were notoriously improvident, they were impatient of law, taxes, merchants, too many children, and too much bad weather. In truth, they were probably grumblers and complainers in the wilds, too, but preferred hunting and fishing to disciplined farming. The third,
Third type described	fugitives from the law, simply found the frontier a convenient escape from jail sentences or heavy fines imposed perhaps for drinking, gambling, bad bets, or other crimes.

Note the ways in which the authors of the next paragraphs classify and order their ideas. Eric Fromm, in his first example from *The Heart of Man: Its Genius for Good and Evil*, discusses two characteristics of mankind:

> Unamuno, in speaking of the necrophilous character of the cry "Long live death," touched

	upon the core of the problem of evil. There is no
Main idea divided into two parts	more fundamental distinction between men, psychologically and morally, than the one between those who love death and those who love life, between the *necrophilous* and the *biophilous*. This
Two parts may overlap	is not meant to convey that a person is necessarily either entirely necrophilous or entirely biophilous.
Explanation of part one	There are some who are totally devoted to death,
Explanation of part two	and these are insane. There are others who are entirely devoted to life, and these strike us as having accomplished the highest aim of which man
Two parts may blend	is capable. In many, both the biophilous and the necrophilous trends are present, but in various blends. What matters here, as always in living
Importance of studying the two parts	phenomena, is which trend is the stronger, so that it determines man's behavior—not the complete absence or presence of one of the two orientations.

Then, through the rest of the chapter, Fromm illustrates the differences and similarities of the "love of death" and the "love of life" phases of man.

Race is one of the most common classifications of man. Eldridge Cleaver in *Soul on Ice* discusses the attitudes in America during slavery days toward two groups:

	Blacks and whites being conceived as mutually exclusive types, those attributes imputed to the
Topic idea divided into two parts	blacks could not also be imputed to the whites—at least not in equal degree—without blurring the line
Explanation of reason for two images	separating the races. These images were based upon the social function of the two races, the
First image explained	work they performed. The ideal white man was one who knew how to use his head, who knew how to manage and control things and get things done. Those whites who were not in a position to perform these functions nevertheless aspired to
Second image explained	them. The ideal black man was one who did exactly as he was told, and did it efficiently and cheerfully. "Slaves," said Frederick Douglass, "are
Reinforcing the point	generally expected to sing as well as to work." As
The two images influence today's classification of men	the black man's position and function became more varied, the images of white and black, having become stereotypes, lagged behind.

Rather than restrict their discussion to one paragraph, writers of exposition usually develop points of classification throughout several paragraphs or an entire essay. That is, if a historian were analyzing four characteristics of history, he might devote a paragraph or more to each. Classification, by the way, is the most helpful when you present three or more categories; otherwise, mutually exclusive stereotypes may arise, as Cleaver points out.

Comparison and Contrast

In comparing and contrasting, the writer depicts likenesses and differences in order to explain or to clarify. Sometimes *analogy* works well. A writer often chooses to compare basically unlike things. Melville, for instance, compared free will and fate in the human destiny to the weaving of a mat, illustrating that chance events frequently alter a man's plans. Analogies can easily be pushed too far, although they are colorful and striking when they are apt.

More commonly, writers compare one event, action, idea, or object to another *to point out advantages and disadvantages* or *to prove a point*. Here is one example:

Topic idea establishes two subjects	The Miss America image of young women conflicts with the Playgirl image of women.
Comparable points	Although both portray the attributes of youth, nubility, cleanliness, and innocence, Miss America
First contrasting points	is cool, queenly, stylized, while the Playgirl is wanton, seductive, and hot-blooded. A retinue of
Contrast extended	chaperones are deployed about the smiling queen, to protect the well-groomed and coiffed virginal quality. The Playgirl, half-clothed, is supposedly accessible in empty rooms, wide couches, deserted
Comparison	beaches. Ironically, however, both images depict
Comparison extended	young women as things to be exploited. Miss America sells cars, dedicates bridges, dispenses lotions, depilatories, and hair sprays. The Playgirl sells sex—but once the product is used, she is disposable, with no encroaching demands. Thus,
Summary; point of argument	both images encourage exploitation of young women; both suggest girls are to be used, rather than be treated as individualized, free human beings.

In his essay "Disenfranchise the Old" in *The New Republic*, Douglas J. Stewart advocates "that all persons lose the vote at retirement or age 70, whichever is earlier. . . . " Preceding his controversial statement, Stewart prepares his audience with a *comparison* of two age groups:

Topic idea initiated	We have no qualms about denying the vote to one group, children, because we see a strong correlation between age and the prevalence of dangerous temptations: giddiness, fatuity and the herd-instinct (even if the voting age is lowered to 18, this would only be an empirical judgment that maturity begins earlier than we thought, and in no

Comparison of temptations of older people to those of children

Authorities as source of support for argument

Comparison of herd inclination of old and young

way disturbs the principle that there is an age below which political responsibility cannot be *assumed*). But the old are subject to a complementary set of temptations. As a class, they are not, as pious belief would have it, wise, benign and tolerant. Aristotle observed with acerb precision in the *Rhetoric* that their chief characteristics are greed, cowardice, resentment over the cheats of life that did not turn out as planned, and the consequent desire to punish somebody for it. One may add, from *Lear*, willful self-deception in the indulgence of soured emotions, envy and vengefulness, a bloc even more certainly herd-inclined than the young, moved, not by a vision of the common good, but by a desire to see old prejudices vindicated.

Arnold J. Toynbee, in the next paragraph from *A Study of History*, contrasts civilizations and primitive societies:

Topic idea establishes two subjects

Definition

Contrast of how mimesis operates in different societies

Explanation of its operation in primitive societies

Effect of mimesis in primitive society

Explanation of its operation in civilizations

Effect of mimesis in civilizations

An essential difference between civilizations and primitive societies *as we know them* (the *caveat* will be found to be important) is the direction taken by mimesis or imitation. Mimesis is a generic feature of all social life. Its operation can be observed both in primitive societies and in civilizations, in every social activity from the imitation of the style of film-stars by their humbler sisters upwards. It operates, however, in different directions in the two species of society. In primitive societies, mimesis is directed towards the older generation and towards dead ancestors who stand, unseen but not unfelt, at the back of the living elders, reinforcing their prestige. In a society where mimesis is thus directed backward towards the past, custom rules and society remains static. On the other hand, in societies in process of civilization, mimesis is directed towards creative personalities who commanded a following because they are pioneers. In such societies, 'the cake of custom,' as Walter Bagehot called it in his *Physics and Politics*, is broken and society is in dynamic motion along a course of change and growth.

Because you must control two subjects at the same time in a comparison-contrast paragraph or essay, you need to limit your topic statement scrupulously so that you can adequately prove your point. Then, to be effective in a full essay, compare or contrast both subjects *item for item*. That is, avoid lumping all points about civilizations together before discussing all points about primitive societies. Your purpose is to create *one essay*, not two.

Cause and Effect

The cause and effect or causation order is another analytical arrangement. Here the dependent relationship between actions or events in time demands primary focus. In cause and effect, the writer usually works inductively, attempting to demonstrate why something is the way it is—what causes led to a particular result. Also, it is structurally acceptable to begin with the present situation and return to its causes. Here is an example of a cause-and-effect paragraph:

Topic idea	The slum child cannot succeed in the middle-class school because of the intellectual and sensory poverty of his environment.
Cause: example of intellectual poverty	The adults in his household do not speak much, especially not to a child, and if they do, the speech is short and grammatically
Effect	simple. Thus, the child cannot follow the long sentences of the teacher, both because he does not understand the vocabulary and because he does not have a well-trained
Cause: another example of intellectual poverty	listening span. Furthermore, since adults in his environment are only irritated by the child's questions and frequently push him
Effect	away, he does not know that he is supposed and encouraged to ask questions of his
Cause: example of sensory poverty	teacher. Similarly, the child has few toys, few pictures, few of anything at home
Effect	except noise and people. Thus, he is not equipped to handle sizes, colors, shapes and textures that the middle-class child already knows and handles. As a result, the slum
Conclusion: overall effect	child is bewildered, upset, and frustrated by the school's intellectual demands upon him, and he fails the first in a long, long procession of failures.

In this excerpt from an address, "The Tragedy of the Commons," Garrett Hardin presents hypothetical causes that could lead to one kind of public effect different from today's way of life. This pattern enables him to emphasize our present condition:

Cause	If each human family were dependent only on its own
Cause	resources; if the children of improvident parents starved to
Cause	death; if, thus, overbreeding brought its own "punishment" to
Effect	the germ line—*then* there would be no public interest in controlling the breeding of families. But our society is deeply

Contrast committed to the welfare state, and hence is confronted with another aspect of the tragedy of the commons.

Next, philosopher-scientist R. Buckminster Fuller discusses factors affecting the intelligence of children in *Utopia or Oblivion: The Prospects for Humanity*, pointing to causes and their effects, as in this paragraph:

Cause   If good books are around the home—though the child cannot as
Effect   yet read them—he senses that those are the kind of books leading
Cause   to greater understanding. Having confidence in his parent's
Effect   determination to learn more, the child also so aspires.

The cause-and-effect pattern, of course, is easy to spot and to develop because certain words—"since," "if," "because," or "a cause for" in the cause section, and "then," "thus," "therefore," "a result is," or "as a result" in the effect section—invariably appear. Notice, too, that the causation sequence may have several causes leading to several effects.

Emphasis

In the emphatic order, the writer arranges his details, examples, and illustrations in ascending importance, listing the least important first and the most important last. He does so to appeal to the reader, to retain his interest, to stimulate his desire for more information. In the following example, the most forceful detail is reserved until the end.

Topic idea   One migrant camp in southern Florida is typical
           of migrant camps in many southern agricultural
Detail about roads counties. The muddy, rutted, littered roads wander
           irregularly among shacks and huts. The buildings
Detail about buildings themselves are reminiscent of the tar paper and
           board shacks made infamous in Steinbeck's *The*
Detail about sanitation *Grapes of Wrath*. The putrid and offensive privies
           are located at least one quarter mile away—too
Detail about workers inconvenient for children. The workers themselves
           appear old, beaten, purposeless, and the children
           scrawny, dulled, covered with sores and insect
Emphatic detail   bites. At the perimeters of the camp stalk the
           overseers—wearing heavy boots and carrying shot-
           guns.

Then, Algerian psychiatrist Frantz Fanon, in this paragraph from *The Wretched of the Earth*, builds detail upon detail about colonial oppression and its effects in order to stress how strapped-in the native feels:

Topic idea   A world divided into compartments, a
           motionless, Manicheistic world, a world of
           statues: the statue of the general who carried
           out the conquest, the statue of the engineer
           who built the bridge; a world which is sure
           of itself, which crushes with its stones the

	backs flayed by whips: this is the colonial
Focus on the oppressed native	world. The native is a being hemmed in; apartheid is simply one form of the division into compartments of the colonial world.
Detail about boundaries	The first thing which the native learns is to stay in his place, and not to go beyond
Detail about natives' dreams to escape boundaries	certain limits. This is why the dreams of the native are always of muscular prowess; his dreams are of action and of aggression. I
Details about personal dreams of freedom	dream I am jumping, swimming, running, climbing; I dream that I burst out laughing, that I span a river in one stride, or that I am followed by a flood of motor-cars which
Emphatic point in the conclusion	never catch up with me. During the period of colonization, the native never stops achieving his freedom from nine in the evening until six in the morning.

Emphasis lends vitality and color to a paragraph. Sometimes *overstatement* or *hyperbole* helps the writer impress his reader with a point. Such exaggeration, as in the following paragraph from *Minority Report*, adds force. H. L. Mencken, a caustic wit, renowned journalist, who championed the dignity of the individual, verbally stabs at the weaknesses of institutions such as law:

	American law has made very little real progress since
Topic idea about American law	the days of Blackstone. In large part it still belongs to the Fifteenth Century. There has been some effort to
English law has progressed some	get rid of its worst absurdities in England, but hardly any in the United States. If medicine had remained as
Overstatement to emphasize the weakness	backward the doctors would still believe in the humoral pathology, and their chief remedial agent would be blood-letting.

Paragraphs therefore offer meaning not only through their words but also through their structure. By arranging his material as he does, the writer attempts to comment either directly or implicitly, and he accomplishes his purpose in the paragraph only when the reader understands the purpose.

THE EXPANDING OF PARAGRAPHS: VARIETIES OF IDEA SUPPORT AND AMPLIFICATION

Succinctness and brevity can be vices or virtues. Readers cannot know the writer's mind. If a writer leaves too much to the reader's imagination, he fails to communicate. A noted linguist, Frances Christensen, has pointed out that offering the needed expansion marks the difference between self-expression and communication. Too few words can be too costly. In general, the beginning writer needs to add *more* proof, more evidence, more details than he thinks necessary. In order to avoid all suspicion of superficiality, the writer needs to assume that his reader is intensely interested and highly critical. Any assertion, any observation, any judgment must be supported if the writer is to be believed. Remembering that the paragraph is an outlined block to be filled in, a writer works usually in terms of four to six sentences that support the topic idea.

Beginning writers frequently are accused of too-sketchy paragraphs. The professor often must write "clarify," "develop," or "expand" in the margins of papers. Obviously, adding more details, more examples, more illustrations is one way of expanding. In addition to the more obvious methods of support and developing paragraphs, writers frequently choose to include these kinds of support:

- Examples
- Statistics, tables, graphs, enumerations
- Interviews
- Anecdotes
- Diagrams, pen-and-ink illustrations
- Quotations from authorities
- Allusions
- Citations of text (literary papers)

Admittedly, such kinds of support may require investigation of some sort—searching the library, taking surveys, polling friends. Buttressing contentions with a variety of kinds of proof is invaluable in strengthening assertions. And variety enlivens a paper.

Think, for instance, of the ways in which any of the previous examples of paragraphs could be expanded.

Paragraph on Primitivism. Expand by quoting from Rousseau; use Hemingway's heroes as an example; interview persons who believe in primitivism; include an anecdote about a hippie commune; allude to Wordsworth or to Romanticism in general.

Paragraph on Frontiersmen. Expand by quoting from early American writers, such as Thoreau, Wecter, or later historians, like Turner or Morison; allude to novels like *The Big Sky*; refer to television's Daniel Boone, or to Lewis and Clark; add examples of their activities before and after pushing West.

Paragraph on Miss America and Playgirl. Expand by polling friends' attitudes, men and women; quote from *Playboy* or the *Miss America* song; research psychologists' opinions, theologians' opinions, sociologists' opinions; quote from former Miss Americas and Playgirls; analyze the exploitative aspects of the two images.

Paragraph on the Slum Child. Expand by researching educators' opinions; cite statistics on failure; give examples of the kinds of language a slum child hears; include examples of kinds of things a child sees but does not know in kindergarten or first grade; include an anecdote; cite authorities' opinions about poverty or race problems.

Naturally, these are not the only ways of expanding—no doubt you can think of other, and perhaps better, ways. For instance, how could the paragraph on the migrant camp be expanded?

Most often, writers do not only rely on one method of expansion. The order differs, the proof differs, the amount and kinds of evidence differ, as the purposes differ. Each writer essentially writes alone; his thinking must be better than anyone else's for his purpose.

COHERENCE: BETWEEN
AND WITHIN PARAGRAPHS

Reading paragraphs and essays without coherence is like listening to a string of firecrackers; one never quite knows when another will go off. The ideas seem disconnected, illogical, jumpy. Coherence is the epoxy that glues the parts together, relating one sentence to another, one paragraph to all the others. A paragraph can be unified; that is, it can carefully stick to one point, but without coherency it may still sound disjointed, unrelated.

This student paragraph resembles a string of firecrackers:

> The Sun Also Rises by Hemingway depicts two members of a lost generation. Some of them had experienced World War I. Jake had suffered an emasculating wound. It suggests a cutting off from the past. Brett was a woman. She lacked traditional values. The nineteenth century believed in marriage and fidelity. They, and others, gathered in Pamplona to indulge their cynical hedonistic desires.

The sentences seem oddly put together, jerky and bumpy. Here is the same paragraph, rewritten to attempt coherency:

> The Sun Also Rises by Hemingway depicts two members of a lost generation, a generation who had experienced World War I. Jake, one of the group, had suffered an emasculating wound during the war, suggesting a cutting off from the past. Brett, the most important woman in the group, rejected the nineteenth century values of marriage and fidelity, choosing a less confining way of life. Jake and Brett, along with others, met in Pamplona to indulge their cynical hedonistic desires.

In this version, a variety of means allows the reader to move easily from one thought to the next. The writer joins the first two sentences by repeating "a generation"; he adds "one of the group" to identify Jake and links two sentences by using a comma and "suggesting." The next three sentences he joins smoothly into one by adding "the most important woman" and compressing the other two by writing "values of" and "choosing." Finally, the writer repeats the names "Jake and Brett" to link the earlier part of the paragraph with the last

If you will return to the sample paragraphs on pages 57–64, you will notice a number of these transitions. Try to evaluate their effectiveness; perhaps some of them seem obtrusive, others necessary. Some writers are rather heavy-handed in their use of transitions; others prefer to let the sentence construction and thought carry the momentum. The right way for each writer is his own way, obviously. But try transitions heavily at first; they do help to straighten out the thinking processes, and you can then see if the parts really do fit as a whole and whether or not the sentences and paragraphs really do cohere.

Repetition and parallelism are not only stylistically effective; repeating and paralleling words and phrases also move the thought smoothly from one part to another. Here is a sample from "Letter to My Nephew" by James Baldwin:

> Let him laugh and I see a cellar your father does not remember and a house he does not remember and I hear in his present laughter his laughter as a child. Let him curse and I remember him falling down the cellar steps, and howling, and I remember, with pain, his tears, which my hand or your grandmother's so easily wiped away. But no one's hand can wipe away those tears he sheds invisibly today, which one hears in his laughter and in his speech and in his songs. . . .

Baldwin is not rigid about his parallelism; the paralleled words and phrases are not always in the same place in each sentence, but the total effect is cumulative, rich to the ear and the mind. Note the "Let him" repetitions, linked with "and I" phrases. And he links "hand" with "grandmother's" and "no one's" though the first use is literal and the last metaphorical. Note, too, how neatly "in his laughter and in his speech and in his songs" refers us again to the opening sentences. These are signs of a master stylist!

Thematic links are the least obvious but the most precise signals of coherence, since linking by theme and idea demands close relationship of meaning. Instances, examples, extensions, and elaborations of an idea can be implied when the idea is all-pervasive and the writer is exercising strict control. The following is a paragraph from *Crisis in Black and White,* by Charles E. Silberman, who does not depend upon obvious transitions but rather links the sentences by their tight relationship to the topic:

> The most striking aspect of the concentration camp inmates' behavior, Elkins writes after surveying the extensive literature on the subject, "was its *childlike* quality." Many inmates—among them mature, independent, highly educated adults—were transformed into fawning, servile, dependent children. Infantile behavior took a variety of forms: "The inmates' sexual impotence brought about a disappearance of sexuality in their talk; instead, excretory functions occupied them endlessly. They lost many of the customary inhibitions as to soiling their beds and their persons. Their humor was shot with silliness and they giggled like children when one of them would expel wind." Dishonesty was endemic; prisoners became chronic and pathological liars; like adolescents, they would fight each other bitterly one moment and become close friends in the next; "dishonesty, mendacity, egotistic actions, . . . theft" were commonplace. This childlike behavior, moreover, was

It is not that Los Angeles is altogether hideous, it is even by degrees pleasant, but for an Easterner there is never any salt in the wind; it is like Mexican cooking without chili, or Chinese egg rolls missing their mustard; as one travels through the sullen repetitions of that city which is the capital of suburbia with its milky pinks, its washed out oranges, its tainted lime-yellows of pastel on one pretty little architectural monstrosity after another, the colors not intense enough, the styles never pure, and never sufficiently impure to collide on the eye, one conceives the people who live here—they have come out to express themselves, Los Angeles is the home of self-expression, but the artists are middle-class and middling-minded; no passions will calcify here for years in the gloom to be revealed a decade later as the tessellations of a hard and fertile work, no, it is all open, promiscuous, borrowed, half bought, a city without iron, eschewing wood, a kingdom of stucco, the playground for mass men—one has the feeling it was built by television sets giving orders to men. . . . (Norman Mailer, *The Presidential Papers*)

There is only one episode in the early years of which I have a direct memory. You may remember it, too. Once in the night I kept on whimpering for water, not, I am certain, because I was thirsty, but probably partly to be annoying, partly to amuse myself. After several vigorous threats had failed to have any effect, you took me out of bed, carried me out onto the pavlatche balcony and left me there alone for a while in my nightshirt, outside the shut door. I am not going to say that this was wrong—perhaps at that time there was really no other way of getting peace and quiet that night—but I mention it as typical of your methods of bringing up a child and their effect on me. I dare say I was quite obedient afterwards at that period, but it did me inner harm. What was for me a matter of course, that senseless asking for water, and the extra-ordinary terror of being carried outside were two things that I, my nature being what it was, could never properly connect with each other. Even years afterwards I suffered from the tormenting fancy that the huge man, my father, the ultimate authority, would come almost for no reason at all and take me out of bed in the night and carry me out onto the pavlatche and that therefore I was such a mere nothing for him. (Franz Kafka, "Letter to His Father")

Man is nothing else but what he makes of himself. Such is the first principle of existentialism. It is also what is called subjectivity, the name we are labeled with when charges are brought against us. But what do we mean by this, if not that man first exists, that is, that man first of all is the being who hurls himself toward a future and who is conscious of imagining himself as being in the future. Man is at the start a plan which is aware of itself, rather than a patch of moss, a piece of garbage, or a cauliflower; nothing exists prior to this plan; there is nothing in heaven; man will be what he will have planned to be. Not what he will want to be. Because of the word "will" we generally mean a conscious decision, which is subsequent to what we have already made of ourselves. I may want to belong to a political party, write a book, get married;

_____

_____

_____

but all that is only a manifestation of an earlier, more spontaneous choice that is called "will." But if existence really does precede essence, man is responsible for what he is. Thus, existentialism's first move is to make every man aware of what he is and to make the full responsibility of his existence rest on him. And when we say that a man is responsible for himself, we do not only mean that he is responsible for his own individuality, but that he is responsible for all men. (Jean-Paul Sartre, "Existentialism")

sentence
strategies

In Chapter IV, we noted that the basic skill in writing is the composing of paragraphs and sentences and that the sentences are to the paragraphs what the paragraphs are to the entire essay. Sentences are extremely elastic. They can be stretched and elongated; combined with other sentences; compacted and compressed. Because they are so elastic, they offer great possibilities for creative fiddling. But maturely thought-out sentences will not simply be fiddled with for fun, although that is part of their pleasure. They will convey facts and ideas clearly, precisely, but interestingly. James Michener, author of *Hawaii* and *The Source*, once wrote, "The American who can write a competent sentence is rare." He means that since the range of sentence patterns is quite large, choosing the most effective pattern requires stylistic skill and awareness. The choice is not always dependent upon subject matter; many times, you will construct your sentences by evaluating your need for emphasis or variety.

Loose and Periodic Sentences

The basic English sentence imitates the "Ned drank vodka" pattern, the simple subject—verb—object arrangement. This arrangement reveals the normal action, subject to verb to object: Ned drank vodka. An alternate possibility reserves some part of the basic pattern until the end, delaying for emphasis:

Ned, who was really too frail to take on the overpowering liquor, drank vodka.

The normal order is generally called *loose*. Most conversational and written sentences are loose, expressing the main idea first, then adding details and modifiers as it moves along. The delayed order we call *periodic*, reserving the main idea until the end. These are loose sentences:

Roses bloom in a profusion of colors.

The fish swim, darting among the shadows of the rocks in the riptide pools.

Now consider the effect of the same sentences when they are restructured into periodic order:

In a profusion of colors, some riotous, some subdued, roses bloom.

Darting among the shadows of the rocks in the riptide pools swim the fish.

Periodic sentences heighten interest since the subject or subject and verb climax the sentence rather than introduce, delaying the completion of the thought. Most loose sentences, no matter what type, can easily be converted into periodic structure by simply rearranging the sentence parts. The value of periodic sentences lies in the emphasis or suspense they create.

SENTENCE TYPES

Sentences are classified by the kind and number of clauses they contain, a clause consisting of a subject and predicate. All sentence types are essentially variations on the basic "Ned drank vodka" pattern, some varying by enlarging, some by combining, some by abbreviating. Here are five sentence types:

simple
abbreviated
compound
complex
compound-complex

The Simple Sentence

The complete simple sentence is the kernel of all sentences, notwithstanding length and complexity. It is grammatically complete, consisting of subject, verb, and usually an object or complement:

Plants bloom.

Fish swim.

Good teachers motivate students.

The writer can, by altering the order, shift the intention of the sentence:

Bloom, plant. (imperative)

Do fish swim? (interrogative)

How well he motivates! (exclamatory)

The basic sentence pattern can be expanded into longer simple sentences by adding phrases, or into compound or complex sentences (see the sections following on those types). Or the basic pattern can be abbreviated by omitting parts (see the section that follows, "The Abbreviated Sentence").

Here are a few examples:

Roses bloom in a profusion of colors, some riotous, some subdued. (expanded by adding phrases)

Fish swim easily, darting among the shadows of the rocks in the riptide pools. (expanded by adding phrases)

Motivate? Him? (abbreviated by omitting parts)

Thus, the simple sentence can perform precisely as the writer intends it should, from short and emphatic to long and labyrinthian. The short simple sentence is best used to emphasize an important fact:

Men with business interests clearly believed that the Secretary of the Interior would capitulate under pressure, thus relieving them of the necessity of installing antipollution measures. The Secretary refused.

He teed the ball carefully, adjusted his stance, and began his backswing while concentrating on that white sphere. But he missed.

Brevity, as the final sentences illustrate, delivers impact.

The Abbreviated Sentence

Sometimes writers abbreviate the basic sentence pattern, compressing meaning by relying upon the context, but without employing the standard subject-verb-object pattern. Such fragments are frequent in conversation: "Good work!" "Now—about the rest of it." "So much for that." In writing, too, the incomplete sentence can simplify or emphasize, especially in these situations:

- *for emphasis*:

  Waves. The sound of them reverberated off the cliffs and rocks, inundating us with rhythmic echoes.

- *in dialogue*:

  "Did you find the passageway?"

  "Yes. But not quickly."

- *for transitions*:

  Thus, the masculinity crisis. But the femininity image needs yet to be defined.

Since most readers expect writing to be carefully complete, you will use incomplete sentences only rarely and judiciously. An intentional and effective one adds snap and sparkle; an unintentional and ineffective one reveals only indifference or, worse, ignorance.

The Compound Sentence

The compound sentence basically unites two simple sentences, or two main, independent clauses. It essentially joins two (or more) simple sentences of equal importance by a semicolon alone or by a conjunction with a semicolon or comma. Stylistically, the compound sentence is rhythmic and smooth, swiftly merging ideas that are closely allied or contrasted, as in these instances:

Zero Population Growth is a movement attempting to stem the population explosion; it encourages limiting family size to two children.

Zero Population Growth is a movement attempting to stem the population explosion; it opposes the old frontier value of large families.

In these instances, a semicolon joins the simple sentences, or clauses, but a compound sentence can also be held together by such *coordinating conjunctions* as *and, but, or, nor, for, yet*:

Universities do not intend to impose duties, but they do intend to offer choices.

The Irish immigrants exhibited strong ethnic chauvinism, and they scorned "wops," "hebes," and "niggers."

Notice that a comma precedes the conjunctions *and* and *but*. A third way of linking parts of a compound sentence is to use a semicolon and a *longer conjunction*, such as *therefore, nevertheless, however,* and *consequently*:

Astrology is immensely popular in Hollywood; consequently, some actors refuse to sign contracts except under favorable stellar conditions.

Andrew Wyeth's paintings are priced beyond the reach of most Americans; however, good reprints are available at nominal cost.

Conjunctions in compound sentences indicate that the basic ideas are equal in importance.

The Complex Sentence

The complex sentence, combining one main clause or simple sentence with one or more dependent or subordinate clauses, stresses one main idea but buttresses that main idea with less important details. In the two simple sentences,

In preparation for childbirth, a woman must learn to relax. She must also learn to control her breathing.

or in the compound sentence,

In preparation for childbirth, a woman must learn to control her breathing; she must also learn to relax.

the two thoughts are of equal weight. But in a complex sentence, either one or the other thought can be emphasized:

When a woman learns to relax in preparation for childbirth, she can control her breathing.

While the main idea is illuminated by its central position in the main clause, the lesser ideas are related by choosing the most exact subordinator. Some express time relationship (*when, while, before, after, until, since, as soon as*), some contrast (*although, whereas, though*), some cause and effect (*because, inasmuch as, since*), some manner or method (*as if, as though*), and some condition (*if, unless*). Some subordinators work as adjectives rather than as adverbs, as *who, whom, which, that.*

The long distance runner who does not train daily fails to develop adequate stamina.

The book that he had assigned was missing.

What I want to know is why must we be plagued with busywork?

A word of caution, however: too many *that*'s, *which*'s, and *whose*'s tend to be wordy, tedious, or overly formal. Most good stylists eliminate as many such subordinators as they can without losing precision and clarity.

The long distance runner, in neglecting to train daily, fails to develop adequate stamina.

I want to know why we must be plagued with busywork.

The Compound-Complex Sentence

Since the English sentence is highly elastic, the types can be combined and lengthened into sentences reflective of sophisticated maturity. The combination

sentence, or compound-complex sentence, artfully joins two or more independent clauses and one or more dependent clauses. As simple sentences,

> I bloom at a party. I feel responsible for its success. Good conversation
> stimulates more than drugs.

the ideas seem prosaic, unleavened. As a compound sentence,

> I bloom at a party; I feel responsible for its success; good conversation stimu-
> lates more than drugs.

the ideas are still undifferentiated. Try them in a compound-complex structure:

> I feel responsible for a party's success; I bloom then, because good
> conversation stimulates more than drugs.

Such a structure allows for both variety and emphasis, while stressing more
precisely the relationship the writer intends.

Mastering the names of the five rhetorical forms of sentences is obviously not
as important as remembering the strategy. The principal thing to note is that
using all forms gives you more control over style than depending on only one or
two of them.

STYLISTIC CONSIDERATIONS: FOCUS, VARIETY, CONCENTRATION, PARALLELISM

Given the sentence's plasticity and flexibility, you can achieve any effect you
want. In deliberately working toward stylistic precision and artistry, you become
increasingly aware of what you want to say. In other words, exploration and
discovery of meaning occur when you play with your sentences, juggling the
pieces and creating different shapes. Each sentence configuration contains its
own nuance, its own implications. Trying out three or four versions allows you
to discover your intentions.

Sentence Structure: Focus

Obviously, you will want to focus your reader's interest on the thought you
consider most important. Since sentences are like building blocks, you can
arrange the blocks, or ideas, to stress them as you wish.

> Jed neglected his daily assignments for several weeks.

If that's all you want to say, the sentence is clearly focused. Nothing detracts
from it. But perhaps you want to include other information:

> Jed's neglecting his daily assignments appalled his parents.

> Jed's parents were appalled at his neglecting his daily assignments.

In these two examples, Jed's neglect has had an effect upon his parents, and the
two ideas are joined. Now suppose you want to coordinate the neglect with
other information equally important:

Jed neglected his daily assignments for several weeks, and his instructor informed him that he might not pass the course.

Neither Jed's neglect of his daily assignments nor his instructor's informing him that he might not pass worried him.

Or you could subordinate Jed's neglect:

Despite Jed's neglect of his daily assignments, he seemed to be a serious student.

While Jed was neglecting his daily assignments, his fraternity brothers were striving for scholastic honors.

Rearranging the ideas, then, gives the writer an opportunity to discover exactly which idea he wants to focus on, which thought he deems important. Furthermore, regulating focus allows the writer to control sentence length.

Sentence Structure: Variety

The power of sentence structure focus allows the writer to regulate sentence length and order. Such control influences variations in syntax (sentence structure).

The ideal of civil equality is still an ideal in our country. Not everyone can vote; not everyone has an equal chance for justice in the courts. Everyone is not educated equally. And certainly not everyone has the same social opportunities.

In this passage, the sentences are nearly all of equal length and essentially all are constructed in the same basic subject-verb pattern. Try for some short, punchy sentences interspersed with long and flowing ones:

In our country, the ideal of civil equality is still only that: an ideal. Justice is not meted out equally. Quality education is reserved for those living in certain residential areas and for those in the upper income brackets. Not everyone can vote. That everyone has the same social opportunities is only a pretense.

Or perhaps you want to focus the attention of the reader upon the similarities:

In our country, the ideal of civil equality is still only that–an ideal. Not everyone can vote; not everyone receives justice in the courts; not everyone is educated equally; not everyone has the same social opportunities.

Here the identical syntactical structure achieves an enlarged focus by its very parallelism. And one sentence is moderately short while the other is long and rhythmical. You will want to try out the periodic sentence, too (see the section "Loose and Periodic Sentences") to vary structure and focus.

Sentence Structure: Concentration

Concentration or economy in syntax is one of the more difficult skills for a beginning writer, probably because in speaking we tend to draw out our sentences in a loose and rambling fashion. And we tend to think that the longer our sentences the more impressive they are. But wastefully long and involved structures dissipate readers' interest and energy, in addition to diluting the content of our thoughts. Here is an example:

> The reason for such wasteful overexpenditures in the defense budget is the lack of careful monitoring of bids and projected costs by the major contractors.

This is a sprawling sentence, spewing its main information in phrases rather than packing it into the main clause. As it is, the main clause says:

> The reason . . . is the lack. . . .

Not very meaty, is it? Had the writer moved the main information to the main clause position, he would have garnered his reader's attention to the major idea in this way:

> The defense contractors' failure to monitor their projected costs caused the Pentagon's wasteful budget overexpenditures.

If a writer allows his main ideas to drop to lower positions in his sentences—from verbs to nouns, from main clause nouns to phrases, from precise modifiers to phrases—his sentences weaken and blur. Wordy and inconsequential openers, like these, are also weak:

> "Now, let me make one thing clear . . . "
> "It seems to this writer . . . "
> "In my opinion . . . "
> "The point I want to make is . . . "
> "The thing that has always seemed obvious is that . . . "

When we revise, we can strike out these deadwood clauses and phrases in order to concentrate the meaning, distilling the essence of our intent. Remember the rule: main ideas belong in the main clause, that is, in the subject-verb-complement position.

Sentence Structure: Parallelism

Symmetry is a way of ordering one's sentences so as to emphasize meaning, show relationships, and demonstrate clarity. It is best achieved by using parallel structure, that is, by repeating or contrasting grammatical elements in a coordinate series:

Nouns: It's a new world of hope,
                                   joy,
                                   love. . . .

Verbs: I disapproved,
                      deplored,
                      derided his faulty logic.

Phrases: He offered to listen to their complaints,
                to redress their grievances,
                to repeal the unjust laws.

Clauses: I came,
              I saw,
              I conquered.

Parallelism develops a rising order in ideas, or groups ideas, or lists items in a series. Furthermore, it is rhythmic, symmetrical, and self-perpetuating; once a rhythm is begun, a writer finds it easy to continue in its use. Parallelism can also contrast, pointing up dissimilarities:

> This tiny war is not the old, hard, personal fight for the means of life; this is a war of foolish self-deluded men.

> The nationalistic states are not physical groups; they are social symbols, chauvinistic and proud.

And parallelism can result in concentrated, terse statements:

> "See no evil, hear no evil, do no evil."

> " . . . of the people, by the people, and for the people."

> "Marriage is popular because it combines the maximum of temptation with the maximum of opportunity." (G. B. Shaw)

Consider this passage from John F. Kennedy's speech "We All Breathe the Same Air":

> What kind of peace do I mean? What kind of peace do we seek? Not a *Pax Americana* enforced on the world by American weapons of war. Not the peace of the grave or the security of the slave. I am talking about genuine peace, the kind of peace that makes life on earth worth living, the kind that enables men and nations to grow and to hope and to build a better life for their children—not merely peace for Americans, but peace for all men and women—not merely peace in our time, but peace for all time.

Parallelism at its best is the most striking of sentence structures; it allows for flashes of insight, for dazzling displays of word arrangements, for bursts of power in ideas. (See also the section "Sounds and Rhythms," in Chapter VII, for additional discussion on parallelism.) But the real aim here is to increase your number of options—to offer innumerable choices so as to convey the most precise nuance of meaning you intend. The best writers, of course, are those who exercise their options carefully, working and reworking sentence after sentence in a paragraph until they accomplish focus, variety, concentration, and parallelism.

LEARNING AIDS

Focus:

1. Take a single bit of information—"The President rejected the education

bill"—and place it in a number of different places in a series of sentences. Try to develop sentence flexibility.

Variety:
2. Revise the paragraph below for greater variety in pattern and length:

> Billy the Kid had many pleasant human qualities. He was bright, alert, quick to sympathize, loyal, and honest. Moreover, he was cheerful, hopeful, unassuming, and courteous. Most women considered him not only handsome but also gentlemanly. But he lacked one major characteristic: he placed no value on human life. He valued no man's, not even his own. He killed whenever and whoever and however he felt like it. Remorse was alien to him.

Concentration:
3. Revise the following sentences so that the important idea is in the main clause position, eliminating deadwood.
   a. There are two requirements which are necessary for success in politics, one of which is the ability to hedge and dodge astute questions, and the other one is the charisma which makes it appear that the candidate is genuinely interested in the questioner.
   b. One thing which makes a student impress his teacher is the avowal by the student that he really works hard.
   c. Improvement of the media's image can be gained by a sincere attempt to report all sides to an issue which is currently in the news.
   d. It seems to me that filmmakers who are attempting to play on the viewer's secret desires for pornographic-like scenes are perhaps guilty of a conduct which could be termed somewhat immoral.

Parallelism:
4. Rework each of the following into several versions, paralleling the structure by using nouns, verbs, phrases, and clauses:
   a. He defeated his opponent by trickery. The party he won by blandishments. His superiors he ignored.
   b. Ralph Nader objects to manufacturing ethics. He also objects to incomplete information in advertising as well as his objections to public indifference and ignorance.
   c. He is a great passer and receiver. He also carries the ball well. But his greatest talent is in calling the plays.

Everyone has problems with writing sentences that are clear and unambiguous, that are punctuated properly and effectively, that are grammatically standard. With a little study and some careful rewriting, however, most writers can avoid glaring problems.

BASIC SENTENCE FAULTS

Sentence Fragments

The most common type of sentence fragment is the detached clause or phrase that should be attached to the sentence preceding it. Some sentence fragments are successful, such as those that answer questions, those that serve as transitions, or those that serve as stylistic variations for emphasis. But usually the fragment appears incomplete and unsuccessful in a beginning writer's work, such as these two examples:

Frag   1.   Washington decided not to attack. Because the British were too well prepared.

Frag   2.   *The Return of the Native* is one of Hardy's most widely admired novels. Not just a tale of illogical coincidences.

The first fragment may be corrected by attaching the detached clause to the main sentence in one of two ways:

Washington decided not to attack, because the British were too well prepared.

Or:

Washington decided not to attack—because the British were too well prepared.

Notice the effect the dash allows. In the second revision, the clause about the British is prominent, while the first revision with a comma does not stress the cause and effect as strongly. To revise the second fragment about Hardy's novel, you might wish to attach the separated phrase to the main sentence, or you might create two sentences in order to offer additional information:

The Return of the Native is one of Hardy's most widely admired novels, not just a tale of illogical coincidences.

Or:

The Return of the Native is one of Hardy's most widely admired novels. Readers realize that it is not just a tale of illogical coincidences.

Another type of sentence fragment is a jumble of words that does not make a sentence and cannot be attached to the preceding sentence. Here are some examples:

1.   A kind of movie I like, though not too often, whether in color or black and white being a western.

2.   Psychology, an interesting subject, not too tedious or hard when one studies it.

These jumbles can be revised into the following complete sentences:

The kind of movie I like is a western, either in color or in black and white.
Psychology, an interesting subject, is not too tedious or hard when one studies it.

Too often, heedless writers create sentence fragments because they mistakenly use *participles*, such as "developing," "expressing," "turning," and "being," in place of verbs. This confusion occurs because participles resemble verbs. Analyze these examples:

1. The novice photographer developing his own film rapidly.
2. The foreign dignitaries expressing their unusual opinions to a startled audience.
3. The investigator turning the tiny dial of the recovered safe.
4. Lions being major attractions at the zoo.

To correct this type of incomplete sentence, the writer has two easy choices. First, he may select some form of the verb "to be" to precede the participle. The alert writer can alter the first two fragments this way:

The novice photographer was developing his own film rapidly.
The foreign dignitaries were expressing their unusual opinions to a startled audience.

Second, the writer could change the participle into a verb; the third and fourth examples then appear this way:

The investigator turned the tiny dial of the recovered safe.
Lions are major attractions at the zoo.

Comma Splice, or Comma Fault

In another type of basic sentence fault, two independent clauses or two sentences that are distinctly separate are joined with only a comma, causing a comma splice, or comma fault. Consider these examples:

CS 1. Formal education is not necessary for high intellectual achievement, Faulkner did not even finish high school.

or 2. The war provided the setting for many novels, three of Remarque's were especially outstanding.

CF 3. The 1883 red-brick church where Antonia was married had changed gradually into a private residence, members of the Willa Cather Pioneer Memorial recently resolved the problem through a restoration project.

To correct a comma splice, change the comma to a semicolon or add a coordinating conjunction (*and, but, for, or, nor*):

Formal education is not necessary for high intellectual achievement; Faulkner, for instance, did not finish high school.
The war provided the setting for many novels, and three of Remarque's were especially outstanding.

The 1883 red-brick church where Ántonia was married eventually became a private residence, but members of the Willa Cather Pioneer Memorial recently restored the original structure.

Fused or Run-on Sentences

Sometimes two sentences are run together with no separating punctuation at all; such sentences are called fused or run-on. Inspect these examples:

FS   1.   Two volumes of this work are now completed the first will be published next year.

or   2.   In ancient times people believed that the full of the moon was the time for planting people now believe that the full of the moon is the time for courting.

RO   3.   Young people become more concerned daily about air pollution water pollution is another concern they wonder how to alleviate these life stranglers.

The writer can revise fused sentences in three ways: (1) he can separate the clauses with either a period or a semicolon; (2) he can subordinate one of the parts; or (3) he can divide the clauses with a comma and coordinating conjunction.

Two volumes of this work are now completed; the first will be published next year.

Although in ancient times people believed that the full of the moon was the time for planting, people now believe that the full of the moon is the time for courting.

Young people become more concerned daily about air and water pollution, and they wonder how to alleviate these life stranglers.

LEARNING AIDS

Revise these sentence fragments into clear, complete sentences:

1. Bees with red, chartreuse, and ivory-colored eyes have been developed. Suggesting that they are prettier than ordinary brown-eyed bees.
2. From the study of patterns of inheritance setting up genetic rules which aid the breeding of gentler bees that produce more honey.
3. Although honey bees are generally industrious compared to human beings.
4. Brazil having replaced the United States as the world's major melting pot.
5. More than twenty nationalities are merging to form the new Brazilian. Prospering because of high coffee prices.

Correct the following sentences containing comma faults, or comma splices:

1. Desert locusts are a plague upon the continents of Africa and Asia, they are called "teeth of the wind" by the natives.

2. Adult locusts eat daily the equivalent of their weight, they are also capable of living four days without feeding.

3. The British government maintains an Anti-Locust Centre, it operates a plague "alert room" in London for the countries about to be invaded by the hungry hordes.

4. The female desert locust usually lays about 200 eggs, it lives about four months.

5. The ordinary green grasshopper in the bush is capable of becoming the desert locust simply by changing colors and behavior, it is probably the creature that caused the Biblical plagues.

Correct these fused or run-on sentences:

1. Conservation-minded gardeners should choose the least toxic insecticide available they should buy the smallest quantity necessary.

2. D. H. Lawrence once characterized the American male as "harsh, isolate, stoic, and a killer" John Wayne likes to portray that kind of character.

3. Wayne became the essential Western hero he is tough to men but kind to women.

4. Wayne's motto in films is don't go looking for trouble if you get in a fight win it.

5. The public loves the John Wayne westerns as morality plays good vanquishes darkest evil and ambles into a gaudy-hued sunset.

Sample Correct Responses to Learning Aids

Sample corrections for grammatical and structural errors in the faulty sentences follow:

Revision of fragments into clear, complete sentences:

1. Geneticists have developed bees with red, chartreuse, and ivory-colored eyes, and this development suggests that such bees are prettier than ordinary brown-eyed bees.

2. From the study of patterns of inheritance, researchers are able to set up genetic rules which aid the breeding of gentler bees that produce more honey.

3. Although honey bees are generally industrious compared to human beings, they concentrate on only one particular task.

4. Brazil has replaced the United States as the world's major melting pot.

5. More than twenty nationalities are merging to form the new Brazilian who is prospering because of high coffee prices.

Revision of comma faults, or comma splices:

1. Desert locusts—natives call them "teeth of the wind"—are a plague upon the continents of Africa and Asia.

2. Adult locusts eat daily the equivalent of their weight, but they are also capable of living four days without feeding.

3. The British government maintains an Anti-Locust Centre where it operates a plague "alert room" in London for the countries about to be invaded by the hungry hordes.
4. The female desert locust, living about four months, usually lays about 200 eggs.
5. The ordinary green grasshopper in the bush is capable of becoming the desert locust simply by changing color and behavior; it is probably the creature that caused the Biblical plagues.

Revision of fused or run-on sentences:

1. Conservation-minded gardeners should choose the least toxic insecticide available and buy the smallest quantity necessary.
2. D. H. Lawrence once characterized the American male as "harsh, isolate, stoic, and a killer"; John Wayne likes to portray that kind of character.
3. Because he is tough to men but kind to women, Wayne became the essential Western hero.
4. Wayne's motto in film is, "Don't go looking for trouble. If you get in a fight, win it."
5. The public loves the John Wayne westerns as morality plays, for good vanquishes darkest evil and ambles into a gaudy-hued sunset.

COMMON SENTENCE CONSTRUCTION PROBLEMS

A good writer does not merely write sentences; he grips and welds his sentence patterns with controlled purpose. Wrestling with the elements of sentences—combining, subordinating, varying the patterns—increases their effectiveness. Watch out for the obvious traps of ineffective sentence happenings.

"There is" and "There are" Constructions

Sentences beginning with "There is" and "There are" are unemphatic and wordy:

Wdy   There are many people who believe that existentialism is a simply defined term.
  Revision: Many people believe that existentialism is a simply defined term.
  There are many symbols in Frost's poetry.
  Revision: Frost's poetry contains many symbols.

Weak Use of Passive Voice

Verbs are *active* when the subject initiates or performs the action; verbs are *passive* when the subject receives the action. The trouble is that the passive verb avoids placing responsibility, and further, most sentences using the passive verb are dull.

Pass Procedural innovations to simplify registration are being taken under consideration by the registrar. (Wordy, dull, passive.)

    Revision: The registrar is considering innovations to simplify registration procedures.

    One student was said to be a natural leader. (Who said?)

    Revision: The athletic director said that one student was a natural leader.

Pass The personality differences of identical twins can be accounted for by varying environmental circumstances.

    Revision: Varying environmental circumstances account for personality differences of identical twins.

Pass Imagination is seen as a superior quality in man's intellect. (Who sees?)

    Revision: Wordsworth and Coleridge see imagination as a superior quality in man's intellect.

Dangling and Misplaced Modifiers

Verbal modifiers should be clearly related to the words they modify. Sometimes modifiers relate to a word that is implied rather than stated, and are called *dangling modifiers*; sometimes modifiers occur in awkward positions, too far from the words they relate to, and are called *misplaced modifiers*.

Dang, In painting four of these pictures, his native wife was used as his model.
or (Can the wife be the painter?)
DM **Revision:** In painting four of these pictures, Gauguin used his native wife as his model.

Dang, By requiring a student to take science courses, the purpose of the class
or is not fully realized. (Who requires?)
DM **Revision:** By requiring a student to take science courses, the faculty who voted the requirement in do not allow the purpose of the class to be fully realized.

MM One early-day western senator distributed campaign cards to the voters pinned together with five-dollar bills. (Were the voters pinned together?)

    Revision: One early-day western senator distributed to the voters campaign cards pinned with five-dollar bills.

Short, Choppy Sentences

A whole string of simple sentences reduces your intentions to the level of the Dick-and-Jane readers; instead, try to subordinate or coordinate such a series, making them into a complex or compound sentence.

    Choppy: Mark Twain wrote *Huckleberry Finn*. It is about a ragamuffin boy. He lived on the Mississippi River. The book is important both as fiction and as a social history.

Revision: Mark Twain's *Huckleberry Finn*, important both as fiction and as social history, is about a ragamuffin boy living on the Mississippi River.

Choppy: Pamplona is best known for its *encierros*. It is a sport. It is also a rite. It begins at 7 A.M. on each day of the fiesta. Bulls and steers are released. They run to the *plaza de toros*. They are unguarded in the streets.

Revision: *Encierros*, best known in Pamplona, is a sport and a rite in which bulls and steers, released each day of the fiesta at 7 A.M., run unguarded through the streets to the *plaza de toros*.

Coordination to Subordination

Compound sentences can be as boring as this one:

I like ice cream, and John likes pie.

The complex sentence, one that subordinates one idea to another, stresses the relationship of one idea to another or emphasizes one, rather than merely linking or joining two equal ideas. The complex sentence is thus more appealing.

The movie is funny, and one remembers the underlying meaning.
Revision: Although the movie is funny, one remembers the underlying meaning.

If the ideas are in fact equal, and a writer wishes to stress their equality, he will choose the semicolon instead of the comma-*and* method:

I went to a movie recently, and it was worthless.
Revision: I went to a movie recently; it was worthless.

The revision is a stronger compound sentence because the semicolon creates a greater degree of separation between the two ideas than the comma.

Lack of Parallelism

Frequently, sentence structure can be improved by carefully paralleling nouns, phrases, or clauses. The sentence then contains rhythm as well as logical clarity. (See earlier discussion of parallelism on pages 80–81.)

//
Paral
My new job was perfect; I had no real work of any kind, nothing to be concerned about, and best of all not having to punch a time clock. (Three phrases should be parallel, but the last one, "having to punch," does not match the previous two.)

Revision: I had no real work of any kind, nothing to be concerned about, and no time clock to punch. ("No real work," "nothing," and "no time clock" are now parallel in noun form.)

Two different kinds of margarine are on the market: those having saturated fats, and with polyunsaturated fats. ("Those having" is not parallel to "with.")

Revision: Two different kinds of margarine are on the market: those with saturated fats and those with polyunsaturated fats.

In addition to series construction, the *not only . . . but also* construction needs careful paralleling:

We not only found a new home but also a new life. ("Not only found" is not parallel with "but also a new.")

Revision: We found not only a new home but also a new life.

Not only will there be new scientific developments but also economic and social changes. (Check the words following "not only" and "but also"; are they parallel?)

Revision: We will see not only new scientific developments but also economic and social changes.

LEARNING AIDS

Correct the following poorly constructed sentences and identify the kind of sentence problem:

1. Returning home from the trip, the home town remains the same but the friends keep changing.
2. At the age of eleven, my taste turned to detective stories.
3. My first interest in hawking, my first hawks, and to reveal all the difficulties take a long time to tell.
4. Not only did we rest for about thirty minutes but also snacked on raisins and dried beef.
5. There are cattle ranches and horse training farms in Montana.
6. There is open space around nearly every town, and the state is frequently referred to as "The Big Sky Country."
7. One goes to the Collegian Room to drink a coke, to chat with friends, or just for the pleasure of taking a break from studying.
8. A painting believed to be by Van Gogh was reported stolen by officials of Zane's art store yesterday.
9. Lincoln realized he was in a war and needing to direct a conflict not between conflicting armies but between societies.

Combine the following sentences to avoid short, choppy ones and to subordinate ideas.

1. Franklin Pierce was the fourteenth president. He was born in New Hampshire, and he was educated at Bowdoin College, Maine.
2. Theseus was the Duke of Athens. Hippolyta was to be his bride. Shakespeare wrote a play about these two figures.

3. Luther fled from Wittenberg. He knew that his life was in danger.
4. There are two cherished papers of the nation. They are the Declaration of Independence and the Constitution. They have been placed in the National Archives Building.
5. *Crime and Punishment* is about a young man who commits a murder. Then his conscience bothers him. A police inspector finally traps the young man. The police inspector is intelligent and psychologically astute.

common grammar and punctuation problems

PUNCTUATION: ESSENTIAL INFORMATION

Punctuation marks are more than mere mechanics; they reflect style by influencing meaning, tone, attitude, structure, creativity. Unfortunately, few persons become intensely excited about the mechanics of punctuation initially. Only when a writer begins to observe other writers' inventive uses of punctuation can he sense that punctuation is a meaningful part of rhetoric, as meaningful as one's word choice, one's sentence structure, one's choice of subject. Correct use of punctuation is, therefore, as essential as any of the other skills of writing.

Two Basic Marks: Period and Comma

The period and the comma can do everything that needs to be done in punctuating. The period is the terminal mark; it finishes a sentence or marks an abbreviation. The comma has two uses: (1) it separates and (2) it sets off or encloses. *Separating, enclosing, finishing—these are the three functions of all punctuation marks.* All other marks of punctuation are simply variations of the period and the comma—the other marks simply separate, enclose, or finish in a slightly different way.

The Finishers: Question Mark, Exclamation Mark, Period

The *question mark* signals the end of a question, or a statement expressing doubt:

> Who would believe that punctuation can be mechanically correct but still creative?

The *exclamation mark* emphasizes strong feeling—such as surprise, alarm, or forceful command—at the end of a sentence or sentence fragment:

> White lower-middle-class people are resentful of aid to other minority groups; they think, "We made it; let them!"
> Come here at once! Now!

The *period* finishes thoughts, either complete sentences or fragments intended as complete thoughts (where some part or parts are omitted but understood):

> Good grief. I thought he'd never finish.

Periods also mark abbreviations (Mr. and Mrs., Dr., Calif., N.Y.P.D., *ibid*.) and aid in typing outlines (A.B.C.). *Note: The period always belongs inside quotation marks*; the question mark and exclamation mark are placed either inside or outside the quotation marks, depending upon the situation.

The Separators: Comma, Semicolon, Colon, Dash*

Obviously, to make a sentence clear, writers need to separate some parts of a sentence from other parts. These are parts that need to be separated:

- Long introductory word groups
- Word groups that introduce quotations, lists, or explanatory material
- Words, phrases, or clauses in a series
- Complete sentences (independent clauses) from other clauses within the same sentence
- Afterthoughts, words or word groups, that are tacked on the end of a sentence

That mark of all seasons, the **comma** can function in any of these ways; that is, it can separate any part from any other part (exception: see Chapter V on the comma fault). The semicolon, colon, and dash are not quite so versatile, although each of them can substitute for the comma in some instances.

The **comma** *separates introductory words or word groups from the rest of the sentence:*

In Australia,[†] the imported hive-bee is rapidly replacing the native bee. Since the imported hive-bee is rapidly replacing the native bee, the local bees are dying off.
Having been replaced by the hive-bee, the native bee is in danger of extermination.

—separates word groups that introduce a quotation from the quotation itself:

She said, "None of the girls is rude or snobbish."
Brecht wrote, "Anyone who wishes to combat lies . . . must manipulate truth as a weapon."

—separates all words, phrases, or clauses in a series (a series consists of three or more elements):

Galileo observed, experimented, and reasoned carefully in order to understand physical phenomena.
Modern man experiences alienation from the community, disillusionment from its mores, and frustration from his attempts to change the system.
The Indians were corrupted by the example of the whites, they were abased by raw whiskey, and they were nearly exterminated by the military.

---

*Exceptions to principles set forth here on "the separators" occur in journalistic publications, but college writers are generally wise to follow these punctuation prescriptions. The purpose is to provide adequate signals in more complex academic writing and thus to effect ease of reading.

[†] Some punctuation authorities say that short introductory phrases indicating place and time need not be set off by commas at all. But we recommend setting off *all* introductory phrases in all but journalistic writing. Such use cannot be judged wrong, and it removes guesswork in comma placement for many while also effecting sentence clarity and reading ease.

—*separates independent clauses* (complete sentences) *joined by* "and," "but," "or," "nor," "for," "yet," *or* "still":

The odds were intimidating, yet he fought on.
Swift loved individual men, but he was appalled by the human race.
Drops of sweat stood out on his face, and his breathing was labored.

—*separates afterthoughts from the rest of the sentence:*

The war has caused much national self-examination, obviously.
Red China looms as the big Communist threat, ready to tip the precarious balance.
The tar remover dulled the finish, even though it was labeled safe for all finishes.

*The **semicolon** separates independent clauses joined without a conjunction or with connectives like* "however," "nevertheless," "moreover," "for example":

The Indians were to remain savages; neither their manners nor their ideas were modified by contact with the white civilization.
Custer was acclaimed a hero by the nation; however, reappraisal of his behavior in the massacre at Wounded Knee reveals him as a glory-hunting murderer.

—*separates groups of words in a series when those groups of words already contain commas:*

During his early years, he lived in Effingham, Illinois; Columbus, Georgia; and Houston, Texas.
His paintings are light, but not without intent; ironic, but not bitter; delightful, but not cloying.

*The **colon** separates an explanatory phrase or sentence from its explanation:*

The civil rights movement rests on one premise: that a minority group deserves equal treatment.
The Protestant ethic consists of one main tenet: work is a spiritual good.

—*separates a group of words that introduces a quotation:*

Marshall McLuhan observes: "The medium is the message."
The Shakespearean quote is apt: "The fault is not in our stars; it is in ourselves."

—*separates an introductory statement from a list:*

We believe in these virtues: truth, honor, courage, dignity.
Man invented new weapons and armor: the helmet, the sword, the buckler, and the javelin.

*The **dash**—two hyphens on your typewriter—separates any emphatic part, replacing the comma for this purpose:*

One of the newest weapons is one many abhor—napalm.
Coyotes are hardy creatures—but they look like mangy, scavenging curs.
Miss America may have replaced the Virgin Mary to the female imagination—but have stringy-haired coeds replaced the Sirens?

The hydrogen bomb possesses fantastic and horrifying power—power to annihilate millions of citizens.

The Enclosers: Commas, Dashes, Parentheses, Quotation Marks

Frequently, sentences are interrupted by words or groups of words that are not essential to the main intent of the sentence but that give additional information. Any element—a word, a phrase, or a clause—can be an interrupter, as in this sentence. *Commas, dashes, parentheses, and quotation marks are used in pairs to enclose such interrupters*, since the interruption in sentence continuity must be set off from the rest of the sentence.

Quotation marks *enclose the exact words of a source or a speaker.*

Vance Packard insists that "people's attitudes are more easily reached through their emotions than through their intellects."

—enclose titles of short poems, short stories, chapters of books, titles of articles, and paintings (all small works or parts of larger works): *

T. S. Eliot's poem "The Hollow Men" contains a reference to Guy Fawkes' day.
"Guernica" was Picasso's commemoration of the Spanish Loyalists' senseless bombing of that town.

Note: Periods and commas always belong inside quotation marks (except in England, where the practice is the reverse). This practice is an editorial standard, but the *other marks of punctuation appear inside or outside the quotation marks, depending upon whether the mark belongs with the original quotation or with the writer's use of the source.*

Single quotation marks *enclose quotations within quotations:*

The author wrote that "the haranguing orator repeated Patrick Henry's famous words, 'Give me liberty or give me death!' "

Commas, dashes, *and* **parentheses** *enclose interrupters by using a pair of commas, a pair of dashes, or parentheses, depending on the intended emphasis:*

The children, wet and hungry, straggled into the kitchen.
The children—wet and hungry—straggled into the kitchen.
The children (wet and hungry) straggled into the kitchen.

In general, parentheses should be reserved for asides or irrelevant information, dashes for emphatic interrupters, and commas in pairs for the majority of interrupters.

---

*Note that *large works (or things) or works that have parts*—books, multi-act plays, feature-length films, ships, TV shows, or long poems—*are underlined (italicized)* although newspapers and magazines sometimes play variations on this principle.

LEARNING AIDS

Punctuate the following paragraph correctly (in a variety of ways if you can). Note as you insert the marks whether the marks separate one part from another, or whether they enclose some kind of interrupter.

The object of the Black Humorists____the Living Theater____*Hair*____and Happenings____is predicated on the effort to breathe life into men who are incapable of true heroism____This is the age of the antihero____life's absurdity is too big for a single man to conquer____so he becomes the victim____like the boy in Bruce Friedman's *A Mother's Kisses* or the young man who is inducted into the military in *Hair*____This antihero is the outsider____the scapegoat____the clown____the rebel without a cause____ the criminal____the poor sod____the fool____the freak____the "hero on a leash____" We are____it seems at times____a race of Willy Lomans of Arthur Miller's *Death of a Salesman*____or so the artists see us____for we seem incapable of deep feeling____of great actions____great dreams____ great goals____The ideals of the past seem closer to us____and yet our artists and youth both____when not raging at the insensitivity and obtuseness of those of us middle Americans who fail to act as individuals____have at the center of their concern the ideals of the past as advanced by Emerson and Thoreau____

The Possession Indicator: Apostrophe

Few marks of punctuation stir less interest than the apostrophe. Many sign painters, menu printers, department store graphic artists, and uninitiated writers skip apostrophes or misplace them with the confidence of ignorance. Actually, Bre'r Rabbit could probably master all there is to know about placing apostrophes properly. Here is the essential tidbit:

To make a word possessive (that is, to show ownership), ask yourself who possesses. If the answer is a word that does not end in *s*, then add *'s*. If it does end in *s*, add only the apostrophe. (Occasionally, if the sound pleases you more, add *'s*, as in *James's toy, Jesus's words, the Peters's home*.)

Who possesses the ticket or tickets?

Boy. Boy's ticket.
Boys. Boys' tickets.
Brother. Brother's tickets.
Brothers. Brothers' tickets.
Marlys. Marlys' tickets. (Or, if it sounds better to you, Marlys's tickets.)

Who possesses the groceries?

Man. Man's groceries.
Men. Men's groceries.
No one. No one's groceries.

Special note for a very common error: *it's* means *it is*. Only *its* (without apostrophe) shows possession.

Cat's food.   Its food.

Contractions:

The apostrophe also indicates the omission of a letter or letters in contractions, the omission of a letter in one word, or, the omission of numbers, as in:

He hasn't succeeded in his third goal.
She doesn't buy non-returnable bottles.
Cruel people dubbed him a ne'er-do-well.
In '64, the Free Speech Movement was born.

Other Uses:

Finally, an apostrophe indicates the plural of letters, words, years, and signs, or symbols, as in:

M's and *O*'s are not mystic symbols.
His *or*'s and *if*'s saturate his conversation.
In formal writing, avoid %'s or ¢'s as symbols.
The 1950's spawned today's leaders of radical youth.

Two Aids in Direct Quotations: Ellipsis, Brackets

You must be exceedingly accurate when you quote someone else's words, and the ellipsis and brackets aid precision.

Ellipsis   Sometimes you will find a quotation that could illustrate your major point, but you consider the quotation too long. When this happens, simply use an ellipsis, three spaced periods (. . .), to indicate omitted words in the quotation, as in this example:

"The new high rise apartment building . . . will accommodate fifty fewer people than advertised in the original plans."

If the ellipsis falls at the end of a sentence, remember to add that sentence's period, too. You will then have *a period and three spaced dots* (the only time you have more than three). Consider this example:

"A core group of interested citizens organized a Ban-the-Can petition to demand the sale of only containers that are recycled be used for pop, juices, beer. . . ."

Brackets   At other times, you might select a quotation that, out of context, has a vague pronoun or a missing reference. In this case, enclose your explanation with penned-in brackets, as in these illustrations:

The newspaper stated, ". . . and at the meeting of nursery school leaders it [*Sesame Street*] was acclaimed an outstanding educational program for pre-schoolers."
"Many of Sinclair Lewis's short stories of that period [1917-1923] are difficult to obtain, since few appear in today's anthologies."

Then, if a misspelling or some inaccuracy occurs in the quotation and you wish to indicate that it is not yours and the quotation is precise, follow the inaccuracy with [sic], as in this example:

> The novice reporter wrote, "The pilots, expecting an icy runway, heard it was alright [sic] to land."

Instead of "alright," the reporter should have written "all right."

LEARNING AIDS

Add or correct apostrophes, ellipsis, or brackets in these sentences or passages:

1. Its a wise child that knows it's own beauty.
2. The students and facultys committees convened to formulate joint proposals on the reforming of dormitory regulations.
3. The bands' and swimming teams' uniforms cost nearly the same price, but the book clubs expenses were minimal by comparison.
4. A weeks feverish work ended in the teams victory and fanned the alumnis hopes.
5. Dick Tracys sleuthing methods are satirized in the comic misadventures of Al Capps Fearless Fosdick, Lil Abners fond dream hero.
6. Xs and Zs are seldom used letters, and #s, @s, and +s are seldom used symbols.
7. The 1920s, referred to as "The Roaring Twenties" or "The Jazz Age," werent his specialty, he claimed, but he seemed to know everything about the financial panic of 28, 29, and 30. Yesterdays' debacle, he observed, led to the relatively safe and sometimes indolent economy of the 1940s and 50s.
8. *Indicate an ellipsis for omitted material:*

   "Liberal," which once connoted a kind of noble concern for minorities and increased freedoms for all people, has come to suggest halfhearted and even ineffective commitment to these ideals. (Omit the words between the commas, beginning with "which" and ending with "people.")

9. *Use an ellipsis to indicate omission of the last part of this sentence:*

   Violence, sex, poverty, filth, aberrations of all kinds—these are literary and film preoccupations in a culture that fears these events but that also wishes to escape from the banality of a protected life, safe in the plush security of clipped-hedge suburbias.

10. *Insert bracketed information at the appropriate places in the following two sentences:* (The information needed is Brasilia for the first one and the cross-Florida canal for the second.)

Brazil's new inland national capital has begun to thrive recently and lure diplomats and the rich from the coastal cities.

Our President has wisely halted the plan in order to protect the ecological balance of the area and avoid an engineering boondoggle.

COMMON GRAMMAR FAULTS

Although few writers in college display flagrant errors in grammar, some inevitably creep into our sentences unnoticed. Generally, close proofreading will detect them quickly.

Faulty Pronoun Reference

A **pronoun**, since it is a word that substitutes for a noun, can have meaning only when it refers clearly to a specific noun, called its antecedent. Faulty reference occurs when a pronoun does not refer clearly to an antecedent. Notice these examples:

He had been vaccinated against typhoid, but it did not protect him. (What? "It" cannot refer to "vaccinated," a verb, and obviously "typhoid" is not intended.)
Revision: His typhoid vaccination did not protect him.

Older people do not understand the younger generation because they have forgotten their own youth. They are just doing what all generations do. (Who are "They"? Does the writer intend "youth," "younger generation," or "older people"?)
Revision: Because older people have forgotten their own youth, they do not understand the younger generation. The young people are just doing what all generations do.

In the nineteenth century, many businessmen exploited the workers, not caring whether they were making a decent wage, but only whether they were getting a lot of money. (Who are the "they's"?)
Revision: In the nineteenth century, many businessmen exploited the

Pro

Ref

workers, not caring whether the workers were making a decent wage, but only whether the employers were getting a lot of money.

If our teen-age generation is irresponsible and immoral, a great amount of this comes from older people. (Great amount of what? "Irresponsible" and "immoral"?)
Revision: If our teen-age generation is irresponsible and immoral, a great amount of the irresponsibility and immorality comes from older people.

Today's young adult finds it difficult to have faith in anything but security, which is profoundly disturbing. (What does "which" refer to?)
Revision: Today's young adult finds it difficult to have faith in anything but security, a fact profoundly disturbing to many.

In the dictionary, they have many words they don't accept. (Who are "they"?)
Revision: The dictionary includes words unacceptable in formal style.

Pronoun and Antecedent Agreement

A pronoun must also agree in number with its antecedent. And if the pronoun is the subject of the sentence, the number of the verb must also agree.

Although the average American believes in justice for all, they sometimes fail to practice it. ("They" does not agree with "American," a singular noun.)
Revision: Although the average American believes in justice for all, he sometimes fails to practice it.

Pro
Agr
Either Dick or Stan will lend you their book. ("Their," plural pronoun, does not agree with "Either . . . or.")
Revision: Either Dick or Stan will lend you his book.

After reading his argument in favor of abolishing property and his argument in favor of state ownership, I found that I was not convinced by it. (Two arguments, not one.)
Revision: After reading his argument in favor of abolishing property and his argument in favor of state ownership, I found that I was not convinced by them.

Subject and Verb Agreement

Subjects and verbs must agree in number. Errors occur usually because of intervening prepositional phrases, of inverted sentence order, or of a compound subject.

A crowd of spectators were standing around the Salem jailhouse. ("Crowd" is singular, requiring a singular verb.)

Revision: A crowd of spectators was standing around the Salem jailhouse.

Here and there a man, such as Columbus, Galileo, and Copernicus, have ventured into the unknown physical and intellectual worlds. ("Man" is singular subject.)

Agr

Revision: Here and there a man, such as Columbus, Galileo, and Copernicus, has ventured into the unknown physical and intellectual worlds.

Across the bay gleams the many lights of the city. (Lights "gleam.")

Throughout the story appears thinly disguised references to the author's own boyhood. (References "appear.")

The original draft of the poem and the version finally published differs in several significant ways. (Draft . . . and version "differ.")

LEARNING AIDS

Correct the pronoun reference, pronoun agreement, and subject-verb agreement in the following sentences:

1. This blending of cultures—of the Romans, the Christians, and the pagan Germans—represent the beginning of Western European culture.
2. The wood shop could be used by each peasant if they gave a definite share of their crops as rental.
3. Most employers do not think much about what nationality or race a future employee belongs to, but rather judges them according to ability and incentive.
4. The development of various automatic controls have made flying less hazardous.
5. Everyone of us may become sick for a long time, and it may take them several years to pay doctors' bills; socialized medicine would prevent this financial problem.
6. *Martin Chuzzlewit* is one of the most enjoyable books I have ever read, and this is the reason I have remembered it so long.
7. Rice is an important crop in Viet Nam, and many of them have little else to eat.

ADVICE ON USAGE

Disagreement over word choices and patterns has led to one of the more unusual battles of our time, the battle over the role of the dictionary as a language authority to label some usages (word choices and patterns) "good usage" and others "bad usage." The dispute eventually centers around the essential issue: Who determines usage? Language purists would like to insist that grammar and usage are codified, standardized by rules and laws set down by traditional grammarians. In fact, however, the purists have lost the battle: usage is its own authority—the ruler, the governing magistrate of language. That is, our only laws are the ways in which language is currently spoken and written. But spoken and written by whom? To whom? And where?

Certainly, discrepancies appear between the English used by professional and educated men and that used by uneducated men, between English used in nationwide broadcasts and magazines and that used in regional and local media. But to label some of these differing usages as right and others as wrong seems unnecessarily rigid and pedantic; *correctness depends upon the occasion*. A young man, for instance, chooses his words differently as he moves from activity to activity: from locker-room language when he is with his buddies, to regional and social dialect when he is on a date, to national dialect when he is interviewed on an NBC news broadcast.

The language patterns chosen by the educated, by those holding higher status, will inevitably be accorded higher prestige than the usage of the disadvantaged and uneducated. "Good English" is, therefore, somewhat like acquiring good manners: both allow one to act socially without appearing or feeling gauche and provincial. If we violate rules, at least let us do so knowingly, with a valid purpose.

The following list does not exhaust common usage problems; it includes only those that seem invisible to many students. For further help, consult a good desk dictionary. *The American Heritage Dictionary of the English Language*, for example, provides some 1,500 notes on usage, and Wilson Follett's *Modern American Usage* (1966) is still another worthy reference tool.

Affect, effect. Both *affect* and *effect* are verbs; *affect* means to influence, *effect* to bring about: "A pay raise will *affect* (concern) your status." "The students *effected* (accomplished, executed) a change in the dorm rules." Pills may *affect* your health; pills may *effect* your complete recovery."
As nouns, *effect* is the common word choice: "The *effect* was to abolish closing hours." As a noun, *affect* is confined to psychology.

Although, though. *Although* and *though* are interchangeable, *although* appearing more frequently at the beginning of clauses, and *though* appearing more frequently between two words or phrases: "*Although* I was not bankrupt. . . . I was wiser *though* poorer."

And, but, or, nor. Any of these conjunctions may be used at the beginning of sentences; this usage is currently appearing in some sophisticated writing: "*And* the consequence was severe."

Because, for, since, as. *Because* is the strongest conjunction indicating a causal relationship: "He remained at home *because* he was ill." The other connectives are less forceful: "He remained at home, *for* he was ill." "He remained, *since* he was ill." "He remained, *as* he was ill."

Between, among. Use *between* for two instances, and *among* for more than two when emphasizing similarities: "He divided the prize *between* Jane and me." "He divided the prize *among* the three of us." Use *between* to stress distinctions and differences, even if referring to more than two: "The meeting *between* three nations. . . . " "The differences *between* the hospitals at Springfield, St. Louis, and Columbia. . . . "

Continual, continuous. Both are frequently used interchangeably, but the difference is helpful: *Continual* means intermittent, repeated at intervals: "The *continual* ringing of the phone. . . . " *Continuous* means uninterrupted, especially in time or space: "The *continuous* vigil, a *continuous* stretch of sand. . . . "

Different from, different than. Cultivated writers use *different from*: "His schedule is *different from* mine." Colloquially, however, *different than* frequently introduces clauses. "My schedule is *different than* what I thought it would be."

Disinterested, uninterested. *Disinterested* means impartial: "A *disinterested* witness. . . . "; *uninterested* means devoid of interest or concern: "The *uninterested* listeners. . . . "

Due to, because of. Most educated persons avoid using *due to* as a substitute for *because of*, especially if the phrase appears at the beginning of a clause: "*Because of* unusual circumstances . . . " is preferred to "*Due to* unusual circumstances. . . . " Colloquially, however, the phrases seem to be interchangeable.

Etc. Practiced writers avoid this Latin abbreviation for *et cetera*, meaning "and so forth," whenever possible, since it seems to appear as an excuse for not offering examples. *And etc.* is redundant.

e.g., i.e. These are Latin abbreviations—*e.g.* for *exempli gratia*, meaning "for example"; *i.e.* for *id est*, meaning "that is." Parenthetical clarifications are introduced by *i.e.*: "Anesthesiologists (*i.e.*, specialists in anesthetics) do not need private practices." Parenthetical examples are introduced by *e.g.*: "Many contemporary novelists (*e.g.*, John Updike, John Cheever, Saul Bellow). . . . "

Imply, infer. *Implying* is the action of the speaker; *inferring* is the action of the listener: "I *implied* that I was hungry, but he *inferred* that I was on a diet."

Like, as. As a conjunction connecting a clause, *like* when inappropriately substituted for *as*, smacks of flip advertising ("Winstons taste good *like* a cigarette should"); such usage is still scorned by most educated writers. The usage is particularly frequent, however, when the clauses are elliptical: "Her gown looked *like* new" ("Her gown looked *as if it were* new"). *Like* is a preposition, though, and should be used as such: "He spoke *like* a demagogue"; "She looked *like* Twiggy"; ". . . looking for a boy *like* him."

Reason is because, reason why. Such usage is obviously redundant; traditional grammar requires *that* instead of *because*; and practiced writers reject the awkward phrasing: "The reason is *that* (not *because*) conservationists deplore such widespread polluting practices." *Reason why* is equally redundant.

So. As an adverb, *so* intensifies: "*So* many colleges. . . . " *So* is also a conjunction, meaning "as a result": "Coleridge hurt his foot, *so* he could not go on the walk with Wordsworth." However, *so* as a substitute for *very* is usually shunned: "I'm *so* happy"; "my date was *so* great." Avoid such usage.

That, which, who.   These relative pronouns are not interchangeable. *Who* refers to persons: "The man *who* . . . ; *which* and *that* to things and animals: "The pencil *which* . . . " and "the dog *that*. . . . " Furthermore, *that* is used for restrictive clauses, providing essential information; "The law *that* the public demanded was quickly enacted." *Which* is used primarily for nonrestrictive clauses, providing only incidental information: "The Edinburgh golf course, *which*, in my opinion, ought to be inundated with water. . . . "

Very, really.   Beginning writers *really* overwork these two words in *really* trying for a *very* unexamined intensity, which is *really very* annoying. Avoid like typhoid.

When, is when, where, is where.   Sentences to define something cannot employ these constructions. Avoid sentences like the following: "A tragedy *is when* (or *is where*) the hero gets killed." "A successful race *is when* everyone finishes." "An instance *is where* my father and I. . . . " Even though the revisions may contain more words, noun-followed-by-noun construction is preferable: "A tragedy is a drama in which the hero dies." "A successful race is one that everyone finishes." "An instance is the evening that my father and I. . . . " (See conventions for defining in Chapter IX.)

choosing words

Each of us greatly values saying the right thing at the right time. Our concern is not so much with the truth or accuracy of what is written or said as with the precise impression we wish to create, as in the following:

"Don't call me a child. I'm fourteen years old!"
"I wasn't trained. I was educated."
"He's not a photographer. He's a picture-taker."
"I'm not a Negro. I'm a Black!"
"This isn't democracy. It's tyranny by the masses."
"That is a cocktail lounge, not a saloon!"
"Okay, he might not be 'fat,' but he is surely plump in the wrong places."

We can use words lazily, adorning ourselves in ready-made words and expressions—called clichés—and thus effect the illusion of thinking. And, we often adopt words that have become identified with certain social classes or political outlooks. Or we can try to hide the facts of reality behind the impersonal mask of bureaucratic prose or jargon, the refuge for those who need to create the impression of cool, professional, detached efficiency and erudition. Or we unconsciously express the myths of our social attitudes. Thus, we can lazily mouth the platitudes of "getting ahead," "being decent," "the good old days," "the phony world," "doing one's own thing," "getting with it," or "paying the price." But, if we are trying to create an impression of detachment and cool professionalism, we might adopt such soaked logs as "an organizational change agent" or "antipersonnel mine," both of which involve human beings in an important way, though this is difficult to perceive.

The words you use and the words used to describe you are really extensions of your true identity, and the way you say things is at least as important as what you say. Our choice of words betrays our attitudes, our special interpretations of reality. The person who perceives himself as receiving a "hand-out" rather than "benefiting from a social welfare plan" loses personal dignity and self-respect. Words can thus demean us or enrich our sense of personal worth. Parents choose names for their children with much thought, knowing that they are thereby laying the cornerstone for individuality. Why "Mark" rather than "Henry"? Or why "Diane" rather than "Clara"?

Whatever social task we have to perform that involves words necessarily leads us to consider what of our attitudes we will reveal and perhaps how much of the "truth" we will release. We are careful, therefore, to consider *how* we preach a sermon, ask for money by letter, write a note of condolence to bereaved relatives, write copy for a news article, or explain the importance of sex education to anxious parents.

Our use of words exposes our inhibitions and prejudices. Do we write "naked" or "unclothed" to describe the appearance of an athlete at the locker-room door? On the one hand, *euphemistic* expressions paint a kind of gloss on reality and often reveal status prejudice, as when we label janitors "custodians," city trash collectors "sanitation engineers," used car salesmen "transportation consultants," military invasions "skirmishes," and bombing "interdiction." How many euphemisms can you recall or create for "death," "dying," "graveyards," "embalmers"?

Then, opposite the agreeable expressions are those venting social contempt, such as "dago," "chink," "gook," "boy," "white trash," "bourgeois," "social climber," or "skinflint"—all of which are defensive weapons to foster our own sense of security. If we know this, we might be more careful, more deliberate in choosing words, for they can have the effect of wounding or strengthening.

Moreover, we use words to express a kind of social vision, to maintain the appearance we wish society to see. This is not so hypocritical as it might seem, because if we told the "truth" at all times without regard for others' sensibilities, or if we failed to detect exaggerations or lies, then we would lead lives of needless confusion. Consider, for instance, two people who are reading an advertisement for a new novel that is touted to be "number one," "provocative," "scintillating," "breathtaking," "shocking," and "best in the decade." Truth? Or exaggerations? It would not be surprising to hear one person say to the other, "Do you suppose it's worth reading?" Such a simple response is a way of reading past the words to the possible reality behind the shouted message. If we misuse or misread words, we can inflict pain, become fools, or perhaps grant undeserved praise.

It should be obvious, therefore, that words are important to us in many ways. They amuse us or deaden our senses; they encourage or repress us; they depress or excite us; they admonish or ennoble us. In fact, we use and enjoy an uncommon number of words. Sometimes, we feel inundated and overwhelmed by them, as though drowning in a sea of verbiage streaming from television, books, parents, friends, instructors, advertising. We must, therefore, know a great many words—both figurative and literal—and use them with deliberation. And it should be no surprise that everyone, from birth to death, can continue to extend his knowledge of words.

Learning words is a never-ending pleasure and one of the most rewarding, for the more words one knows and the more expressions he can create, the greater his ability to think new thoughts and express his thoughts accurately and memorably. As a kind of investment in this pleasure, we therefore provide here a brief tussle with words you might meet while reading a textbook, listening to a lecture, or reading a popular magazine meant for educated people, such as *Harper's* or *Newsweek* magazine. If you do not know some of the words—or even some of the words which serve as definition choices—then you could begin your own private dictionary of new found words. For this quiz, circle the word or phrase that most nearly matches the italicized word:

1. A *panacea* for social ills
   - a. explanation
   - b. partial remedy
   - c. breeding ground
   - d. cure-all
2. incredibly *gauche*
   - a. powerful
   - b. haughty
   - c. impolite
   - d. cynical
3. to participate in *chicanery*
   - a. frivolity
   - b. ceremony
   - c. debate
   - d. deception
4. *gregarious* animals
   - a. living in groups
   - b. flesh-eating
   - c. languid
   - d. immobilized
5. the charge of *genocide* against Germany
   - a. slaughter of the wealthy
   - b. slaughter of cattle
   - c. extermination of a race
   - d. slaughter of children
6. to *inculcate* ideas of right
   - a. oppose
   - b. instill
   - c. explain
   - d. teach
7. a *quixotic* deed
   - a. strange
   - b. rapid
   - c. individualistic
   - d. impractical
8. The *recalcitrant* witness
   - a. obstinate
   - b. hostile
   - c. evasive
   - d. silent
9. a literary *fiasco*
   - a. experiment
   - b. parade
   - c. failure
   - d. avidity
10. an *addled* freshman
    - a. corrupted
    - b. cynical
    - c. vehement
    - d. confused
11. a *potpourri* of ideas
    - a. mixture
    - b. scarcity
    - c. dearth
    - d. plethora
12. a *platonic* relationship
    - a. ideal
    - b. vulgar
    - c. spiritual
    - d. occult
13. *banal* criticism of the poetry
    - a. aesthetic
    - b. adverse
    - c. technical
    - d. hackneyed
14. a *soporific* lecture
    - a. bemused
    - b. trivial
    - c. sleep-inducing
    - d. compelling

15. a small *coterie* of people
  a. queue   b. social set   c. union
  d. list
16. a *perfunctory* performance
  a. done mechanically   b. done with zeal   c. scheduled
  d. done by stealth
17. *dilatory* behavior
  a. puerile   b. troublesome   c. slow
  d. dejected
18. an effective *parody*
  a. burlesque   b. zenith   c. gamut
  d. genre
19. a *scurrilous* comment
  a. vulgar   b. genteel   c. redundant
  d. furtive
20. *esoteric* information
  a. raw   b. abstruse   c. extant
  d. exigent
21. an *innocuous* compromise
  a. harmless, ineffective   b. critical, crucial   c. flat, vapid, empty
  d. irascible, choleric

Are you among the cognoscenti in your knowledge of words or are you a verbal duffer? Consult the quiz key at the bottom of this page.

The quiz probably contains some words you were not familiar with, or some words you were unsure of. Although there is no one simple way of learning words, try these sources for improving and increasing your word power:

Dictionary The dictionary, an alphabetical reference list of words, is an indispensable tool for you, but many of us use it haphazardly and ineptly. Carefully study all the information about a word:

  a. spelling
  b. pronunciation (pronounce it out loud, several times)
  c. irregular forms
  d. meanings
  e. level of use (not in Webster's Third International)
  f. etymology (derivation and development of words)
  g. synonyms and antonyms

Also, do not forget the separate lists at the back of some dictionaries, such as "A Pronouncing Biographical Dictionary" and "Geographical Gazetteer."

You should own a hardback abridged or collegiate dictionary, such as

Webster's Seventh New Collegiate, Webster's New World, New College Standard, The American College, or *The American Heritage Dictionary of the English Language.* A small paperback dictionary for spelling during tests or writing in class is helpful, too.

If your collegiate dictionary does not suffice, use an unabridged one in the library.

Roget's Thesaurus   The thesaurus, a word-finder, must be used with care. It presents a number of central ideas or concepts and groups words and expressions in some way related to that concept. The words are neither *synonyms nor antonyms*; since the words in the groups are only related, *you must discriminate with care*, checking the dictionary for precise definitions.

Webster's New Dictionary of Synonyms (hardback) or *Soule's Dictionary of English Synonyms* might be more helpful to you than a thesaurus. The words in these books are arranged alphabetically, rather than by concepts, and the words are thus easier to locate. Further, the editors include meanings and then lists of synonyms. We recommend that you use one of these intensively also.

Vocabulary builders   These books are fun to use. You can progress at your own rate, spending fifteen minutes or an hour and a half as your schedule permits. We recommend two:

Wilfred Funk and Norman Lewis, *Thirty Days to a More Powerful Vocabulary*

Cedric Gale, *Building an Effective Vocabulary*

SELECTION: PRECISION AND CLARITY

An able writer is as clever about the choice of words for his essay as he is about its structure and organization. He chooses words for precision and clarity of meaning and for artistic expression. You, too, will want to be exacting in meaning and at the same time as colorful as possible so as to strike fresh interest in jaded tastes. George Orwell, in his fine essay "Politics and the English Language," warns against choosing the automatic phrases that come to mind when he writes: "Prose consists [for too many writers] less and less of words chosen for the sake of their meaning, and more and more of phrases tacked together like the sections of a prefabricated henhouse." He also writes in the same essay of the dangers of thinking prefabricated thoughts:

> You can shirk the trouble of thinking clearly by simply throwing your mind open and letting the ready-made phrases come crowding in. They will construct your sentences for you—even think your thoughts for you, to a certain extent—and at need they will perform the important service of concealing your meaning even from yourself.

In other words, make every word count; precise, apt, picture words sparkle in finely honed writing.

Vague, Abstract Words to Particular Words

Generalities are like Orwell's henhouse: the walls are there, but the chickens have flown. Generalities are largely made up of abstractions. Such abstract words as "freedom," "peace," "democracy," "the equality of men," "honesty," "activity," "selfishness," "personality," or "human nature" are vague when used alone because they do not focus on particular instances or cases. Your job as a writer is to help your reader know exactly what kind of freedom or peace you refer to. Thus, instead of writing, "We need more freedom in college," write a particularized statement: "We need the freedom to elect a physical science." Or, "We need the freedom to set our own dormitory hours." If you use abstract, vague words, you must also employ concrete details to be clear and precise about your meaning. Consider these questions, noting how these descriptive expressions clarify abstractions:

> When does *patriotism* (abstraction) become chauvinistic, Machiavellian, pharisaical, philistinistic, or iconoclastic?
> Is a *man's behavior* (abstraction) sadistic, quixotic, hedonistic, stoic, narcissistic, erotic, or Byronic?
> Is our *American Dream* (abstraction) Dionysian, Apollonian, Janus-faced, protean, Spartan, or Gargantuan?

Add examples and illustrative information to make the abstractions even more specific. Granted, such inclusion invariably lengthens your sentences and paragraphs, but you are not really sacrificing economy; instead, you are gaining in clarity and precision. Consider, for instance, this statement:

> The candidate changed parties.

What candidate? What parties? More specifically, the writer could say:

> The candidate for Congress, Ted Jamhouse, switched his political affiliation from the Republican Party to the Democratic Party.

Here is another vague sentence:

> Both candidates, vying for election, are alumni of the same college.

A better version:

> Both candidates, Ted Jamhouse and Ed Jellyfish, vying for election to the U.S. House of Representatives as Congressman from the Third District of Kansas, are alumni of Fort Hays Kansas State College.

Another bland, say-nothing statement:

> Ted Jamhouse announced his platform.

Rewritten explicitly:

> Ted Jamhouse announced that he would work for parity for the Kansas farmers, an equitable tax basis, and equal treatment for Kansas in military expenditures, education, and welfare.

Here are other samples:

> A philosopher wrote against women.
> **Revision:** Arthur Schopenhauer, a 19th century German philosopher, denounced women as being childlike, irresponsible, and nonintellectual in his treatise "On Women."
>
> A child, hunting for a toy, found money.
> **Revision:** A six-year-old girl, searching for a lost baton, discovered $600 in twenty-dollar bills behind an abandoned barn.
>
> A great advance in science occurred when doctors began using a simple test.
> **Revision:** A great advance in cervical cancer control occurred in the 1960's when gynecologists and obstetricians began using the Pap smear test, the examination of a bit of cervical fluid for cancer cells.

Adding specific details, then, achieves precise information instead of abstractions. The trick is to change general words and phrases to specific terms. Try replacing general words with specific ones in these sentences:

1. The football player ran a great play.
2. We made it to the big event.
3. The lawyers tried a new tactic.
4. The tool wouldn't work.
5. His big dream vanished with that bit of bad luck.
6. He likes some types of music.

Wordiness to Economy

Wordiness and redundancy commonly creep in when a writer fails to prune away dead, needlessly repeated words. Notice how phrases and sentences, heavy with superfluous matter, can be revised for explicitness:

Dull, Unnecessarily Wordy or Redundant	Economically Explicit
"Today, in our modern world, people tend to believe that . . . "	"Today, some Americans believe that . . . "
"Refer back to the previous paragraph."	"Refer to the previous paragraph."
"Whatever he decided to do, he did it well."	"Whatever he did, he did well."
"There are several of our neighbors who teach in the sociological field."	"Several of our neighbors teach sociology."
"He is delighted to discuss any enigma of an astrological nature."	"He discusses delightedly any astrological enigma."

| "In the case of the Peace Corps volunteer, her colleagues spoke only Portuguese." | "The Peace Corps volunteer's colleagues spoke only Portuguese." |

Writers generally do not intend to be verbose, but sometimes the attempt to be a flashy stylist fails. Usually wordiness occurs when you replace a simple word with a larger one, as "move" with "to make a motion," "state" with "to present a statement," or "significance" with "the factor of largest important significance." (Notice that the inflation of words here does not convey meaning more precisely. Refer to the "Allusions, Foreign Words, and Polysyllabic Words" section in this chapter for a discussion on substituting plain words with specific words for a clearer meaning.)

You can stumble into verbosity, too, when you add *vague* qualifiers or adjectives to other modifiers:

very obviously
somewhat diffident
quite attractive
rather poor
interestingly phrased
fabulously tangy
remarkably rich

Similarly, a list of adjectives can be wordy: "She was *proud, haughty, conceited, and vain*." These four adjectives overlap too much to be effective. Try "She was haughty . . . ," and then portray the queenly woman as she produces her effect.

Likewise, simply wallowing in redundancy, that is, repeating the meaning, adds to wordiness:

first basic principle
blend together
in the last final analysis
a local shop in our town
the primary essentials
great huge towering buildings
throughout the whole book
repeat over and over
free gratis
petite in size

Of course, deliberately repeated or paralleled words and phrases, a style called anaphora, help emphasize sentence or paragraph meaning. (See Martin Luther King, Jr.'s speech on page 127.) Certainly it is better to be clear and emphatic than sketchy and vague, but perhaps you are like countless others who struggle to achieve clarity. We recommend that you write some *aphorisms*, which, incidentally, is a fine American pastime that Benjamin Franklin probably first popularized. Perhaps you remember his aphorisms "Stay ahead or you'll find yourself behind" and "Fish and visitors stink in three days." The very rhythm of these statements aids memory. We could say that brevity is the better part of clarity. Our hope would be that, by punning gently on the rhythm of Falstaff's statement "Discretion is the better part of valor," the alert reader might store that idea away more easily than if we had explained it in full. Students of ours have produced hundreds of aphorisms and have enjoyed slicing fat off wordy sentences. Here are three that might set you scrambling to better them:

"Empty beer cans rattle the loudest."
"Love is like war; it has no true explanation."
"People who poke fires often get burned."

Such statements invoke idea overtones through their aptly chosen images. The point is that condensation is a joyful process when it produces such rewards.

Denotation and Connotation

Most students are familiar with the overtones of words, the ways in which words imply additional meanings beyond the literal. Denotation refers to the literal meaning of a word, as "ass" means "donkey." Connotation, however, refers to the emotional content, or the listener's associations with the word. What emotional content surrounds the word "ass" when most people hear it? The word "thin," on the other hand, is a relatively neutral word; that is, it has a specific denotation but not much connotation. "Skinny" is less neutral, usually indicating disapproval, while "lean" carries an approving connotation.

To many college rebels, as another example, the word "anarchy" connotes individual freedom from society's repression; to older persons, the word connotes lawlessness and wanton behavior. During the infamous trial of Sacco and Vanzetti, Vanzetti used "anarchy" in a letter to denote its theoretical meaning of personal freedom, but the judge, jury, and populace reacted to the usual connotations of "anarchy." Think of other words with equally inflaming connotations: "military-industrial complex," "leftist," "cops," "napalm," "pigs," "rioters," and the like.

Objective analysis requires neutral terms, words that do not play on the reader's emotional associations. "Young radicals" as a substitution for "effete snobs," for instance, tones down or neutralizes a reference to youthful dissenters. What associations arise from these Agnewisms: "covey of confused congressmen," "hopeless hysterical hypochondriacs of history," "nattering nabobs of negativism," and "troubadors of trouble"? Obviously, alliteration, the repetition of sounds, accomplished Spiro Agnew's political intent of denouncing those opposed to his views. We have to watch news stories, as well as politicians, for their use of connotation, since emotionally-laden words fail to provide accurate information and honest reasoning.

Here is a paragraph about television from *The New Republic*. Notice all the italicized [ours] words which express approval or disapproval. Then try to neutralize the paragraph by substituting words that do not carry feeling:

Proctor and Gamble, Bristol-Myers—all the *big* sponsors—turn their sales *problems* over to Mad Ave; Mad Ave hires dozens of *scholars* like Louis Harris to *ferret out* and *tame* significant public norms; and the *tube people* themselves feel the *popular pulse* with the *tenderness of a specialist waiting on a queen.* All the *lovely characters* who *manipulate* the *tube's* world view thus *deny* that they are *manipulators*; they are merely *'umble servants* of something (freedom or a *buck*) or someone (a *divinely average* someone; a norm). *Nobody is in charge* as the TV window *fills with lies,* with *grotesque* and *simplistic images* of middle-class life, with *phony cuteness.* Nobody is in charge, yet the nobody is *insatiably preoccupied* with *chasing* (and therefore creating) the *faddish* relevance that keeps *half of America* continuously thinking about the *same* things in the *same* way at the *same* time.

Revise the neutral description in this paragraph so that it becomes connotatively approving and then again so that it is disapproving:

Dr. Walters came in with eyes red from traveling at a hard pace, placed his attaché case and well-worn Bible on the table behind him, and addressed us. His grey hair shone with some sort of hair creme; his suit was rumpled; his shoes were muddy and worn at the heels. This is the man whose voice sounds over 730 radio stations on "The Gospel Hour" in sermons against modern life and communism. He links the Cross and the Flag in the typical John Bircher manner. He is a large man, rotund, with an aquiline nose, cleft at the end. His voice is resonantly sonorous and well-modulated.

One hint: if you are uncertain about a word's connotation, check a collegiate dictionary. (See page 111 for a list.) Following the definition of a word, a good dictionary will differentiate the meanings of the word's synonyms under the section headed *Syn.* See a standard dictionary of synonyms for a full explanation of connotations for various words.

Slang to Longer-Lived, Less Ambiguous Words

Slang words are fun to use in conversation, especially among our friends. As a rule, however, they do not serve well in essays because they are too timely. They change meaning with hand gestures, with a raised eyebrow, with tone and stress, with time. Because of their shifting nature, slang words are ambiguous in writing, and they do not survive in "deathless prose."

Such slang expressions as "cool," "hepped up," "far-out," "neat," "right on," "groovy," "cop-out," "putting me on," "uptight," "a hang-up," and "the in-group" are often colorful and effective when we can observe the speaker's mannerisms and hear his tone, but in writing they lack precision. Further, they carry more emotion than logic, more general ideas than specific ones. And finally, slang words suggest the chatty, too informal pose, and thus fail to persuade. "Arlo is like really together" does not convince your reader that contemporary music has some value.

Trite Expressions and Clichés to Inventive Phrases

Words and phrases that once were bright images often become so encrusted with rust that they belong in a trash heap. Many beginning writers recognize the cliché phrases, expressions limp from overuse, and avoid using them. Still, the ready-made expression often endures in the sharpest of imaginations and surfaces in our writing. Only a keen and persistent eye can spot those aging clichés and then replace them with inventive substitutes that charm the reader's interest and inform him at the same time.

Noticing the banal image is one thing, but replacing it with a refreshing and appropriate equivalent is yet another. Try limbering up your own verbal imagination by examining these possible replacements for tired clichés:

Trite Expressions or Clichés	Inventive Replacements
clear as a bell	clear as a hawk's eye
	clear as a mountain stream
cool as a cucumber	cool as an ice cave
green as grass	green as new alfalfa
good as gold	good as an all-day sucker
a wet blanket	a soaked log
	a limp noodle
spur of the moment decision	a mid-flight decision
a diamond in the rough	a buried treasure

Ironic reversals are also possible:

Usual Trite or Cliché Expressions	Inventive Ironic Replacements
clear as a bell	clear as red barn paint
cool as a cucumber	cool as a Mexican jumping bean
bright as a penny	bright as a cinder
a plain Jane	a plain Playmate of the Month
the depths of despair	the depths of hilarity

You will surely be able to improve on the suggested replacements. Please do. But if you find that such limbering-up exercise reveals a creaky imagination, this is only testimony to the stiffening effect of society's thought patterns on you. Like running and swimming, however, the more you exercise, the easier and faster you can move. We propose the following list of trite expressions and clichés for you to improve the ease and speed of your creative abilities:

Trite Expressions and Clichés	Your Inventive Replacements— Ironic or "Straight"
he tossed his hat in the ring	_____
black as night	_____

in all seriousness   _____

goes without saying   _____

As one further stretch of your imagination, list here some of the trite expressions *you* have noticed and then invent your own replacements:

_____   _____

_____   _____

_____   _____

_____   _____

Jargon, Social-Sciencese to Widely-Understood Words

Far too many writers pack their sentences so densely with technical words that the reader feels not only overwhelmed but uninformed. Jargon and pseudo-literary or pseudo-psychological or sociological words usually obscure meaning—or, worse, hide a lack of knowledge. The readership should provide the criterion for word choice here; a linguist chooses words other linguists know if the essay is aimed at professional linguists; space engineers communicate effectively with technical words to other engineers. What we are concerned with is pretentious usage. Leonard Ashley, in an article entitled "A Guided Tour of Gobbledygook," quotes this example of military jargon:

> We have locked on to operationally significant quantities of practicable equipment to zero in on optimum capabilities if the aforementioned philosophy materializes. Conceptional imponderables will be minimized by programming on the mach so as to firm it up and cream it off.

Obviously, this passage is verbose, vague, and pretentious. We cannot really decipher the language unless we have been inducted into the near-Martian world where such verbal goulash abounds. Here is a sociologist's statement: "A network is a social configuration in which some, but not all, of the component external units maintain relationships with one another." Although other sociologists will understand this writer, the general reader will not. "External units" are *people*; "social configurations" are friendships, personal relationships. Thus, you can see that one of the dangers of social-sciencese is its tendency to reduce persons and their activities to abstract, almost nonhuman "units." Likewise, a student who employs literary terms like "symbol," "existential concerns," "oxymoron," and "foil" without precisely understanding or illustrating these terms also fails to communicate. A passage from the Bible contains the point succinctly:

> Except ye utter by the tongue words easy to be understood, how shall it be known what is spoken? for ye shall speak into the air. (1 Cor. 14:9)

Consistency and Tone

An effective writer maintains a consistent level of word choice throughout his essay, determined by the purpose of his essay and its intended audience. It is helpful here to identify three levels of diction—*formal, informal, and colloquial.* The more formal the purpose and more educated the readers, the more likely you will include less familiar words and avoid contractions, local idioms, and the impersonal "you." The resulting tone is impersonal, serious. Consider Vannevar Bush's formal discussion of the formative stages of our mother earth in his essay "Science Pauses":

> The first men who pondered did so on a small earth, which did not extend far beyond the horizon, for which the stars were mere lamps in the skies. Now, we are no longer at the center; there is no center. We look at congeries of stars by light that left them before the earth had cooled. Among the myriads of stars we postulate myriads of planets with conditions as favorable to life as is our earth. We puzzle as to whether the universe is bounded or extends forever; whether, indeed, it may be only one universe among many. We speculate as to whether our universe began in a vast explosion, whether it pulsates between utter compression and wide diffusion, whether it is self-re-newing and thus goes on unchanged forever. And we are humble.

Informal writing consists of relaxed diction, less tightly constructed sentences, some contractions, perhaps some idioms, and sometimes the impersonal "you" addressed to the reader. The tone is lighter, somewhat subjective, less detached. Adam Smith chose the informal level for his national best-selling book *The Money Game*:

> The strongest emotions in the market place are greed and fear. In rising markets, you can almost feel the greed tide begin. Usually it takes from six months to a year after the last market bottom even to get started. The greed itch begins when you see stocks move that you don't own. Then friends of yours have a stock that has doubled; or if you have one that has doubled, they have one that has tripled. This is what produces bull market tops.

The colloquial level is one you are familiar with because you use it in your personal letters. Slang, "you," contractions, popular and ordinary words and phrases, simple sentences, or even sentence fragments are colloquial. Here the tone is breezy, personal, immediate. The following excerpt from "Prelude to Love—Three Letters" by Eldridge Cleaver in *Soul on Ice* illustrates the colloquial level. Cleaver is answering the woman's fear that both of them may only be pretending to love. The letter is effective precisely because of its level:

> Your persistent query, "How can he tell? He has no choices," deserves an answer. But it is not the type of question that can be answered in words. It . . . involves making ourselves vulnerable to each other, to strip ourselves naked, to become sitting ducks for each other—and if one of the ducks is shamming, then the sincere duck will pay in pain—but the deceitful duck, I feel will be the loser. (If both ducks are shamming, what a lark, what a fiasco, what a put-on, what a despicable thought! . . .)

Listen: Your letter is very beautiful, and you came through with rockets on. You came through and landed on your feet, with spiked shoes on, right on my heart. It is not that we are making each other up and it is not ourselves alone who are involved in what is happening to us. . . .

Cleaver's letters are effective because he has diminished nearly all distance between himself and his reader by his choice of images, his hushed tone, and his "private" language—all characteristics of highly informal writing.

Most of today's writing, the most imaginative and appealing writing, manages to combine the best qualities of all three levels: the careful logic and serious intent of the formal, the less detached tone and the mixed diction of the informal, and the immediacy of the colloquial. Writers like John Steinbeck, Norman Mailer, or James Baldwin manage to combine the levels into their unique, articulate, and effective prose. But they are careful writers, careful not to let one tone conflict with another, careful not to jar the serious intent with flippancy and irrelevancy. Your task is thus to harmonize the diction and tone of your essays with your intent.

LEARNING AIDS

Rewrite these sentences, avoiding clichés, wordiness, vague expressions, jargon:

1. Like a shot out of the dark, Tom found himself a wet blanket; all asked him to put himself to the acid test. Although he was as tired as a dog, and flat broke, he came through with flying colors. It turned out that he was only a diamond in the rough.

2. Dear Mom and Dad,
   College is just fantabulous! The girls are all swingy, and my roommate is the greatest. My room is groovy now with our decorations. The food is blah, but then you can't have everything.

3. We will develop the great society. With enthusiasm, we will tackle all of America's problems, and there will be freedom and peace for all.

4. It should be clear that this does not mean that in any given instance we have arrived at knowledge which is absolute or beyond doubt.

5. Whenever the statistical method of measuring definitely gains the ascendancy, the number of students of a high intellectual level who are attracted to sociology tends to fall off considerably.

6. Conceptual imponderables will be minimized by programming on the practicable equipment, honing in on the optimum capabilities so as to utilize and finalize all socioeconomic motivations.

7. It is not now generally acknowledged by most people today that we live in a calm, contented, peaceful, and nontroubled world.

8. One of our trained sales personnel representatives will soon call upon you shortly to establish your own personal private credit account service.

9. The woman who said she was Mrs. Shirley Drew wore the newest in latest fashionable garb which was a coat made of artificial simulated patent vinyl adorned with gold-colored buttons and military epaulets.
10. To take the matter one step further, I should cautiously advise that we handle the matter in as discreet a fashion as humanly possible.
11. These technological problems have already been solved; or they will be, or these problems will inundate and overwhelm us with their magnitude and complexity.

Refer to Chapter VIII on types of essays for fuller explanation of purposes and styles, and evaluate the word strategies in the introductory paragraphs of the exemplary essays.

ARRANGEMENT: THE ARTISTRY OF DESIGN

In the previous section, we considered ways to transform inscrutable prose into effective communication, ways to jettison dead words, and ways to harmonize diction with purpose. In this section, we are still concerned with precision and clarity, but now we will begin to mix the colors of our word palette, brightening a drab prose. You need to imitate, if not be, an artist, choosing luminous words and arranging phrases and sentences that compel the reader to change his indifference or mild aversion to delighted response.

Allusions, Foreign Words, and Polysyllabic Words

Although you will not want your essays to be so decorated with frothy and fanciful words that the meaning is obscured, you can enliven an otherwise grey landscape of dry plainness and monotony. You may choose, therefore, to enrich your vocabulary with allusions, foreign words, or polysyllabic words.

Allusions are words or phrases referring to or drawn from famous people, places, historical events, or literary works that have become familiar to educated persons. For instance, the word "sadism," which comes from the Marquis de Sade, now means "a delight in cruelty." Likewise, the word "quixotic" is derived from Cervantes' *Don Quixote* and means "idealistic and impractical." Then, from the downfall of Napolean in 1815, at Waterloo, Belgium, comes the historical allusion "met his Waterloo," which means "a decisive defeat." Expressions such as these pack meaning into a small space.

Mythology, too, has inspired a wide choice of words with diverse implications:

Words of Mythological Origin	Meaning
narcissism	egoism; love of one's own body
tantalize	to tease by keeping a desirable item in view but out of reach

aegis	protection; sponsorship
protean	variable
meander	to follow a winding course; to ramble
Adonis	a beautiful youth whom Aphrodite loves
aphrodisiac	food to excite sexual desire
chimera	an illusion
morphine	a narcotic-based sedative
bacchanalian	pertaining to a drunken revelry or orgy

The mythological stories about Narcissus, Tantalus, Zeus, Proteus, Adonis, Aphrodite, Morpheus, and Bacchus have shed seeds for the above words and innumerable others.

Biblical allusions are unusually rich resources for extending the connotative dimensions of your prose:

Words of Biblical Origin	Meaning
Jezebel	a shameless woman
babel	a confusion of sounds
jeremiad	a prolonged complaint
mammon	material wealth of a debasing influence
pharisaical	having hypocritical censorious self-righteousness
samaritan	an individual who generally aids those in distress
philistine	a person led by material rather than intellectual or artistic values

To delve into the interesting Biblical, mythological, and modern history of words, consult a book of etymology.

Foreign words and phrases also add a cultural depth to your prose. Use them, sparingly, when there is no direct English equivalent and when your readers either are familiar with them or can infer the meaning from the context. Consider the effective uses of these possibilities:

Foreign Term	Meaning
ad nauseam	to nausea, to a sickening degree
non sequitur	it does not follow
avant-garde	vanguard, pioneers
aficionado	a fan, a devoted follower of a sport
faux pas	a social blunder
beau geste	a magnanimous gesture
nom de plume	pen name

Too many allusions and too many foreign words and phrases will stamp the writer as pretentious or pompous, so use them as you would garlic, with great care.

Polysyllabic words, or "big words," are those words of Greek or Latin origin. Anglo-Saxon words are short, hard-hitting words. You will use both in your writing. However, vocabulary that is only Anglo-Saxon can appear too simple, too elementary, although we do not want to be pseudo-Miltonic, choosing only the heavy Latinate words. But polysyllabic words contrast effective'y and excitingly with simple words. They are also more precise. Evaluate your verbs and verb phrases: are they short or polysyllabic? Such verbs as "think," "make," "put," "show," "tell," "have," "get," and "do" suggest a variety of synonyms, slightly different in meaning, out of the ordinary and precise. Notice that the following list contains specific verbs rather than abstract ones:

Think. reflect, meditate, dream, muse, contemplate, deliberate, determine, imagine, conceive, plot, design, deem, surmise.

Make. create, frame, mould, shape, construct, execute, secure, compose, form, contribute, compel, constrain, force, require.

Show. exhibit, display, flaunt, parade, divulge, proclaim, demonstrate, discover, blazon, disclose, instruct, elucidate, interpret, define.

Put. deposit, impose, plant, inflict, oblige, compel, incite, entice, induce, utter, express.

Tell. describe, narrate, define, delineate, orate, exhort, advise, relate, report, enumerate, disclose, divulge, confess, apprise, betray, discover, declare.

Verb phrases, too, can be specific:

Put away. discard, reject, expel, divorce, renounce.

Put down. repress, crush, quell, baffle, overthrow, degrade, disconcert, humble, shame.

Put off. discard, renounce, defeat, frustrate, defer, procrastinate, reject.

Put out. offend, displease, anger, extinguish, emit, protrude, extend.

To develop the power to insert appropriate polysyllabic words into otherwise sixth-grade sentences, a dictionary of synonyms and a vocabulary builder are invaluable tools to increase your word stores.

LEARNING AIDS

The following are some sentences that contain allusions, foreign words, and polysyllabic words. Identify them, evaluate their effectiveness, and consider the author's intent:

1. To Black Americans, soul is the catchword of the new racial narcissism, something that elates them and ignites them, something they have for no other reason but for the color of their skin; something all their own; something only a pariah Whitey can have—yet only if he waxes black, and only if he plays in reverse the same debasing color game Negroes have had to play for two hundred years. (Mel Ziegler, "James Brown Sells His Soul")

2. The malady [mumbling] is one part laziness, one part a perverted shyness, perverted because its inarticulated premise is that it is less obtrusive socially to speak your thoughts so as to require the person whom you are addressing to ask you twice or three times what it was you said. A palpable irrationality. If you have to ask someone three times what he said and when you finally decipher it you learn he has just announced that the quality of mercy is not strained, or that he is suffering the slings and arrows of outrageous fortune, you have a glow of pleasure from the reward of a hardy investigation. (William F. Buckley, "What Did You Say?")

3. Good and evil we know in the field of this world grow up together almost inseparably; and the knowledge of good is so involved and interwoven with the knowledge of evil, that those confused seeds which were imposed upon Psyche as an incessant labour to cull out, and sort asunder, were not more intermixed. It was from out the rind of one apple tasted, that the knowledge of good and evil, as two twins cleaving together, leaped forth into the world. And perhaps this is that doom which Adam fell into as knowing good and evil, that is to say of knowing good by evil. (John Milton, "Areopagitica")

4. The Roman hordes were more civilized. Their gladiators asked them whether the *coup de grâce* should be administered or not. The *pièce de résistance* at the modern prize fight is the spectacle of a man clubbing a helpless and vanquished opponent into complete insensibility. (Paul Gallico, "A Large Number of Persons")

Develop your own cache of precise words for these "weak" verbs and verb phrases:

have _____.

get _____

do _____

see _____

get in _____

get out _____

get around _____

get by _____

see into _____

see through _____

No two words are exactly alike in meaning, so it is wise to extend your ability to use more precise words by trying them out in sentences in which they are appropriate. Select words in the above lists with which you are not highly familiar, look them up in a dictionary, and write at least one sentence in which you use each word correctly.

Figurative Expressions: Metaphors, Analogies, Images

Figurative language is language that *compares*, that transfers our associations from something abstract or not familiar to something familiar and concrete. It can be frilly and decorative, but in its best use, it is unusually strong, practical, and picturesque. Similes are explicitly stated comparisons, as "We replied, like a trained Greek chorus." Metaphors are implied comparisons, as "Our trained Greek chorus reply was. . . . " An analogy is an extended comparison, useful in clarifying, but not in persuading, as in the sentence "A beginning writer can be likened to Charles Lindbergh, readying himself for his first solo flight." Expository prose at its best is not completely isolated from descriptive writing—both kinds of writing should appeal to the reader by clarifying, by illustrating, by comparing. Furthermore, by nature, we think figuratively and seem to enjoy it. Consider the italicized figurative expressions in these sentences: "The house looks *like a cracker box*," "The assignment *weighed* me down," "The bulldozer *chomped up* yards of dirt," "Our old car *gagged* before it started," or "If he smiled, he'd *fracture* his face." Why not write figuratively, then? Because many young writers are afraid to experiment with language. But that is precisely what you should be—experimental. Try out your wings. Fly. Perhaps, like Icarus, you will fail; but perhaps, like Pegasus, you will soar where ordinary, unimaginative writers would not dare. Two cautions you need to observe are to avoid mixing metaphors and to avoid dead or trite metaphors. Here are some absurd mixtures:

Her flood of tears was nipped in the bud by his sharp tongue.

Three metaphors there, all dead too: "flood," "nipped in the bud," and "sharp tongue."

The leeching Communist threat claws at each mutilated country in order to swim closer to the next one.

Again, the combination of "leeching," "claws," "mutilated," and "swim" is inconsistent with nature.

You might begin a conscious effort to add color to your writing if you create at least two metaphors for every page of your next essay. Consider the effectiveness, the color, the precision of your figurative substitutions. Use images as adverbs, adjectives, verbs, as well as whole phrases. Find and examine for effectiveness the metaphors and images in the following passages:

1. The fetishes of the witch doctor may be shown to be made of nothing more than dogs' teeth and colored ink—but still the people will go to him; as today the people continue to tolerate, and to patronize, schools and colleges and universities which treat their children like half-rational bio-

logical mechanisms, whose highest ambition in life is to develop in such a fashion as to render glad the rotarian heart in Anytown, U.S.A. (William F. Buckley, "The Aimlessness of American Education")

2. Grant was the modern man emerging; beyond him, ready to come on the stage, was the great age of steel and machinery, of crowded cities and a restless vitality. Lee might have ridden down from the old age of chivalry, lance in hand, silken banner fluttering over his head. (Bruce Catton, "Grant and Lee: A Study in Contrasts")

3. From my experience, not one in twenty marries the first love; we build statues of snow, and weep to see them melt. (Sir Walter Scott)

4. ... and we thought, in the decisive syntactical way we reserve for such occasions, how all water is in passage from purity to purity. Puddles, gutters, sewers are incidental disguises: the casual avatars of perpetually reincarnated cloud droplets; momentary embarrassments have nothing to do with the ineluctable poise of H_2O. Throw her on the street, mix her with candy wrappers, splash her with taxi wheels, she remains a virgin and a lady. (John Updike, "Spring Rain")

Sound and Rhythm

Previously, we have considered single words and phrases primarily, choosing diction that is clear and precise and at the same time colorful, a little strange, delightful, imaginative. Now we need to consider the artistic arrangement of sentences. Sound, rhythm, and parallelism are strategies that public speakers and master prose stylists deliberately design.

Sound and rhythm are closely connected; poets explore sounds of individual words, such as "slide," "slither," "slink," "gabble," "clatter," "boggle." Although your chief interest in words is not *primarily* in their sound, but rather in their meaning, you will notice that sounds of words and the rhythm in the sentences intrigue our ears and our sense of movement. Here is Herbert Gold, from an essay entitled "A Dog in Brooklyn, a Girl in Detroit: Life Among the Humanities," speaking of his role as instructor in a college classroom:

Shame. I feel shame at this ridicule of my authority in the classroom. A professor is not a judge, a priest, or a sea captain; he does not have the right to perform marriages on the high seas of audio-visual aids and close reasoning. But his is more than an intercom between student and fact; he can be a stranger to love for his students, but not to a passion for his subject; he is a student himself; his pride is lively. . . .

The rhythm is cumulative, dependent upon the sounds of the phrases and words: "at this ridicule," "of my authority," "in the classroom." The short words, such as "judge," "priest," "sea captain," and the repeated "s" sounds in "shame," "classroom," "seas," "student," "stranger," and "subject" appeal to our sense of rhythm.

Here is a passage about African natives in Laurens van der Post's *The Dark Eye in Africa*:

> But having destroyed their natural defences, we then denied them our own. Having taken away their way of life, we then made it impossible for them to acquire any other. Having supplanted their law by ours, we then gave them no right to live as our law demanded but rather forced them to drift suspended in dark acceptance of a state of non-being.

Clarity and rhythm characterize this passage through repeated words and phrases, such as "having destroyed," "We then ... having taken," "we then ..., having supplanted," and "we then. ... " Obviously, one highly effective way to compose rhythmically and to play upon the sounds of words is to construct phrases and sentences in a balanced fashion, called *parallelism*. (See the section "Sentence Structure: Parallelism" in Chapter V.) Surprisingly, the sentences do not become redundant or wordy; on the contrary, they become much clearer, much more precise *because* of the repetition. Consider this selection from another part of Gold's essay:

> There is power to make decisions, power to abstain, power to bewilder, promote, hold back, adjust, and give mercy; power, an investment of pride, a risk of shame.

Gold not only repeats words and sounds—"p" sounds and the word "power"—but also capitalizes on the rhythm of the short verbs and verb phrases. The sound and arrangement amplify the force of the sentence and ease the reading of a complex idea.

Listen to political speeches or to oratory of any kind, and notice the balancing of phrases, the deliberate toying with sound, and the paralleling of clauses for rhetorical effect. Martin Luther King, Jr.'s speech entitled "I Have a Dream" is a good one for study:

> I have a dream that one day this nation will rise up and live out the true meaning of its creed . . . that all men are created equal.
> I have a dream that one day on the red hills of Georgia the sons of former slaves and the sons of former slaveowners will be able to sit down together at the table of brotherhood . . .
> I have a dream that my four little children will one day live in a nation where they will not be judged by the color of their skin but by the content of their character . . .
> I have a dream today . . .
> I have a dream that one day every valley shall be exalted, every hill and mountain shall be made low, the rough places will be made plain, and the crooked places will be made straight . . .

The following is a famous sentence of Francis Bacon, imperfect in parallelism, but rhythmic and balanced:

Histories make men wise; poets witty; the mathematics subtle; natural philosophy deep; moral grave; logic and rhetoric able to contend.

Here the compressed, choppy phrases suggest a rhythm and balance that is as compelling as the longer phrases we considered previously.

In short, experiment creatively, imaginatively, perhaps even wildly. Grope for apt images, hunt for the unexpected word, but shelve the first phrase that sneaks into your head until you can compare its value with others. Design your sentences deliberately, varying the length, arranging and rearranging for the most emphatic balance, the most appealing display. In so doing, you will be benefiting yourself as well as the reader.

LEARNING AIDS

1. Appraise the essays in the "Exemplary Essays" section, following Chapter VIII, for their artistry in the use of allusions, precise words, figurative language, and rhythmic and parallel sentences. Try to discover how the words, phrases, and sentences are effective, noting especially the ways in which they make the meaning clearer and more specific.
2. How would you describe an owl? What are the usual words that tumble into your head? Here is a professional writer's description:

    He was small when he arrived, and has never grown above six inches tall, but the full measure of him is much larger than that. He is a feather filtering through the sunlight here, a humiliated cat over there. He is a *chirr* sound, he is a nibble on the toe, he is a sudden whoosh, he is a missing chicken neck. But most of all, he is HEX. (William Service, *Owl*)

    Spot the words that convey the sense of "owlness." Can you think of such words to describe a cat, a frog, or the first moon landing?
3. Write a few sentences using bright metaphors to describe the following:
    a. the appearance of the moon on a clear night
    b. a campus building (of your choice)
    c. a biology laboratory
    d. courage, truth, or hate—or some other abstract quality.
4. Write a short series of sentences in which you deliberately repeat the sounds of particular letters, such as "m," "c," or "s." Try to blend the idea of the passage with the sound you repeat.
5. Invent metaphors or personifications for the following literal phrases, using the first two examples as a pattern:

Literal phrase or sentence	Figurative substitute
a. Literature is a more powerful force than coercive weaponry.	a. The pen is mightier than the sword.

b. A ten-hour bus journey through the mountains is an arduous undertaking.

b. <u>A ten-hour bus journey is like two days in a stream bath.</u> (This is all right if exaggeration is appropriate to the passage.)

c. The large bouquet of orange gladiolas was a colorful and beautiful sight.

c. _____

_____

_____

d. Little children can be delightful and full of surprises.

d. _____

_____

e. Science has been the means for new and useful—if not marvelous—inventions.

e. _____

_____

6. Invent similes (with your choice of verb) for the following situations. Invent as many as you can (try for at least five) for each item. The point, again, is to stretch the imagination until you find the image you want. One example serves to launch your imagination. Finish each sentence as it becomes appropriate to do so.

verb
↓

Big city traffic <u>thunders</u> as loud as <u>10,000 jack hammers</u> at five o'clock rush hour.

Modern art <u>resembles</u> _____ .

Supermarkets _____ as _____ as_____ .

Modern Romance magazines _____ as _____ as _____ .

Contemporary morality is like _____ .

Dormitory living _____ as _____as_____ .

essay forms

When Neil Armstrong, Edwin Aldrin, and Michael Collins returned from the moon and prepared to write about their exploration, they needed to choose quite deliberately the form in which they described their experiences. They chose, of course, the essay, that moderately brief prose discussion of a restricted topic, and published their account in *Life* magazine (August 22, 1969). Millions of readers were waiting to learn what the moon looked like, how it felt to walk about on the moon, and how the astronauts were able to accomplish their mission—all new experiences to earthlings and, thus, more difficult to relate accurately.

It is to the astronauts' credit that they chose their essay form wisely—*the personal* (informal) *essay*. Had they chosen to write of their experiences in a *formal essay*, they might have seemed less than lively human beings elated over their feat. And they might not have retained the world's sympathy for their efforts, because their prose form would have lost them many readers who wanted to feel close to them. Likewise, if the astronauts had chosen to report their findings in a *research article*, they would have risked losing more readers through a numbing succession of data reports and impersonal summaries. Finally, a *critical essay* was out of the question, since this was the task of those experts who were to evaluate the success of the mission in retrospect.

The central concern of this chapter, then, is *form*, the approach to the subject and the arrangement of the material within the essay. Essay writing is basically explaining, even though the writer might choose to argue, to describe, or to narrate in order to explain. As explained in Chapter III, writers like Armstrong, Aldrin, and Collins must judge their readers' expectations, experience, and attitudes and then decide which kinds of explanation will best serve their purposes. The college writer should recognize and develop four essay forms as part of his own writing repertoire:

The formal essay
The personal essay
The critical essay
The research article

Each form is a strategy for a different audience, a slightly different set of purposes, and a different distance from the reader and the material. Although other forms exist, they are more variations in style than variations in form.

Although you will very likely use the same patterns of preparation explained in Chapter II in writing these essays, you will necessarily work within a definite framework that writers have followed for many years. The able writer relies on certain conventions of the common essay forms, for these conventions are familiar to the readers' thinking processes, the familiarity having developed, probably subliminally, through years of experience in our culture. You might regard these frameworks as inhibiting to free individualistic expression, but adhering to a form has the advantage of meeting the expectations of the readers.

And if the writer wishes to grope for new forms, he is still committed to paying close attention to the conventions of the older forms, for he might confuse the reader about the quality of his credentials as a writer on his particular subject. In any event, the writer can choose among several approaches.

THE FORMAL ESSAY

The form which the writer adopts for his essay derives from the occasion and the purpose of the essay itself. For the *formal essay*, the occasion is one that moves the writer to a significant statement addressed to a serious-minded readership on a subject that is important for the time. Serious concerns of modern man—like the nature of democracy, infringements on individual freedom, air pollution, war, men's liberation, or the role of art in the mind of man—identify the nature of the formal essay. The exemplary formal essay at the end of this chapter reveals a further example. If you examine the essay, you will find that it educates and enlightens—as opposed to entertaining or delighting.

Also, the formal essay length can vary considerably. *Time* essays must fit into a two-page, four-column maximum length, while an essay in *Atlantic Monthly* is considerably longer. Indeed, some formal essays approach chapter length or, sometimes, book length—as in C. P. Snow's book *The Two Cultures and the Scientific Revolution*. The dominant characteristics of the formal essay, therefore, are these:

- *Serious purpose*, indicated by the significance of the subject and the writer's effort to encourage long-term attention to the subject
- *Emphasis on fact or theory*, indicated by its close reasoning and thorough attention to providing verifiable information
- *Logical, unified progression of ideas*, indicated by its obvious signals for orderly movement from one phase of the discussion to another
- *Public character*, indicated by its dealing with social, political, moral, or cultural issues quite openly—as if in a public debate or speech where the reader is treated as a fellow citizen rather than a confidant
- *Dispassionate style*, indicated by its careful avoiding of personal references, emotional language and argument, or casual and colorful language

Calmness, dignity, wisdom, perspicacity, significance—all these traits combine to identify the formal essay at its best.

The formal essay is thus likely to reveal a writer who is pondering a significant subject openly, with detailed information, closely reasoned theoretical observations, or scientific conclusions used for idea support. The formal essay writer wants to broach a subject that may cause the reader to doubt the certainty of some ideas he has held for some time about his own life, his environment, his beliefs, or the human condition. The writer's aim is perhaps a simple one: He wants his reader to say, when finished with reading the essay, "That's true. I must think more about this subject."

A possible danger is to assume that such writing is lethargic, unexciting, or thick and hard-to-read. Formal essays achieve their common purpose by a subtly witty and graceful manner of expression—carefully avoiding distracting language or overstatement. Common instances of formal essays read aloud for public occasions include sermons, presidential inaugural addresses, scholarly lectures, and speeches for serious public occasions like an address to Congress or commemorations of historical events.

Theoretically, any subject could be used in a formal manner, but an essay titled "My Life and Hard Times" and "Roommates and How They Grow" are too personal for a formal essay. Better subjects might be "The Nature of 'Found Art'" or "American Symbols, American Dreams." A good example of the even-tempered, factual, serious voice of the formal essayist appears in the following excerpt from a 1969 *Time* essay. The purposes of the essay are to call attention to the real dangers of chemical and biological weaponry experimentation and to suggest future courses of action by government and military agencies. Note the factual, but attention-demanding, effect of the passage:

> Aside from these Strangeloveian virtues, the weapons present a major problem of control. A 1968 test of nerve gas at the gigantic Dugway Proving Grounds in Utah went awry when an airborne aerosol device failed to shut off, and winds spread the deadly agent some thirty miles past the target area, killing 6,000 sheep. Germs may be so potent and long-lasting as to threaten indefinite overkill. During World War II, the British infected Gruinard Island in the North Atlantic to test anthrax, an often fatal disease. The anthrax spores remain virulent to this day; experts say that the island is still uninhabitable, and will probably remain so for 100 years. Controlling germs and gases even inside laboratories and plants can prove difficult. Even so, the overall safety records of such facilities far surpass those of civilian industries and highways. In 26 years of biological experimentation of Fort Detrick, there have been 420 accidental infections, resulting in only three deaths.

There. We are supplied a long string of verifiable facts, indicating the size of the problem and muting the possibility of a reader's thinking it a biased appraisal of the dangers of the situation. That is the effect of a good formal essay.

The formal essayist is a special kind of writer. He is not only perceptive and unswervingly rational; he is also literate and thoughtful about his audience and purpose. Most often, he writes in the third person singular, even using such words as "one" or "he" or "a man"—all dating perhaps from the nineteenth-century origins of the formal essay, but persevering because of the objectivity that such language provides. Only an occasional use of the editorial first person plural ("We seldom experience the pleasures of adult-level television programs. . . .) invades the impersonal, public voice of the master formal essayist. And the use of first person singular is even more rare, for it is used only when the writer is a prominent authority in a certain subject and when he writes from that particular knowledge. ("When I asked Congress to reduce foreign aid allotments, the result was. . .") Thus, the distance the writer stands from his subject and his reader derives from the formal essay conventions, as well as his consideration of the occasion, the audience, and his purpose, as in all deliberate writing.

THE PERSONAL ESSAY

The essay as a literary type began nearly three hundred years ago when the French philosopher Montaigne retired from active life to one of study and contemplation. For a while he recorded witty sayings, such as proverbs, aphorisms, or maxims, but eventually he expanded his efforts to express his own personality through longer pieces, first published in 1580. He called this collection of writings *Essais* and thus invented the word which we now use to label short prose discussions, the art form that nearly every educated person must master as the chief mode of written ideas and opinions. The word "essay" means "attempt," for Montaigne tried to differentiate his tentative or incomplete prose discussions from the more thorough and formal philosophical writings that were the dominant forms of written discourse in his day. Thus, Montaigne's contribution was not only to coin a word but also to add the personal element, the tone of the intimacy of a *tête-à-tête* to the short moral lessons contained in the earlier collections of maxims and aphorisms.

The occasion for the *personal essay* is, therefore, one of expressing a personal view on a subject that is a part of the lives of all men. Thus, the early personal essays (variously called the *informal essay* or the *familiar essay* in its history) had titles like "Of Idleness," "Of the Education of Children," or "Of the Inconsistency of Our Actions." The effect is to create autobiographical accounts of opinions, experiences, and impressions that reveal a particular individual and no one else. The personal essayist fancies himself speaking on behalf of all men, but he writes as no other man could write. The qualities that personal (or informal) essays exhibit are:

- *A confidential manner*, revealing individual tastes and experiences, expressed in the first person
- *Humor and wit*, expressed in self-deprecation, clever allusions or syntax, ironic thrusts at the human scene, or whimsical and skeptical in treatment
- *A graceful, relaxed style*, made so by a conversational idiom, spontaneously organized structure, and a distinctive choice of words that reveals the individual writer on this occasion—never simply correct, not perfunctory, stiff, or affected
- *A suggestive and incomplete treatment of the subject*, indicating that the subject of the essay is probably beyond formal explanation and analysis
- *Literary tone*, revealed through the obviously well-read, speculative, and observant mind
- *Limited length*, usually, because of the demands of periodical publications

The personal essay is thus a work of art, marked by a sprightly, individualistic, clever, relaxed style, and incomplete and speculative in its effects.

At the root of it is a civilized man whose sensitivity substitutes for that of everyman but who is eminently qualified to speak for those qualities of life to which every man might aspire. Such writers as John Ciardi, James Thurber, E. B. White, Joseph Wood Krutch, Archibald MacLeish, E. M. Forster, Sheila Graham, Loren Eisely, Harry Golden, and Art Buchwald have contributed greatly to the perpetuation and popularity of this form today. Notice the urbane and lively imagination, the individualistic and witty use of language in this passage from Ciardi's "The Slush Pile," in which he describes the basis for discarding the weak poetry submissions to *Saturday Review* into the wastebasket, "the slush pile":

> . . . from the current reject basket I have hauled back a sheaf of poems that happened to be on top. All of them went into the reject basket in the first place because they were obviously silly. Here are their openings, along with some parenthetical clues for the soulful who may be charitably slow to identify silliness:
>
> "Sun drenched sand between my toes . . . " (Are those his feet or are they a couple of starfish?) "Lying naked in the sand,/The heat oppresses me . . . " (An odd place for the heat to be lying naked.) "When staring up at the foliage above . . . " (Yes, that's the right direction to look for "above.")

Ciardi's voice is confident and informed, but also ironical and entertaining, as he attempts the modest task of eliminating some of the world's written mediocrities.

On the other hand, a writer like Forster produces a good deal of urbanity through allusions, smoothly asserted statements, and closely reasoned observations, for wit and irony do not serve the more serious subject—individualism—so well. Notice the voice of a highly civilized, well-read, and forceful intelligence in the following passage:

> Personal relations are despised today. They are regarded as bourgeois luxuries, as products of a time of fair weather which is now past, and we are urged to get rid of them, and to dedicate ourselves to some movement or cause instead. I hate the idea of causes, and if I had to choose between my country and betraying my friend, I hope I should have the guts to betray my country. Such a choice may scandalize the modern reader, and he may stretch out his patriotic hand to the telephone at once and ring up the police. It would not have shocked Dante, though. Dante places Brutus and Cassius in the lowest circle of Hell because they had chosen to betray their friend Julius Caesar rather than their country Rome.

Examine the passage. Where is it "urbane," "individual," "literary," "intelligent," or "closely reasoned"? Such sanity and calm grace befit the humanist that Forster represents in his essay on behalf of the heart of man. The personal essay reveals a man "writ large" for the entertainment and the enlightenment of his readers.

THE CRITICAL ESSAY

Both formal and personal essays derive their conventions from the social context and the social purpose they serve. The *critical essay* is no different, for the primary function is to unload criticism—to praise the worthy, to correct society's ills, to scourge the dangerous, to encourage the promising. Every part of the essay is used to this end, even when providing information about the particular work, event, or phenomenon under critical scrutiny. Increasingly, twentieth-century man depends on the critical essay to guide him through the blizzard of cultural institutions, books, films, plays, concerts, fashions, exhibitions, performances, feats, which most people do not have opportunity to experience, or, perhaps more important, have the ability to judge.

It is not surprising that the expression "Well, I know what I like and what I don't—and that's good enough for me" has come of age in this century as a kind of self-defense against a barrage of new art forms, new tastes in fashion, or even new subject matter—as well as new looks at traditional institutions and manners. The critical essay has, therefore, arrived at a time when more and more people need a cultural Baedeker for standards and models of judgment-making, for the stories behind the scenes, for aid in avoiding the unworthy, and for reasons to devote time to the beneficial.

The critic thus plays an important role in the advancement of his culture, or any part of it, in one direction or another. Because of this importance, the critic must have explicit criteria by which he forms his judgments. Two main considerations aid the writer as critic. They are *function* and *basis*. That is, what is the main function or group of functions of the essay in question? And second, on what basis does the critic seem to rest his critical judgment? Here are several functions that a critical essay can perform, though not necessarily all in one piece:

To Explain.   Often the critic must *make known the essential ingredients and underlying principles* before making a judgment, if this is done at all. Indeed, criticism as explanation may be an attempt to justify the thing criticized, since the critic assumes that the readers are uninformed or perhaps prejudiced against the subject under discussion. Such a critical approach characterizes any number of essays on subjects as nudity in films or plays, political conventions, scientific achievements, or obscene literature.

To Analyze.   Here, the critic is primarily interested in *probing the nature of the work, event, or phenomenon* under scrutiny by focusing on the subject itself and providing a thorough analysis of its parts and their organization. Subjects of criticism like novels or plays, new forms of art (like Happenings or Found Art), and events or phenomena which have phases (like rock festivals or beauty pageants) are open to analysis as the chief critical function.

To Advertise. Some critical pieces, while they might be masked as explanations or as analyses, are actually advertising for the event or work in question. Exhibitions, fashions, films, plays, and other such events are frequently "criticized" in advance of their opening in order to attract an audience and help launch their enterprise. State prisons, colleges, or social programs might invite criticisms of a specific kind in order *to publicize their worth* in an acceptable manner.

To Interpret. In addition to explaining, analyzing, or advertising, a critical essay contains interpretive comment, especially if the *meaning of a work, an event, or phenomena* is not easy to deduce. Interpretation is an important function, though the important consideration for the reader to notice is on what basis the interpretation is made. Is the interpretation of the meaning of a rock festival, a ballet, a play, a film, or a fashion trend made on a moral, political, historical, social, or personal basis? The acceptability of the interpretation will depend largely on the acceptance of the basis for criticism.

To Evaluate. Perhaps the most pervasive function of the critical essay is to provide *an appraisal of the worth* of the subject. Such a function can be performed in various ways: by comparing the subject under discussion with others like it, by assessing its historical connection to its predecessors, by discovering inconsistencies or lapses in the form or the performance, or by exploring possible social consequences and judging the significance. All subjects of critical essays—from circuses to riots to modern high schools (see the Friedenberg essay in the "Exemplary Essays" section which follows this chapter)—are open to these sorts of considerations.

To Express Personal Opinions. It may surprise many persons to learn that some critical essays exist *to make known the personal opinions and feelings of the critic himself.* The critic poses as a kind of supersensory, superintelligent consumer of the subject under criticism; he is a kind of brilliant stand-in for the common man. Ordinarily, the critic does not inject himself into his essay, except when he has some significant experience or first-hand information to use. Today, as a critic becomes more extraordinary, this seems to occur more often.

Thus, whether the critical essay entertains or instructs, it still must provide the reader with observations and information for him to make an immediate judgment or for him to experience the work, event, or phenomena under discussion with some informed background information and trial judgments.

While these functions are the most important considerations, it is well to devote some attention to the basis on which a critic writes his essay. Here are several possible bases with brief discussions of their judgment processes:

The Moral Basis. The strength of moral criticism depends on the acceptability of the implicitly or explicitly stated ideas about what is good and what is bad. Thus, the reader needs to beware of unknowingly accepting assumptions about what human beings ought to be. He may find himself accepting a judgment that films which depict sex and violence are immoral—while, in fact, the opposite might be true if different assumptions about morality are used.

The Historical Basis. Here, the critic bases his evaluation of a subject on considerations of historical antecedents. Works of art are examined in this way, but the Apollo moon flight was also judged by a historical comparison to Columbus' voyage to America.

The Aesthetic Basis. Here the critic asks, "How well was the work, event, or phenomena performed? What could have been done better?" The emphasis is on the *appearance* of the work or its performance, using artistic standards, as in judging a painting or recital or play.

The Social Basis. The worth of an event or work is often judged by what it will contribute to the life of human beings, either immediately or in the long run. Thus, the moon shot, the Eighty-ninth Congress, the work of a Presidential administration, labor strikes, student protests, civil rights marches, and other events are evaluated on the basis of their implications for the quality of human life. Such judgments are therefore implicitly political, depending on one's assumptions about the nature of men and about the nature and purposes of society and government.

The Personal Basis. Perhaps the critic depends on one source for judgment: his own personal feelings about any given subject for criticism. The reader's acceptance of criticism offered on this basis depends on how much one identifies with the critic. Norman Mailer's criticism of the two political national conventions in his work called "Chicago and Miami," which won a Pulitzer Prize for journalistic writing, assessed the conventions on largely personal grounds. What made this work so appealing, however, was the large reading audience that identified closely with Mailer's feelings about the workings of such conventions as part of the process by which Presidents are chosen.

Perhaps other bases by which a subject can be criticized might be lumped under "the judicial basis," for *the critic can approach his subject with a definable set of standards that he explicates or in some way indicates as the mark or the purpose against which the subject should be judged.* In judging a musical work, a sculpture, a designer's fashion show, a sports event, a poem, an architectural work, a city plan, the quality of a college program, an actor's performance, or a television talk show, separate sets of standards are used that have evolved from the character and purpose of the works or events themselves. Such standards are definable and may or may not coincide with other bases, such as those named above.

Whatever the function, whatever the basis, the critical essay is simply the medium by which a critic states his reactions to the subject before him. His object may change from paragraph to paragraph, and he may have ulterior motives, but these are matters that the wary reader must be alert to as he reads the essay.

Ordinarily, the critic avoids certain types of observations or arguments that the man of reason should reject. Thus, the critical essay typically is *not* characterized by the following:

- Use of irrelevant criteria, such as attacking the character of a composer (an *ad hominem* argument) rather than examining his work—or, applying a moral or political judgment to a college program because of a history course on communism or a literature professor's assignment of *Love Story* and *The Story of O*.
- Reporting or summarizing alone, since the critical essay must contain some stand, some judgment on the subject being examined.

Thus, the critic should present a balanced view of the subject, some explanation or interpretation, an identifiable criterion or set of criteria, and an explicit judgment on the subject. Critical essays thus occur as reviews, editorials, and even as journal articles—wherever artistic or cultural diagnosis and appraisal is needed.

The style, furthermore, can be formal and academic or light and familiar. Depending on the audience, the subject, and the purpose, the style could even be rollicking, ironic, or flip. An example of the latter, where the style is the essence of the criticism is Calvin Trillin's *Life* book review of Irving Wallace's novel *The Seven Minutes*. Trillin deliberately avoids mentioning any detail of the several-hundred-page-long novel and instead talks about a conversation that he and his wife had about the meaning of the title. At the end, he claims to have written the review in exactly seven minutes. Such a review is an extreme example when compared to a more conventional kind like this excerpt from a review by Charles Thomas Samuels on E. S. Connell, Jr.'s novel *Mr. Bridge*. Samuels clearly commits himself to a particular set of standards in this passage where he judges harshly, though he later praises the novel for its strong qualities:

> However, *Mr. Bridge* shares faults with its companion novel [*Mrs. Bridge*]. The glimpse-of-life form produces redundancy, and Connell is not selective enough. Though the book is scrupulously realistic, melodrama occasionally obtrudes, as when the secretary makes her ludicrous confession of love.

Samuels thus bases his criticism on a set of standards (selectivity, realism, no redundancy) applied to the novel as a form, and the reader is rationally informed about the worth of the work as quality fiction. Trillin's essay on *The Seven Minutes* uses a personal basis for making judgments, and the reader is thus emotionally warned away from the book.

The critical essayist must, therefore, know thoroughly the subject he is to criticize, and he must be aware of his function and his standards for judgment. Without these, he is a lion without teeth. What is more, nearly every professional person, if he rises near the top of his profession, will be called upon to write a critical essay at some time in his life. He might be a physician, a professor, a writer, a general, a film or play director, a dean, or a research scientist.

Whatever he is, he will need to be aware of the expectations of his reading audience, and he will very likely follow this process of preparing to write: After determining the kind of readership, the available space, and the nature of the subject, he might jot down some notes about details, first impressions, and central features of the subject. After deciding which points to emphasize as strong and which as weak (according to a deliberately chosen set of standards), he should organize the essay by first identifying the subject, then making known his overall opinion, providing necessary background information, a summary of the events or central characteristics of the subject, and then an assessment of the specific strengths and weaknesses. Finally, the usual reviewer will develop his central criticism of the subject under consideration and draw a general conclusion or recommend a particular idea or action. While different critical essayists might use a different order, these are the essential ingredients of most critical essays.

THE RESEARCH ARTICLE

Of the forms that a piece of writing might take, the research article is probably the most demanding of the writer, especially in terms of the close reasoning, the verfiable evidence, and the preparation. Further, we have used the term "article" rather than "essay" for two reasons: first, research writing can take several forms, all of which can be independent parts of longer works; laboratory reports, research chapters in books, scholarly papers, monographs, and research papers (see Chapter X) are all variations in length or style of the research article. Second, it is often the means by which professionally educated persons talk to one another when they are basing their observations on impartially discovered research findings. The occasion for the reasearch article is therefore one where preserving knowledge is the chief function, for research information needs to be accessible in the future. Thus, its dignity and permanence rise with its functions—that of communicating knowledge and reporting research in order to preserve it.

Some research articles report mainly systematically derived research findings; among these are *the survey, experiment, laboratory test, statistical measure, archeological probe, interpretive examination, or historical inquiry*. Still another kind of research article, less common but still quite helpful, is the piece of writing that brings together various sets of research findings found in many articles in order to place the subject under discussion in perspective or to draw an overall conclusion about the research. Both varieties of research exhibit a number of features that distinguish the research article from other kinds of writing. The chief characteristics are these:

- *Emphasis on verfiable findings*; reports as the result of systematic inquiry into or collection of facts that could, most often, be duplicated if another researcher were to follow the same process

- *Critical inquiry into a problem or testing of a hypothesis*, whereby the research method is explained in detail and the problem is solved or not solved or the hypothesis is upheld or rejected
- *A subject that appeals, most often, to somewhat specialized interests*, even though—as in the research article "The Heroic Style in America"—the research sometimes appeals to a wide audience. (Relevance is often not a concern in the research article, for the subject has its own appeal to the person who wants more significant information.)
- *Impartiality, or an objective, philosophical attitude* where the writer wishes to explore thoroughly a worthwhile subject that has puzzled or baffled him and others in the past
- *Limited scope*, usually by the demands of the subject itself, since the research question must be narrowed so that data can be gathered and explained in a short space
- *Informative nature in contrast to persuasive*, though the researcher wishes to persuade his readers to see the subject the way he sees it
- *Highly-structured format* (particularly in articles that report findings from an experiment)
- *Plain style (most often)*, primarily voiceless and leavened with a professional vocabulary (The author subordinates his own feelings and identity, except in the rare instance where the research article is disseminated beyond a particular profession, as in the example at the end of this chapter.)
- *Close documentation*, whereby footnotes and bibliography are necessary as the conventions for indicating borrowed ideas, words, or facts (Sometimes textual documentation—where author and work are named in the text—is combined with the more usual footnote.)

Although these conventions might seem to limit the writer's expression in the research article, it is the natural means for professionally-educated people to speak to each other. Confusion, emotion, and ambiguity are thus virtually prevented from entering and causing misinterpretation or misjudgment. For this reason, research articles are generally written in third person, though first person is now occasionally used to dilute the possibility of pedantry or stilted prose. While scholarly writing is somewhat more relaxed than it once was, it is still a studied medium of expression that serves academic, technological, and scientific inquiry the world around.

The structure of the research article deserves a bit more explanation. Several structures are common, but among the sciences and social sciences, writers generally follow this pattern:

First, the writer announces the precise nature of the subject, indicates the problem or hypothesis he investigated, and then discusses significance.

Second, he states the limitations of his research effort—the restricted subject he chose because of the need for information, time limitations, the methodology, the scarcity of information, or whatever.

Third, he provides background information, such as related research, speculations on the subject, or the history of interest in the research subject.

Fourth, he explains the methodology he employed to obtain the results that he reports in the article. He relates the step-by-step procedures he used, the kinds of authorities he might have consulted, or the kinds of specific analyses he might have applied to the subject.

Fifth, he presents the important findings that result from the kind of methodology he used. These are organized according to their relevance to the point that he makes rather than according to their interesting features, though these most often coincide.

Finally, the article ends with a summary and an interpretation of the findings, with inquiry into the implications of the findings for other research or for human action or life in general.

The sum effect of this is an article that can be read and understood in the same way today as it will be if it is read far into the future. Thus, original thinkers communicate their findings and thoughts to countless unknown others who need to understand the findings and observations of the writer in the same way he discovered and explained them.

Researchers in the humanities or social sciences and natural sciences generally follow a less sharply defined process, though the purpose of reporting and preserving knowledge is the same. Generally, such writers begin their research articles with an explicit statement of the subject and an announcement of the main observation they wish to make in the research inquiry of the article. Next, they proceed through a step-by-step discussion of the report or the argument, presenting *ample convincing evidence* of various kinds along the way, as it becomes appropriate. Finally, there is the necessary explanation of the meaning and significance of the findings and a considered judgment of the implications. By such a process, new interpretations of a literary work emerge, additional historical findings contribute to existing annals, puzzling musical or artistic phenomena become explicated, or philosophical quandaries are untangled for the advancement of knowledge about human beings in all their pursuits. Writers of such articles follow prescribed reasoning processes of analysis, argument, and judgment, for their standing in the intellectual company of their peers depends on the effectiveness of their reasoning abilities.

Researchers go about gathering information and preparing their writing in many ways, depending on the demands of the specific discipline, but, in general, they follow the process which we explain in considerable detail in Chapter X, "The Research Process." The types of research, the research process, documentation, and using the library constitute the significant kinds of information which should be second nature to research writers or readers, for they must understand and use such information as educated persons in a world that will make increased use of this knowledge.

exemplary
essays

FORMAL ESSAY

Leonard R. Sayles is Professor of Business Administration at the Graduate School of Business, Columbia University. He is a specialist in both business administration and social science and has written essays on such subjects as business organization, industrial sociology, applied anthropology, and labor relations. He is author and co-author of many books, including *The Local Union: Behavior of Industrial Work Groups; Personnel: Human Behavior in Organizations; Managerial Behavior;* and *Individualism and Big Business.* Such writing indicates his special ability to provide unusual and broad perspective on the announced subject of the following essay: the man who works in and whose behavior is modified by the organization.

Professor Sayles makes no impassioned pleas, marshals no armada of detailed scientific findings, and ponders rather than argues—all traits of the formal essay. The implications of this formal presentation of information and thoughtful observation might lead his readers to write other essays, such as a personal essay, a research article, or a critical essay, in order to take up where he leaves off. His calm assessment of man as manager and as member of business organizations prompts his readers, quite likely, to check his observations against what we know about our parents or relatives or ourselves—as members of organizations. Even Willy Loman, from Arthur Miller's *Death of a Salesman*, or Sloan Wilson's "man with a gray flannel suit" are appropriate referents to explore the larger significance of the essay as a guide to our own thinking.

THE ORGANIZATION MAN: HOW REAL A PROBLEM?*

Leonard R. Sayles

Recently we have witnessed a new variation on the old theme that business destroys (or at least eats away) the souls of those who come within its grasp. The eating-away process used to refer to ethics and morality. Caught up in the

*This material was presented at the Arden House conference and later published in Eliot D. Chapple and Leonard R. Sayles, *The Measure of Management.* New York: The Macmillan Company, 1961. Copyright 1961 by The Macmillan Company, and reprinted with their permission.

profit-making system, men who otherwise might dedicate themselves to a life of unselfish service sought instead a far tinnier Holy Grail—the almighty dollar. Although as generalizations about an entire system these condemnations embodied exaggerations, they had the virtue of sensitizing the community to excesses. A growing sense of business responsibility and protection against willful discharge and sweatshop servitude may to some extent be due to their harsh repetition. If this is true, then there may be a virtue in what is otherwise a somewhat puzzling new accusation: Life in the business organization induces excessive conformity and dependence.[1]

The critics do not mean that people caught up in the soulless web of the corporation are converted into money-grubbing robots or ever-fearful wage slaves. They say, rather, that contemporary organizations are a threat to the psyche. Employees and managers in our large companies lose their sense of independence, their pluck, and their daring. Instead of devoting themselves to highly individualistic programs of self-improvement (money-grubbing?), they become dedicated to the seductive goals of being accepted and even being liked by boss and colleague. These are the organization men.

The highly negative fear of losing acceptance becomes the dominating motive, to replace the more positive goal of conquering new frontiers. The critics argue that conforming to the group and kowtowing to the boss absorb all the energies which might be more healthily devoted to constructive development of personality and the corporate and community balance sheet. The result must be slow but sure destruction of national character.

Perhaps the generous reception given to the organization-man image is a hallmark of our steady progress in humanizing the conditions of work and the position of the subordinate. Rather than the callous, over-demanding boss who gets what he wants regardless of the human cost, we are apparently now concerned with his diametric opposite—the group thinker who is more concerned with social cohesion than he is with profit. Surely we have now come around the full circle. Less than two decades ago Elton Mayo's fear about the lack of administrators who could banish the sense of individual isolation (or "anomie," the concept he drew from Durkheim) was the accepted tenet of faith.

As more adherents join a bandwagon that has the additional lure of playing a quasipsychiatric theme, one is reminded of the extremes of "progressive" education and child rearing. Not long ago, the home and the school were the villains. Both at the hearth and at the blackboard our young were being repressed, their

---

[1]Two of the most extensive nonfiction works representing this new critique of business are William H. Whyte, Jr., *The Organization Man* (New York, Simon and Schuster, Inc., 1956); and (with a very different point of view) Chris Argyris, *Personality and Organization* (New York: Harper & Row, Publishers, Incorporated, 1957). A recent fictionalized account of the debilitations induced by the large corporation is Alan Harrington's *Life in the Crystal Palace* (New York: Alfred A. Knopf, Inc. 1959).

individualism squashed long before it could flower. The reasoning was much the same—humans flourished best in an unfettered, unrestricted, free-to-do-as-they-please environment. Fixity of structure, it was insisted, must produce rigidity of mind. The extremists felt, as does the organization-is-an-inhibitor school of thought, that discipline and controls, externally imposed goals, hurt the individual who both desired and needed complete freedom.

Parenthetically, we might ask why the concept of an "organization man" has had such wide and immediate appeal. Is it not the perfect self-rationalization for those individuals whose success has not measured up to their ambitions? They are reassured by the belief that group thinking and conformity have so won over the decision makers in our large corporations that the individual who stands out from the crowd cannot get ahead. Some who use this ready-made excuse confuse the lip service given by companies to presently popular clichés like "teamwork" and "participation" with an actual description of what management expects. Platitudinous statements concerning objectives, values, or goals may bear little resemblance to the types of activities in which a company engages. The organization, as we shall be observing, both needs and rewards distinctive, and unique personality characteristics such as high energy, initiative, and the ability to tolerate unfriendly responses. They may talk about a good "team man," but the uncommon men are the ones who will get ahead and eventually reach the top-level positions.

OPPOSITE FINDINGS FROM RESEARCH

Students of man cannot help but be amused by this whole surprising trend in the critique of business. There are no studies that show man in some Eden-like status of complete independence. In the most primitive state and in all the records of history, man has sought and flourished in tribes and clans, communities, and associations. If half a dozen people are placed in a room with a common task, we can predict they will quickly evolve common routines of behavior and even a self-imposed organization structure. The latter will include leadership to initiate instructions, and the group will penalize deviations from approved standards of behavior. Conformity will be expected, and dependence will be readily forthcoming. The street-corner gang, like the office clique, makes such excessive demands for conformity in thought and action with an impunity that makes the routines of the organization and the demands of its authority pale by comparison.

Man apparently neither wants nor has experienced this postulated state of complete autonomy. People have always demanded structure in their lives. With few exceptions, men depend on human relationships, some fixity of structure, routine, and habit to survive psychologically. Although we do not like to admit it, most of us flee from a vacuumlike absense of structured relationship. Students of business organization know well that one of management's basic problems is to find enough people with characteristics of leadership who will take initiative and who can operate in a relatively unstructured situation. The demand of subordinates for situations in which they can be dependent, not the supply of overbearing authority, is frequently the problem. Companies seeking to make decentralization operative discover, to their sorrow, that unwillingness to accept responsibility or to take initiative, and the desire to have each decision sanctified by the boss's OK are ever-present blocks to successful delegation.

What about the emotional needs of the man on the work level? Is it not true that extremes of the division of labor and autocratic, dominating supervisors rob the individual of any real sense of accomplishment and satisfaction in his job?

Put in these terms, this concern might also be shown to be misplaced. Many workers voluntarily choose the simplest, most routine, most subdivided task. While job enlargement must appeal to some, for many it is a threat to the more idyllic assurance of untroubled working hours, free for daydreaming, social chatter, and strategic planning to "beat the rate." Employees certainly do not always seek additional responsibility and decreased dependence.

THE NATURE OF ORGANIZATION

Contemporary fiction, sermons, and social science have become enamored of their moans over the fate of the individual in the large organization. Unfortunately, the eagerness with which the term "organization man" has been adopted has resulted in substantial confusion, a good portion of which stems from its original promulgation. The essence of organization, of organizational behavior, involves learning to follow routine procedures. Of necessity the organization must be a predictable system of human relationships, where rhythm and repetition are the vital components. This may come as a rude shock to those who think of managers as constantly improvising new activities. Chester Barnard once commented candidly that during a year as president of the New Jersey Bell Telephone Company he had to make only *one* decision that was, in fact, a real choice between alternatives. The preponderant elements of organizational behavior consist of matters such as Joe's knowing that he must check Bill's activities two or three times a week, must be available when Al gets into trouble, and must sit with his boss at least an hour a day to work through plans for the following day. The combination of work-flow imperatives and personality needs provides the raw material for these predictable and rhythmical patterns of interaction.

It must be remembered that in speaking of an organization we imply some degree of permanence—the need for predictable repetition, self-maintenance, assured continuity, and regulated activity. Only when the regular business of an organization is functioning properly—following the *routines* of acquisition, processing, and distribution (of ideas, materials, or paper)—can individuals apply, or are they likely to be permitted to apply, their rational, creative talents to the challenge of new, unsolved problems. Imagination, innovation, and intellectual vigor cannot prosper where individual energies are fully utilized in handling recurring crises.

In this regard, the president of the Brookings Institution recently observed:

> If admnstrators are asked to nominate the aspects of the task that are most time-consuming and frustrating to the exercise of their responsibilities, they will agree that they are preoccupied with distractions; with inconsequential little things that push themselves ahead of important issues; with the tyranny of the telephone; with the relentless flitting from one issue to another; with the ceaseless procession of interviews and ceremonials; with the pressure of circumstance and deadlines; and with the absence of time to collect one's wits, much less to think or reflect. Only a superb or a hard-boiled administrator can cut through this daily morass to concentrate on the important responsibilities that he cannot shirk.[2]

Although Barnard's statement may well be something of an exaggeration, among the most crucial problems of any organization are those concerned with the development of predictable routines. Frayed tempers, suppressed and not so suppressed hostility, and individual frustration resulting from ineffective organization destroy individual competence.

In other fields in which organization plays a part we are not so shocked by this. The most dramatic and best known is sport. Baseball and football teams are the most common examples of organizations where the interrelation of the work routines (the plays) is dependent upon the careful adjustment of players to one another and to the coaches. Here complicated plays and split-second coordination cannot be executed unless the organization is made up of individuals well adjusted to one another. The job of the coach is to see that this is accomplished, to select a series of plays best fitted to the capacities of his materials, and to fit together players who can supplement each other's abilities. To develop a smooth-working organization, he must handle personalities so skillfully that good teamwork becomes almost second nature. As a result, the experts and the fans discuss learnedly whether coach A is getting the most out of his material, whether catcher B can handle his pitchers, whether star C is wrecking the morale of the team.

Business organizations are like teams, but vastly more complicated. The same factors of plays and personalities combine to make an organization, and the adjustment that goes on from day to day determines whether the company is to have effective coordination or will constantly suffer from personnel dissatisfaction, labor disputes, and inefficiency.[3]

[2] Robert D. Calkins, "The Decision Process in Administration," *Business Horizons*, vol. II, no. 3 (Fall, 1952), 20.

[3] We hope the reader will not think we are indulging in the old stereotype of the company president in exhorting his co-workers, "We're all on the same team, boys." We are not talking about "togetherness," but the development and synchronization of a complex set of plays (organization) by which the company operates.

Does this necessity create "organization men"? Members of outstanding instrumental groups like the Budapest String Quartet have developed almost perfect coordination; they can count on each other for completely predictable behavior. It is doubtful that this coordination has destroyed their individuality. Off the job, in the full development of their personalities and interests, they live very different lives. Great athletic teams have consisted of people who had little liking for one another—e.g., "Tinker to Evers to Chance"—amply demonstrating their uncongeniality in their personal lives. Nevertheless, they learned the skills and routines essential for the successful conduct of their organizational affairs.

One would hazard a guess that a great deal of excitement about conformity is due to the *absence* of knowledge concerning what is required for effective organizational activity, like the primitive tribe that does not understand the movements of the heavenly bodies and the occurrence of thunderstorms. Not knowing how to assess Jones's contribution to effective management, we evolve irrational fetishes and taboos. The striped tie, the ivy-league suit, the sheepskin, the appropriate tone of voice, automobile, wife, and home location, even the testing programs designed to exclude all but the "safe" pedestrian types. These are all manifestations of imperfect knowledge about how to evaluate an executive or a new employee. They are not the inevitable products of life in a large organization.

As we develop more understanding about methods of improving the mastery of organizational behavior, we can believe that the nonsensical elements will disappear just as rain dances have fallen into disrepute in most civilized locations. Fitting personalities together to evolve coordination and sound structure does not require fixed patterns of thought and of family and community life.

We must be careful to urge businessmen to deal with real problem areas, not those that may be the easiest to sell during a period when terms like *conformity* are so popular. The human relations problems of business will not be solved by extreme, sweeping assertions and accusations, any more than the field of mental health will be improved by arguments that neuroses are enveloping us all. It has always been good sport to beat at our sources of institutional power, including business, and one of the strengths of Western democracy has been this permissive climate. But we must not confuse sermons with science. We readily concede that there are problems of large scale in contemporary life. Mass communications, for example, in our type of society raise serious questions concerning opportunities for individual expression, privilege in democracy that we rightfully cherish. Further, living with authority, of course, has never been easy. Philosophers undoubtedly will continue to struggle with one of the persistent problems of life: freedom versus authority. The balance is always a tenuous one. Life in the presence of other human beings involves cooperative endeavors and government, and consequently necessitates authority. We must always live with an uneasy balance between the inevitable personal restrictions and our ambivalent needs for both dependence and freedom. The problem neither began nor will it end with the corporation.

THE MODERN MANAGER VERSUS
THE BUSINESS BUCCANEER

As an alternative to this straw man, the organization man, the old-style business buccaneer is having a renaissance. In the current swing to idolize the swashbuckler even the robber baron has had a resurrection. After all, weren't these the true believers—the nonconformists who allowed neither codes nor public disapproval nor built-in inhibition to stand in the way of their single-minded objectives? By contrast, the contemporary manager, concerned with public and industrial relations and with an organization structure to maximize human effectiveness, at best casts only a faint shadow. Or so the critics would have us believe.

It is strange indeed that the contemporary manager is now being maligned for what is his greatest challenge and potential accomplishment. The maintenance of effective human relationships in large-scale organizations is one of the marvels of our age. The skills of administration required to direct and control tens of thousands of people with differing backgrounds and interests, in order to produce coordinated effort directed toward predetermined objectives, tower above the achievements of the business buccaneers of an earlier age. They dealt with a few, simple variables primarily in the market place. Their apparent bravery and daring were more a product of the simplicity of their problem than of extraordinary skills or brute native courage. The diverse and complex responsibilities of the modern business offer a challenge many times more exciting to human abilities than an uncomplicated "inner-directed" objective of maximum personal profits.

PERSONAL ESSAY

Dorothy Lee, Greek by birth, is an anthropologist who has explored the philosophical issues of freedom, existence, and perception in her book *Freedom and Culture* (1961). Now Lecturer in Anthropology and Research Anthropologist at Harvard University, she has also held positions at Vassar College and the Merrill-Palmer School. Although she can write ably of the Hopi, Wintu, Tikopia, Trobriand, and other cultures, she is concerned in the following essay with the social and imaginative parameters of the individual in suburban culture.

Perhaps her main achievement in this essay is her ability to merge her anthropologist's experience in many cultures with a personal concern for the lives of her children and herself in a dominant form of American culture. Her tone resembles a warm, personal talk. She uses relatively short sentences and personal experiences to underscore the relevancy of her main point. She blends her knowledge of the scientific study of man with her humanitarian regard for the welfare of her—and our—children and the meaning and use of "free time." The result is a revelation about the life that many Americans lead, a revelation of the unseen drain on our potential freedom of imagination and of the unnecessary shackles on our social behavior.

SUBURBIA RECONSIDERED: DIVERSITY AND THE CREATIVE LIFE*

Dorothy Lee

Is the suburb a "paradise regained?" Yes, certainly one image of paradise: the paradise of harp players agreeably getting along with one another; a paradise of lights without shadows, of virtue rather than of vibrant good; a paradise where people do the right, the acceptable, perhaps even what they ought to do. But it is not a paradise which is the "blooming, buzzing confusion" of the senses.

At one time I had thought of the suburb as a good place to bring up my children. There was the country for my children to know, to see, to feel, to incorporate

> . . . the gay
> great happening illimitably earth.

There would be available to them the kind of music I liked, the kind of people I liked, the kind of experience I liked. I did not take my children to a suburb, but I did take them to a homogeneous community in the country, to the edge of the

---

*From *Man and the Modern City*, edited by Elizabeth Green, *et. al.*, copyright 1963. Reprinted by permission of University of Pittsburgh Press.

Vassar College campus, near the woods and hills, the brooks, the ponds, the fields, where they could be with deer, and rabbits, and woodchucks, and all the wild growing things. After some years, at tremendous personal expense, and against my children's resistance, I fled from this paradise. I fled, not from the country, but from the filtered experience which I had been providing for my children. We went to where the children could be tempted to join street corner society, where they could see brute poverty, and vice and exultation, and the bewilderment of the rejected immigrant; where they could be exposed to bad English and despicable music. I took them where they could meet taste that had not been labeled good or bad, so that they could make their own decisions about it; where their associates had not been implicity preselected and prelabeled as desirable.

After a period of disorientation and anguish, my children were all glad of the move. We mourned the loss of the country, we had to get it in the summer alone. But, of course, this loss is not relevant to a discussion of suburbs, because if we had been living in a true suburb the country would have been lost to us in time in any case.

In many respects the culture of the suburbs is only an intensification of the official American culture—the culture implicit in the curricula of the schools of education, expressed in the structure and the teaching of our public school system; the culture underlying all policy-making, and even the appeal we make in our advertising and in the mass-oriented movies produced in Hollywood. It is this culture which the urbanite takes to the suburbs with him and finds there in his children's school. But here the suburb with its relative homogeneity approximates a closed system and intensifies certain aspects of culture.

I would like to consider suburban culture from the following point of view: to what extent does suburban life make it possible for the individual to grow, to maintain inner consistency, to exercise autonomy? What is the range of experience, the variety of society which it offers for the transaction of the self? I should like to discuss the prerequisites for personal growth and strength as offered on the one hand by the city and on the other hand by the suburb.

I shall take up first the subject of the strength of the self. To what extent is the individual enabled and incited to excel, not in a comparative sense, but rather in the sense of exercising all the muscles of his person, intellectual, emotional, physical, with joy and pride? Does suburban living help the individual find and give expression to his own peculiar pattern to the minutest detail, and beyond that, to transcend his potential?

To my mind, one essential for the strengthening of the self is the presence of diversity. The self needs variety of experience directly for its own growth for richer transaction. Diversity is also needed indirectly so that an individual can exercise his powers of perception and discrimination in the area of making a choice, so that in making his own choice he can be an agent in creating his own experience. In fact, I believe that the exercise of one's agency is one way to excellence, and I use "exercise" here in the sense that I exercise my muscles. In the suburbs, diversity is largely absent as compared with the city. David Riesman speaks of this lack of diversity in the paper which he entitles "Suburban Sadness." And I agree with him that this is sad. Sometimes the homogeneity happens without deliberate intent, though people are naturally guided by their own likes. In the case of the establishment of Crestwood Heights, it seems to have been done with deliberation. The authors who, in *Crestwood Heights: A Study of the Culture of Suburban Life*, describe this pseudonymous community write that the establishment of the suburb was for the purpose of creating "a smaller area in which they and *others like* them" (the italics are added) could agree on a policy.

Now there is a second aspect in which diversity can contribute to, in fact is necessary for, the strength of the self, and that is through making conflict possible. Conflict may be bad when it is overwhelming; but it can evoke an answering strength, and through the exertion of this strength, can mean the growth of the self through experience, an experience which demands the output of all that is available to the self. A lawyer was speaking to me recently about his early years in this country. He arrived from Greece as a boy of eleven and went to live in an industrial city as an immigrant, as a poor boy, as the nephew of a man who owned a pool hall and who employed the little boy as an assistant. He said to me that when finally he managed to go to Princeton, he had deplored this experience of his as poverty stricken. But now, after years of living, thinking, and experience, he sees these early years of conflict as the years which had made it possible for him to grow from strength to strength. This is the kind of experience which a city does provide usually and which is generally not available to the child growing up in the suburb.

In fact official American culture in general tends more and more to view conflict as bad and to eliminate it. Two years ago I was teaching a seminar in which vigorous discussion of freedom was taking place when suddenly a student asked that we agree on a definition of freedom, that we abandon our differences so that we could all be able to state the same thing. Diversity was happily present in this seminar. The members had come from all over the world. But this diversity, the contrapuntal discussion which created the theme in its rich variety of ramifications, threatened the American student's value of "getting along."

Somehow in the official American culture, harmony, the symphonic unification of diversity, has been reinterpreted to mean monotony. In the name of agreement difference is being eliminated—certainly not fostered—giving place to sameness and to agreement as a desired good. There is a trend toward eliminating difference in taste, in values, in standards, in education, in ways of living. And this trend, I believe is at its strongest in the suburb, because here there is a feedback from the relatively homogeneous situation. But in eliminating diversity we deprive ourselves of the opportunity to strengthen ourselves in our own stand, and, in fact, to create our own position. We have little opportunity to learn to respect difference, or knowing the difference, to despise it or reject it according to our own act of decision.

The city at least does offer more diversity. Cities, of course, vary in idiosyncracy and in the degree of differentiation which they offer. Yet, it is in the city that we meet the extremes, the immigrant as well as the old American, the laborer and the president of the corporation. Here is where we encounter the thrill of the refugee who for the first time lays eyes on the Statue of Liberty or sets foot on American soil. It is here that we meet the hardship, the sordidness, as well as the gracious living of the established. Here to some extent existence is not quite filtered for the growing individual. This is not to say that a girl in the city would end up by having a different assortment of friends than she would have had in the suburb. The point I want to make is that in the city she would have arrived possibly at the same kind of friends after having lived through the experience of choice, through perhaps the anguish of rejection and the doubts revolving around selection, and thus would have grown as a person, would have strengthened her own idiosyncratic pattern. In a sense, she would have created her own experience, and she would have been an agent in her own existence.

Yet whatever the actuality, the idea of official American culture is that of overcoming differentiation. Agreement is "good," because it is the sign of "getting along." To "get along" is one of the goals of living offered to the growing child in the school, whether in the city or in the suburb. When I analyzed manuals for the teachers of Family Life Education and of Home Economics, I found the emphasis on "getting along" strong in a variety of the situations discussed. These manuals represented suggestions for teachers across the country. In one lesson on Family Relationships, the term "get along" was found to occur seven times. Under the heading of Personality, in the chapters which were actually concerned with teaching the student how to be pleasing to others, "getting along" was also given a high ranking. Getting along means agreement; and as a matter of fact when it was used in connection with one's family relations, it spelled the elimination of diversity, the by-passing of conflict rather than living through conflict or facing the situation of conflict.

Thus agreement is good in itself. It is also good because it is the elimination of conflict. Conversely, conflict must be eliminated in the name of agreement. However, there is another sanction which supports the elimination of conflict. This is the sanction against competition.

The aim of the schools is to teach cooperation; cooperation is seen as good and competition as the enemy of cooperation. Yet competition has been decried without enough reflection and understanding. There is one competition that is seen as leading to a standard of success. There is, however, the other competition, the competition that demands a good and strong antagonist, a respected antagonist so as to make exertion of the self possible. Take a chess player. He needs a strong chess player if he is to play well at all. Or take a tennis player. Not only does he need an antagonist, he also needs a strong one, possibly one stronger than himself, a player who calls forth skill and the strength which cannot emerge without this strong competition. In fact, in my experience, a tennis player prefers to play against a competitor who will defeat him rather than against one who, being weak, will not call for an answering strength and will be defeated as a matter of course.

Now the suburbs are often criticized for the competitive life they offer. But in my opinion it is the other kind of competition, the rivalry within approximate sameness, within a similarity of standards, which rages in the suburbs. The contrapuntal competition which calls forth the hidden forces of the self and helps create a new whole, this is thrown away along with the undesired diversity. Agreement engenders at least a surface placidity. And it often is achieved by means of a Procrustean bed, and—to mix my metaphors—establishes the comfortable, rigid ceiling of the golden mean.

In fact, the exertion itself has ceased to be a value; both exertion and the agency of the self. Writers now deplore the fact that things "happen to us" instead of "our doing them." To my mind, they have reason to do so. I have heard of a suburb in New York where the parents became aware of this and decided they would find some way to get their children to do things for themselves. One of the obvious ways was to have the children walk to school instead of being driven by their parents. But when the parents tried to put this into practice, they found it was impossible. The passivity, the non-exertion, had been built into the suburb. There were no sidewalks anywhere except in the one or two blocks of the shopping district.

I have been speaking of diversity as necessary to the growth of the self in affording situations of choice, in offering an agentival role, and, through providing conflict, in encouraging the exertion which is a dimension of commitment and engagement. In addition to this, diversity in the sense of the "blooming, buzzing confusion" is, I believe, the prime requisite of creativity. The individual must create from the source. He must see the peas roll for himself, to use Fromm's illustration, not depend on someone else's experience. It is imperative that he create his own experience, perceiving his own pattern in the chaos. This, I believe to be true of all creative work. Even in the area of law, according to Charles P. Curtis, the language of law is vague (and I should say deplorably bewildering) so as to give an opportunity to each lawyer to recreate the law for himself in terms of the specific situation. It is certainly true of poetry where "naming an object suppresses three-quarters of the enjoyment of a person about it . . . "; and where "an author knows he will give the reader more only by getting him to do more, to take a larger share in the creation." The unfinished evokes because everything is not organized and on the surface.

Now—if I may continue to generalize—all this is lacking in the suburbs; or, rather, what is offered is just the opposite. The suburbs do name the object for their denizens. Experience is offered, organized, prelabeled, preselected, prefabricated. Stephen Birmingham in his "Commuter's Lament" dreams of going back to New York and "wasting" time doing things like taking a ride on the Staten Island Ferry. He wonders "is it still a nickel" and rushes to say, "don't tell me, I want to find out for myself." This freedom to find out for himself he associates with the city, not with the suburbs. This is the tune that Robert Paul Smith sings in his book *Where Did You Go? Out* . . . when he compares his own growing up in New York with the life of his children in a New York suburb. He says, "My kid went to play soccer the other day. The way you play soccer now is this: you bring home from school a mimeographed schedule for the Saturday morning Soccer League. . . . There are always exactly eleven men on each team, the ball is regulation size, the games are played on a regulation-size field with regulation-sized soccer balls, and there is a regulation-sized adult referee." In contrast, he describes his own life. "When I was a kid, the way we got to play baseball was this: we . . . grabbed a beat-up fielder's glove, went out on the block and met a friend who had an old first baseman's mitt, a ball, went down the block a little and hollered at the kid who had the bat. . . . We went to the vacant lot and played a game resembling major league baseball, only that it was played with a bat and bases. It was fun. . . . You see it was our game. I think my kid was playing someone else's game."

Of course the father in his own childhood was wasting a lot of time trying to find the bat and ball, rounding up the kids, getting to the vacant lot. In the suburb, there is efficiency, at least in Birmingham's and Smith's description of suburban life. There is no waste of time; and indeed, at least for the commuting fathers, there is no time to waste. When two or three or more hours of commuting are added to the regular day's work, the remaining very few hours of the waking day have to be utilized in an organized and efficient way. Birmingham, in his "lament," writes of this aspect of suburban life. He says that you can tell the suburbanite by the fact that he drives around in New York. The New Yorker likes to walk because he likes to look around, to smell the smells, to discover what is going on. But then his day is longer; there is more time in it. Perhaps this is why he has not moved to the suburbs. It is not clear here which is the chicken and which is the egg; but I would agree that this stress on efficiency, organization, this battle against wasting time, though a part of official American culture, is perhaps intensified in suburban living. Certainly when I spent three and a half hours on the road commuting, my very few "free" hours had to be rigidly goal-oriented. There was no time to waste on exploration which had not been already mapped and diagrammed and robbed of all creativity.

I must repeat here that this is only an intensification. Throughout our society today there is an emphasis on the streamlined, the efficient. We give our students bibliographies, not so that they may explore, but so that they may save time, so that they may take the shortest route between two points and never have a chance to take a wrong turning and wander around the countryside. In this way they need not "waste" their time looking through poor articles and discovering the inadequacy for themselves, or even in forming their own standards by which to judge a book (and, of course, reading fewer "good" books). We give them a map, not a compass, and quite often we substitute the map for the territory. Now that they have the map, now that they know what other people thought of this book, or of the Renaissance, why should they have to discover for themselves?

A teacher in one of the leading colleges told me how at one time she asked a class in literature to read a book about which they had never heard, and report on it. More than half the class came to her and asked her whether it was a "good book"; because, without knowing this, they did not know how to read it, how to relate to it, what to think of it.

This is the picture I found in the manuals for the teaching of Home Economics which I analyzed in 1954. According to these, the students were to be guided to use even their leisure time with the utmost efficiency. For example, it was suggested that they drive out in the country for a purpose, such as "in order to see the sunset." They were urged to read a book "that had been recommended." They were urged to investigate the radio programs first and then to turn on only the program which had been branded as good. No wandering about, no vagary of the spirit, no sudden exultant discovery of something which had not been approved by a superior beforehand. Here the self is not clearly recognized. It has no validity. Someone outside makes the decisions, clears away the underbrush, smoothes the road, and allows the self to move on only as a zombie, protected against its own mistakes, deprived of its own experience.

This treatment of the self as not significant is seen also, for example, when parents prepare a room for an "eight-year-old boy"; not for John, not for *this* boy. The authors of *Crestwood Heights* speak among other things of the rumpus room and the children's room, "meticulously fitted to what decorators and the furniture trade consider the taste of a child." That is, the child does not create his own room out of the ragged, dreadful bits and treasures that go into the making of his own personal history, the things which eventually produce a room that could be an expression only of his own self and no one else's self.

The Crestwood Heights house in general is described as lacking idiosyncracy. The authors write that it is "reminiscent of a series of department store windows, charmingly arranged, harmoniously matched in color." This statement reminded me of a generalization which a French informant in the Columbia Research Project for Contemporary Cultures said about the French living room, in which one found "the habits, the reminders, the family pictures, the family furniture," a room that grew with the family. This would be a living room uniquely expressing the history, the idiosyncracy of this particular family.

I would say then that for a suburbanite more so than for a city dweller experience comes filtered and preordered. The range of experience has been preselected and highly narrowed. The goal of efficiency is more than elsewhere realized here. And, in the suburb, no less than in the city, the individual is viewed and dealt with as a representative of a category rather than as a person in his own right.

If we are to speak in the language of the existentialist, I would say that all this spells alienation to me. The individual is set on a track which leads and moves him away from encounter with the heterogeneous data of experience. He is provided with a life which does not evoke the exertion of the self, a life which does not call forth commitment. Since experience comes to a large degree prefabricated, the individual is not incited to engage himself in the process of living, to take on his responsibility of choice, and his role as agent. This I believe to be more true of the suburbs than of the city. If suburban life is "paradise regained," it is, to my mind, the wrong kind of paradise.

CRITICAL ESSAY

Edgar Z. Friedenberg was Professor of Sociology at the University of California at Davis when he wrote this essay on the modern high school. He is the author of *The Vanishing Adolescent* (1959), *The Dignity of Youth and Other Atavisms* (1965), and *Coming of Age in America* (1965), in which the following essay appears in a longer version. His particular interest is in adolescent socialization, especially the effects of schooling and other means of socialization on human growth and development. As a social scientist, his ability to write for a wide readership is a kind of blessing that attracts readers to his cause—the reexamination and revision of American high schools.

His special gift for language allows him to sustain a sympathetic but ironic voice throughout the entire book as he describes the clash between high school and adolescent. He is particularly distressed at the commercial and hypocritical values of our mass culture as they invade the schools and promote a kind of "custodial control" of the student, stripping away the humanizing "concepts of dignity and privacy." His prose rasps his readers' consciences, provoking them to attend to the problems he identifies; gone is the "objective scientist" who reports on his visits to teenage America much as though he just returned from a safari to study Masai warriors in darkest Africa. Volumes of abstract reports on this same subject have not moved many people to act on the findings, but Friedenberg's writing, with its admitted personal bias, advantageously stirs smoldering embers of interest in high school education at a time when passions are running high on the subject of youth in colleges.

THE MODERN HIGH SCHOOL: A PROFILE*

Edgar Z. Friedenberg

Not far from Los Angeles, though rather nearer to Boston, may be located the town of Milgrim, in which Milgrim High School is clearly the most costly and impressive structure. Milgrim is not a suburb. Although it is only fifty miles from a large and dishonorable city and a part of its conurbation, comparatively few Milgrimites commute to the city for work. Milgrim is an agricultural village which has outgrown its nervous system; its accustomed modes of social integration have not yet begun to relate its present, recently acquired inhabitants to one another. So, though it is not a suburb, Milgrim is not a community either.

Milgrim's recent, fulminating growth is largely attributable to the rapid development of light industry in the outer suburbs, with a resulting demand for skilled labor. But within the past few years, further economic development has created a steady demand for labor that is not so skilled. In an area that is by no means known for its racial tolerance or political liberalism, Milgrim has acquired, through no wish of its own, a sizable Negro and Puerto Rican minority. On the shabby outskirts of town, a number of groceries label themselves Spanish-American. The advanced class in Spanish at Milgrim High School makes a joyful noise—about the only one to be heard.

Estimates of the proportion of the student body at Milgrim who are, in the ethnocentric language of demography, non-white, vary enormously. Some students who are clearly middle-class and of pinkish-gray color sometimes speak as if they themselves were a besieged minority. Most responsible staff members produce estimates of from 12 to 30 percent. Observations in the corridors and lunchrooms favor the lower figure. They also establish clearly that the non-whites are orderly and well behaved, though somewhat more forceful in their movements and manners of speech than their light-skinned colleagues.

What is Milgrim High like? It is a big, expensive building, on spacious but barren grounds. Every door is at the end of a corridor; there is no reception area, no public space in which one can adjust to the transition from the outside world. Between class periods the corridors are tumultuously crowded; during them they are empty. But at both times they are guarded by teachers and students on patrol duty. Patrol duty does not consist primarily in the policing of congested throngs of moving students, or the guarding of property from damage. Its principal function is the checking of corridor passes. Between classes, no student may walk down the corridor without a form, signed by a teacher, telling where he is coming from, where he is going, and the time, to the minute, during which the pass is valid. A student caught in the corridor without such a pass is sent or taken to the office; there a detention slip is made out against him, and he is required to remain after school for two or three hours. He may do his homework during this time, but he may not leave his seat or talk.

There is no physical freedom whatever at Milgrim. During class breaks, the lavatories are kept locked, so that a student must not only obtain a pass but find the custodian and induce him to open the facility. Indeed Milgrim High's most memorable arrangements are its corridor passes and its johns; they dominate social interaction. "Good morning, Mr. Smith," an attractive girl will say pleasantly to one of her teachers in the corridor. "Linda, do you have a pass to be in your locker after the bell rings?" is his greeting in reply. There are more classifications of washrooms than there must have been in the Confederate Navy. The common sort, marked just "Boys" and "Girls," are generally locked. Then there are some marked, "Teachers, Men" and "Teachers, Women," unlocked. Near the auditorium are two others marked simply, "Men" and "Women," which are intended primarily for the public when the auditorium is being used for some function. During the school day cardboard signs saying "Adults Only" are placed on these doors. Girding up my maturity, I used this men's room during my stay at Milgrim. Usually it was empty; but once, as soon as the door clicked behind me, a teacher who had been concealed in the cubicle began jumping up and down to peer over his partition and verify my adulthood.

He was not a voyeur; he was checking on smoking. At most public high schools, students are forbidden to smoke, and this is probably the most common source of friction with authorities. It focuses, naturally, on the washrooms which are the only place students can go where teachers are not supposed to be. Milgrim, for a time, was more liberal than most; last year its administration designated an area behind the school where seniors might smoke during their lunch period. But, as a number of students explained to me during interviews, some of these seniors had "abused the privilege" by lighting up before they got into the area, and the privilege had been withdrawn. No student, however, questioned that smoking was a privilege rather than a right.

The concept of privilege is important at Milgrim. Teachers go to the head of the chow line at lunch; whenever I would attempt quietly to stand in line the teacher on hall duty would remonstrate with me. He was right, probably; I was fouling up an entire informal social system by my ostentation. Students on hall patrol also were allowed to come to the head of the line; so were seniors. Much of the behavior that Milgrim depends on to keep it going is motivated by the reward of getting a government-surplus peanut butter or tuna fish sandwich without standing in line.

The luncheon itself is a major learning experience, which must make quite an impression over four years' time. There are two large cafeterias which are used as study halls during the periods before and after the middle of the day. The food, by and large, is good, and more tempting than the menu. The atmosphere is not quite that of a prison, because the students are permitted to talk quietly, under the frowning scrutiny of teachers standing around on duty, during their meal— they are not supposed to talk while standing in line, though this rule is only sporadically enforced. Standing in line takes about a third of their lunch period, and leaves plenty of time for them to eat what is provided them. They may not, in any case, leave the room when they have finished, any more than they could leave a class. Toward the end of the period a steel gate is swung down across the corridor, dividing the wing holding the cafeterias, guidance offices, administrative offices, and auditorium from the rest of the building. Then the first buzzer sounds, and the students sweep out of the cafeteria and press silently forward to the gate. A few minutes later a second buzzer sounds, the gate is opened, and the students file out to their classrooms.

During the meal itself the atmosphere varies in response to chance events and the personality of the teachers assigned supervisory duty; this is especially true in the corridor where the next sitting is waiting in line. The norm is a not unpleasant chatter; but about one teacher in four is an embittered martinet, snarling, whining, continually ordering the students to stand closer to the wall and threatening them with detention or suspension for real or fancied insolence. On other occasions, verbal altercations break out between students in the cafeteria or in line and the student hall patrolmen. In one of these that I witnessed, the accused student, a handsome, aggressive-looking young man, defended himself in the informal but explicit language of working class hostility. This roused the teacher on duty from his former passivity. He walked over toward the boy, and silently but with a glare of contempt, beckoned him from the room with a crooked finger and led him along the corridor to the administrative office; the tall boy rigid in silent protest, the teacher, balding and stoop-shouldered in a wrinkled suit, shambling ahead of him. The youth, I later learned, was suspended for a day. At some lunch periods all this is drowned out by Mantovani-type pop records played over the public address system.

What adults generally, I think, fail to grasp even though they may actually know it, is that there is no refuge or respite from this: no coffee break, no taking ten for a smoke, no room like the teachers' room, however poor, where the youngsters can get away from adults. High schools don't have club rooms, they are organized gym and recreation. A student cannot go to the library when he wants a book; on certain days his schedule provides a forty-five minute library period. "Don't let anybody leave early," a guidance counselor urged during a group-testing session at Hartsburgh, an apparently more permissive school that I also visited. "There really isn't any place for them to go." Most of us are as nervous by the age of five as we will ever be, and adolescence adds to the strain; but one thing a high-school student learns is that he can expect no provision for his need to give in to his feelings, or swing out in his own style, or creep off and pull himself together.

The little things shock most. High-school students—and not just, or even particularly, at Milgrim—have a prisoner's sense of time. They don't know what time it is outside. The research which occasioned my presence at Milgrim, Hartsburgh, and the other schools in my study required me to interview each of twenty-five to thirty students at each school three times. My first appointment with each student was set up by his guidance counselor; I would make the next appointment directly with the student and issue him the passes he needed to keep it. The student has no *open* time at his own disposal; he has to select the period he can miss with least loss to himself. Students well-adapted to the school usually pick study halls; poorer or more troublesome students pick the times of their most disagreeable classes; both avoid cutting classes in which the teacher is likely to respond vindictively to their absence. Most students when asked when they would like to come for their next interview, replied, "I can come any time." When I pointed out to them that there must, after all, be some times that would be more convenient for them than others, they would say, "Well tomorrow, fourth period" or whatever. But hardly any of them knew when this would be in clock time. High-school classes emphasize the importance of punctuality by beginning at regular but uneven times like 10:43 and 11:27, which are, indeed, hard to remember; and the students did not know when this was.

How typical is all this? The elements of the composition—the passes, the tight scheduling, the reliance on threats of detention or suspension as modes of social control are nearly universal. The usurpation of any possible *area* of student initiative, physical or mental, is about as universal. Milgrim forbids boys to wear trousers that end more than six inches above the floor, and has personnel fully capable of measuring them. But most high schools have some kind of dress regulation; I know of none that accepts and relies on the tastes of students.

There are differences, to be sure, in tone; and these matter. They greatly affect the impact of the place on students. Take, for comparison and contrast, Hartsburgh High. Not fifteen miles from Milgrim, Hartsburgh is an utterly different community. It is larger, more compact, and more suburban; more of a place. Hartsburgh High is much more dominantly middle class and there are few Negroes in the high school there.

First impressions of Hartsburgh High are almost bound to be favorable. The building, like Milgrim, is new; unlike Milgrim's, it is handsome. External walls are mostly glass, which gives a feeling of light, air, and space. At Hartsburgh there is none of the snarling, overt hostility that taints the atmosphere at Milgrim. There are no raucous buzzers; no bells of any kind. Instead, there are little blinker lights arranged like the Mexican flag. The green light blinks and the period is over; the white light signals a warning; when the red light blinks it is time to be in your classroom. Dress regulations exist but are less rigorous than at Milgrim. Every Wednesday, however, is dress-up day; boys are expected to wear ties and jackets or jacket-sweaters, the girls wear dresses rather than skirts and sweaters. The reason is that on Wednesday the school day ends with an extra hour of required assembly and, as the students explain, there are often outside visitors for whom they are expected to look their best.

Students at Hartsburgh seem much more relaxed than at Milgrim. In the grounds outside the main entrance, during lunch period, there is occasional horseplay. For ten minutes during one noon hour I watched three boys enacting a mutual fantasy. One was the audience who only sat and laughed, one the aggressor, and the third—a pleasant, inarticulate varsity basketball player named Paul—was the self-appointed victim. The two protagonists were portraying in pantomine old, silent-movie-type fights in slow motion. The boy I did not know would slowly swing at Paul, who would sink twisting to the ground with grimaces of anguish; then the whole sequence would be repeated with variations, though the two boys never switched roles. In my interviews with Paul I had never solved the problems arising from the fact that he was eloquent only with his arms and torso movements, which were lost on the tape recorder, and it was a real pleasure to watch him in his own medium. This was a pleasure Milgrim would never have afforded me. Similarly, in the corridors at Hartsburgh I would occasionally come upon couples holding hands or occasionally rather more, though it distressed me that they always broke guiltily apart as they saw me or any adult. One of my subjects, who was waiting for his interview, was dancing a little jig by himself in the corridor when I got to him. This was all rather reassuring.

It was also contrary to policy. There is a regulation against couples holding hands and they are punished if caught by the kind of teacher who hates sexuality in the young. The air and space also, subtly, turn out to be illusions if you try to use them. Hartsburgh High is built around a large, landscaped courtyard with little walks and benches. I made the mistake of trying to conduct an interview on one of these benches. When it was over we could not get back into the building except by disturbing a class, for the doors onto this inviting oasis can only be opened from inside, and nobody ever goes there. Since the courtyard is completely enclosed by the high-school building, this arrangement affords no additional protection from intruders; it merely shuts off a possible place for relaxation. The beautiful glass windows do not open enough to ventilate the rooms, in which there are no individual controls for the fiercely effective radiators. Room temperature at Hartsburgh is a matter of high policy.

Teachers do not hide in the washrooms at Hartsburgh; but the principal recently issued a letter warning that any student caught in the vicinity of the school with "tobacco products" would be subject to suspension; students were directed to have their parents sign the letter as written acknowledgment that they were aware of the regulation and return it to school. Staff, of course, are permitted to smoke. At Hartsburgh a former teacher, promoted to assistant principal, serves as a full-time disciplinarian, but students are not dragged to his office by infuriated teachers, as sometimes happens at Milgrim. Instead, during the first period, two students from the school Citizenship Corps go quietly from classroom to classroom with a list, handing out summonses.

Along with having a less rancorous and choleric atmosphere than Milgrim, Hartsburgh seems to have more teachers who like teaching and like kids. But the fundamental pattern is still one of control, distrust, and punishment. The observable differences—and they are striking—are the result almost entirely, I believe, of *structural* and demographic factors and occur despite very similar administrative purposes. Neither principal respects adolescents at all or his staff very much. Both are preoccupied with good public relations as they understand them. Both are inflexible, highly authoritarian men. But their situations are different.

At Milgrim there is a strong and imaginative district superintendent, who is oriented toward the national educational scene. He likes to have projects, particularly in research and guidance. Guidance officers report through their chairman directly to him, not to the building principal; and the guidance staff is competent, tough, and completely professional. When wrangles occur over the welfare of a student they are likely to be open, with the principal and the guidance director as antagonists; both avoid such encounters if possible, and neither can count on the support of the district office; but when an outside force—like an outraged parent—precipitates a conflict, it is fought out. At Hartsburgh, the district superintendent is primarily interested in running a tight ship with no problems. To this end, he backs the authority of the principal whenever this might be challenged. The guidance office is vestigial and concerned primarily with college placement and public relations in the sense of inducing students to behave in socially acceptable ways with a minimum of fuss.

In these quite different contexts, demographic differences in the student bodies have crucial consequences. At Milgrim, the working-class students are not dominant—they have not got quite enough self-confidence or nearly enough social savvy to be—but they are close enough to it to be a real threat to the nice, college-bound youngsters who set the tone in their elementary and junior high school and who expect to go on dominating the high school. These view the rapid influx of lower-status students as a rising wave that can engulf them, while the newcomers, many of whom are recent migrants or high-school transfers from the city, can remember schools in which they felt more at home.

The result is both to split and to polarize student feeling about the school, its administration, and other students. Nobody likes Milgrim High. But the middle-class students feel that what has ruined it is the lower-class students, and that the punitive constraint with which the school is run is necessary to keep them in line. In some cases these students approach paranoia: one girl—commenting on a mythical high school described in one of our semi-projective research instruments—said, "Well, it says here that the majority of the students are Negro—about a third" (the actual statement is "about a fifth").

The working-class students are hard-pressed; but being hard-pressed they are often fairly realistic about their position. If the Citizenship Corps that functions so smoothly and smugly at Hartsburgh were to be installed at Milgrim, those who actually turned people in and got them in trouble would pretty certainly receive some after-school instruction in the way social classes differ in values and in the propensity for non-verbal self-expression. At Milgrim, the working-class kids know where they stand and stand there. They are exceptionally easy to interview because the interviewer need not be compulsively non-directive. Once they sense that they are respected, they respond enthusiastically and with great courtesy. But they do not alter their position to give the interviewer what they think he wants, or become notably anxious at disagreeing with him. They are very concrete in handling experience and are not given to generalization. Most of them seem to have liked their elementary school, and they share the general American respect for education down to the last cliché—but then one will add, as an afterthought, not bothering even to be contemptuous, "Of course, you can't respect *this* school." They deal with their situation there in correspondingly concrete terms. Both schools had student courts last year, for example, and Hartsburgh still does, though few students not in the Citizenship Corps pay much attention to it. Student traffic corpsmen give out tickets for corridor offenses, and these culprits are brought before an elected student judge with an administrative official of the school present as advisor. But Milgrim had a student court last year that quickly became notorious. The "hoody element" got control of it, and since most of the defendants were their buddies, they were either acquitted or discharged on pleas of insanity. The court was disbanded.

The struggle at Milgrim is therefore pretty open, though none of the protagonists see it as a struggle for freedom or could define its issues in terms of principles. The upper-status students merely assent to the way the school is run, much as middle-class white Southerners assent to what the sheriff's office does, while the lower-status students move, or get pushed, from one embroilment to the next without ever quite realizing that what is happening to them is part of a general social pattern. At Hartsburgh the few lower-status students can easily be ignored rather than feared by their middle-class compeers who set the tone. They are not sufficiently numerous or aggressive to threaten the middle-class youngsters or their folkways; but, for the same reason, they do not force the middle-class youngsters to make common cause with the administration. The administration, like forces of law and order generally in the United States, is accepted without deference as a part of the way things are and work. Americans rarely expect authority to be either intelligent or forthright; it looks out for its own interests as best it can. Reformers and trouble-makers only make it nervous and therefore worse; the best thing is to take advantage of it when it can help you and at other times to go on living your own life and let it try to stop you.

This is what the Hartsburgh students usually do, and, on the whole, the results are pleasant. The youngsters, being to some degree ivy, do not constantly remind the teachers, as the Milgrim students do, that their jobs have no connection with academic scholarship. Many of the teachers, for their part, act and sound like college instructors, do as competent a job, and enjoy some of the same satisfactions. The whole operation moves smoothly. Both Milgrim and Hartsburgh are valid examples—though of very different aspects—of American democracy in action. And in neither could a student learn as much about civil liberty as a Missouri mule knows at birth.

What is learned in high school, or for that matter anywhere at all, depends far less on what is taught than on what one actually experiences in the place. The quality of instruction in high school varies from sheer rot to imaginative and highly skilled teaching. But classroom content is often handled at a creditable level and is not in itself the source of the major difficulty. Both at Milgrim and Hartsburgh, for example, the students felt that they were receiving competent instruction and that this was an undertaking the school tried seriously to handle. I doubt, however, that this makes up for much of the damage to which high-school students are systematically subjected. What is formally taught is just not that important, compared to the constraint and petty humiliation to which the youngsters with few exceptions must submit in order to survive.

The fact that some of the instruction is excellent and a lot of it pretty good *is* important for another reason; it makes the whole process of compulsory schooling less insulting than it otherwise would be by lending it a superficial validity. Society tells the adolescent that he is sent to school in order to learn what he is taught in the classroom. No anthropologist and very few high-school students would accept this as more than a rationalization. But rationalizations, to be at all effective, must be fairly plausible. Just as the draft would be intolerable if the cold war were wholly a piece of power politics or merely an effort to sustain the economy, so compulsory school attendance would be intolerable if what went on in the classrooms were totally inadequate to students' needs and irrelevant to their real intellectual concerns. Much of it is, but enough is not, to provide middle-class students, at least, with an answer when their heart cries out "For Christ's sake, what am I doing here?"

But far more of what is deeply and thoroughly learned in the school is designed to keep the heart from raising awkward, heartfelt issues—if design governs in a thing so subtle. It is learned so thoroughly by attendance at schools like Milgrim or even Hartsburgh that most Americans by the time they are adult cannot really imagine that life could be organized in any other way.

First of all, they learn to assume that the state has the right to compel adolescents to spend six or seven hours a day, five days a week, thirty-six or so weeks a year, in a specific place, in charge of a particular group of persons in whose selection they have no voice, performing tasks about which they have no choice, without remuneration and subject to specialized regulations and sanctions that are applicable to no one else in the community nor to them except in this place. Whether this law is a service or a burden to the young—and, indeed, it is both, in varying degrees—is another issue altogether. As I have noted elsewhere, compulsory school attendance functions as a bill of attainder against a particular age group. The student's position is that of a conscript, who is protected by certain regulations but in no case permitted to use their breach as a cause for terminating his obligation. So the first thing the young learn in school is that there are certain sanctions and restrictions that apply only to them; that they do not participate fully in the freedoms guaranteed by the state, and that *therefore, these freedoms do not really partake of the character of inalienable rights.*

Of course not. The school, as schools continually stress, acts *in loco parentis*; and children may not leave home because their parents are unsatisfactory. What I have pointed out is no more than a special consequence of the fact that students are minors, and minors do not, indeed, share all the rights and privileges—and responsibilities—of citizenship. Very well. However one puts it, we are still discussing the same issue. The high school is where you really learn what it means to be a minor.

For a high school is not a parent. Parents may love their children, hate them, or like most parents, do both in a complex mixture. But they must nevertheless permit a certain intimacy and respond to their children as persons. Homes are not run by regulations, though the parents may think they are, but by a process of continuous and almost entirely unconscious emotional homeostasis, in which each member affects and accommodates to the needs, feelings, fantasy life, and character structure of the others. This may be, and often is, a terribly destructive process; I intend no defense of the family as a social institution. But children grow up in homes or the remnants of homes, are in physical fact dependent on parents, and too intimately related to them to permit their area of freedom to be precisely defined. This is not because they have no rights or are entitled to less respect than adults, but because intimacy conditions freedom and growth in ways too subtle and continuous to be defined as overt acts.

Free societies depend on their members to learn early and thoroughly that public authority is not like that of the family; that it cannot be expected—or trusted—to respond with sensitivity and intimate perception to the needs of individuals but must rely basically, though as humanely as possible, on the impartial application of general formulae. This means that it must be kept functional, specialized, and limited to matters of public policy; the meshes of the law are too coarse to be worn close to the skin. Especially in an open society, where people of very different backgrounds and value systems must function together, it would seem obvious that each must understand that he may not push others further than their common undertaking demands, or impose upon them a manner of life that they feel to be alien.

After the family, the school is the first social institution an individual must deal with—the first place in which he learns to handle himself with strangers. The school establishes the pattern of his subsequent assumptions as to what relations between the individual and society are appropriate and which constitute invasions of privacy and constraints on his spirit—what the British, with exquisite precision, call "taking a liberty." But the American public school evolved as a melting pot, under the assumption that it had not merely the right but the duty to impose a common standard of genteel decency on a polyglot body of immigrants' children and thus insure their assimilation into the better life of the American dream. It accepted, also, the tacit assumption that genteel decency was as far as it could go. If America has generally been governed by the practical man's impatience with other individuals' rights, it has also accepted the practical man's determination to preserve his property by discouraging public extravagance. With its neglect of personal privacy and individual autonomy the school incorporates a considerable measure of Galbraith's "public squalor." The plant may be expensive—for this is capital goods; but little is provided graciously, liberally, simply as an amenity, either to teachers or students, though administrative offices have begun to assume an executive look.

The first thing the student learns, then, is that as a minor, he is subject to peculiar restraints; the second is that these restraints are general, not limited either by custom or by the schools' presumed commitment to the curriculum. High-school administrators are not professional educators in the sense that a physician, an attorney, or a tax accountant are professionals. They do not, that is, think of themselves as practitioners of a specialized instructional craft, who derive their authority from its requirements. They are specialists in keeping an essentially political enterprise from being strangled by conflicting community attitudes and pressures. They are problem-oriented, and the feelings and needs for growth of their captive and unenfranchised clientele are the least of their problems; for the status of the "teen-ager" in the community is so low that even if he rebels, the school is not blamed for the conditions against which he is rebelling. He is simply a truant or a juvenile delinquent; at worst the school has "failed to reach him." What high-school personnel become specialists in, ultimately, is the *control* of large groups of students even at catastrophic expense to their opportunity to learn. These controls are not exercised primarily to facilitate instruction, and particularly, they are in no way limited to matters bearing on instruction. At several schools in our sample boys had been ordered— sometimes on the complaint of teachers—to shave off beards. One of these boys had played football for the school; he was told that, although the school had no legal authority to require him to shave, he would be barred from the banquet honoring the team unless he complied. Dress regulations are another case in point.

Of course these are petty restrictions, enforced by petty penalties. American high schools are not concentration camps. But I am not complaining about their severity; what disturbs me is what they teach their students concerning the proper relationship of the individual to society, and in this respect the fact that the restrictions and penalties are unimportant in themselves makes matters worse. Gross invasions are more easily recognized for what they are; petty restrictions are only resisted by "troublemakers." What matters in the end is that the school does not take its own business of education seriously enough to mind it.

The effects on the students are manifold. The concepts of dignity and privacy, notably deficient in American adults folkways, are not permitted to develop here. The school's assumption of custodial control of students implies that power and authority are indistinguishable. If the school's authority is not limited to matters pertaining to education, it cannot be derived from its educational responsibilities. It is a naked, empirical fact, to be accepted or controverted according to the possibilities of the moment. In such a world, power counts more than legitimacy; if you don't have power, it is naive to think you have rights that must be respected. . . . Wise up. High-school students experience regulation only as control, not as protection; they know, for example, that the principal will generally uphold the teacher in any conflict with a student, regardless of the merits of the case. Translated into the high school idiom, *suaviter in modo, fortiter in re* becomes "If you get caught, it's just your ass."

Students do not often resent this; that is the tragedy. All weakness tends to corrupt, and impotence corrupts absolutely. Identifying, as the weak must, with the more powerful and frustrating of the forces that impinge upon them, they accept the school as the way life is and close their minds against the anxiety of perceiving alternatives. Many students like high school; others loathe and fear it. But even the latter do not object to it on principle; the school effectively obstructs their learning of the principles that, we boast, distinguish us from totalitarian societies.

Yet, finally, the consequence of continuing through adolescence to submit to diffuse authority that is not derived from the task at hand—as a doctor's orders or the training regulations of an athletic coach, for example, usually are—is more serious than political incompetence or weakness of character. There is a general arrest of development. An essential part of growing up is learning that, though differences of power among men lead to brutal consequences, all men are peers; none is omnipotent, none derives his potency from magic, but only from his specific competence and function. The policeman represents the majesty of the state, but this does not mean that he can put you in jail; it means, precisely, that he cannot—at least not for long. Any person or agency responsible for handling throngs of young people—especially if he does not like them or is afraid of them—is tempted to claim diffuse authority and snare the youngster in the trailing remnants of childhood emotion which always remain to trip him. Schools succumb to this temptation, and control pupils by reinvoking the sensations of childhood punishment, which remain effective because they were originally selected, with great unconscious guile, to dramatize the child's weakness in the face of authority. "If you act like a bunch of spoiled brats, we'll treat you like a bunch of spoiled brats" is a favorite dictum of sergeants, and school personnel, when their charges begin to show an awkward capacity for independence.

Thus the high school is permitted to infantilize adolescence; in fact, it is encouraged to by the widespread hostility to "teen-agers" and the anxiety about their conduct found throughout our society. It does not allow much maturation to occur during the years when most maturation would naturally occur. Maturity, to be sure, is not conspicuously characteristic of American adult life, and would almost certainly be a threat to the economy. So perhaps in this, as in much else, the high school is simply the faithful servant of the community.

There are two important ways in which it can render such service. The first of these is through its impact on individuals; on their values, their conception of their personal worth, their patterns of anxiety, and on their mastery and ease in the world—which determine so much of what they think of as their fate. The second function of the school is Darwinian; its biases, though their impact is always on individual youngsters, operate systematically to mold entire social groups. These biases endorse and support the values and patterns of behavior of certain segments of the population providing their members with the credentials and shibboleths needed for the next stages of their journey, while they instill in others a sense of inferiority and warn the rest of society against them as troublesome and untrustworthy. In this way the school contributes simultaneously to social mobility and to social stratification. It helps see to it that the kind of people who get ahead are the kind who will support the social system it represents, while those who might, through intent or merely by their being, subvert it, are left behind as a salutary moral lesson.

RESEARCH ARTICLE

Marshall Fishwick is Professor of History and American Studies at the University of North Florida, in Jacksonville. He has served as a professor or as a visiting lecturer at a number of universities, including Minnesota, Delaware, Lincoln (of Pennsylvania), Copenhagen, Maine, and Krakow, and has been president of the American Studies Association. He has written or edited seventeen books, including *American Studies in Transition; Faust Revisited; Remus, 'Rastus, and Revolution;* and *The Hero, American Style,* and he has contributed numerous research articles to many scholarly publications.

As a writer of a research article, Professor Fishwick does not use a special jargon understood only to his professional peers. He is obviously writing for a diverse, but also well-read, audience. His precise and sprightly vocabulary, his wide span of references and allusions, his carefully documented borrowing from others' research, his objective, philosophical tone, his close reasoning, and his blending of information with his point of view combine to produce an accomplished scholarly paper.

THE HEROIC STYLE IN AMERICA*

Marshall Fishwick

> I want to live in a world that is able to get on to the questions that belong to the twentieth century.
> —Donna Mickleson, A Student Look at America

America's heroic style evades chronology, but not contour. We assign the swashbuckler to the seventeenth century only to have Doug Fairbanks leap onto the twentieth-century scene, sword in hand. We think we've seen the last of the cavaliers who sat proudly on their horses and dashed toward Gettysburg—only to find General Patton atop his tank turret, dashing toward Germany. Fairbanks and Patton inherited their style from earlier epochs of swashbucklers and cavaliers. They reflect contours of an earlier time, as the rear-view mirror reflects the landscape behind.

Other heroes anticipate epochs yet to come. Cool ones dominate the twentieth century; but there was also something wonderfully cool about sixteenth-century Sir Francis Drake, "singeing the beard of the Spanish king" by sailing right into the harbor at Cadiz; or laconic, eccentric, professor-turned-Civil-War-soldier "Stonewall" Jackson, saying quietly to his aides, "If the enemy is still standing at sunset, press them with the bayonet." The history of heroes echoes and re-echoes statements and styles down the corridors of time.

In that history, repetition and revolution exist side by side. The red badge of courage for today's youth is long hair; nothing signals popstyle more decisively. Old boys moan the new barbarism and shagginess in the same terms as did Thomas Hall in 1654:

> Go, Gallants, to the Barbers go
> Bid them your hairy Bushes mow.
> God in a Bush did once appear
> But there is nothing of Him here.[1]

What the newly emerging bushy-headed hero stands for, no one can yet say. He is not, Ihab Hassan notes, exactly the liberal's idea of the victim, nor the conservative's idea of the outcast, nor the radical's idea of the rebel. He finally appears as an expression of man's quenchless desire to affirm, despite the pressures of our age, the human sense of life.[2]

Some of America's most colorful paragons were heroes in homespun—products of a genuine, orally transmitted folklore that did not scorn the grass-roots idiom:

> Beefsteak when I'm hungry,
> Corn likker when I'm dry,
> Pretty little gal when I'm lonesome,
> Sweet heaven when I die.

Diligent collectors have found examples of ballads, dance and game lyrics, blues, spirituals, work songs, hymns and white spirituals, Indian chants and prayers, trickster tales, local legends, tall tales, adapted European stories. There is no shortage in America of superstitions, sayings, proverbs, occupational jokes, and an infinite variety of games, dances, riddles, and rhymes. The distilled experience of generations of birth, life, and death are universal themes with local habitations and names.

What changes is locale, personnel, circumstances. In America the hero moved steadily westward, until he reached Hollywood. Later, he went into orbit. Popular favorites advanced from the open forest to the big tent to the nightclub to the discotheque. European oldstyle was left behind as American folkstyle took root in the rich virgin land. Farmer-planters like Thomas Jefferson, George Washington, and William Penn set our pattern in politics. The myth of the garden, summarized at the end of the nineteenth century by Frederick Jackson Turner, coupled with the Jeffersonian ideal of the family farm to provide the chief theme of American history. Karl Marx also used the struggle between country and city as a major theme in *Das Kapital*. Simultaneously, American ballad-makers complained:

---

[1] Thomas Hall, *The Loathesomeness of Long Hair . . . With an Appendix Against Painting, Spots, Naked Breasts, Etc.* (London, 1654).
[2] Ihab Hassan, *Radical Innocence: Studies in the Contemporary American Novel* (New York: Harper and Row, 1961), p. 6.

The farmer is the man
Lives on credit till the fall;
Then they take him by the hand
And they lead him from the land
And the city man's the man who gets it all.

What happened to the country man in a rapidly changing economy is paralleled by the history of one of his best-loved songs. "Home on the Range." Written by Brewster Highley in 1873, it was picked up as a folksong by John A. Lomax in 1908. In the 1930's city people made it into a popular "hit." The state of Kansas declared it the official state song in 1947. In 1954, Kansas politicians turned Brewster Highley's log cabin, where he allegedly wrote the song, into a shrine. By then, rural sociologists acknowledged that their field had virtually ceased to exist.[3]

So had the traditional ballads, full of oldstyle and folkstyle heroes. In earlier form they had been handed down from the past without known individual authorship; showed evidence of variation in content; had a compact and concise narrative; made much of repetition and refrain.[4] Instead of going to such native folk material, early American writers preferred to return to European precedents. Washington Irving, the first widely accepted professional American writer, made a fairyland of the Hudson Valley by importing tales from the Rhine, changing distant Otmar into nearby Rip Van Winkle.[5] In so doing he became a founding father of American fakestyle, which eventually overshadowed both oldstyle and folkstyle.

Fakestyle impetus also came directly from Europe, where the "artsy-craftsy" ideas of Neo-Medievalists like John Ruskin and William Morris enjoyed a wide vogue. Hatred of early machine civilization, best exemplified in their native England, caused them to retreat to mythical Camelot—a kingdom John F. Kennedy would covet in the twentieth century. While the English were condemning machines, Americans were using theirs to produce dime novels and give fakestyle an enormous boost. The key date here is June 1860, when the first example of this new vulgarism, a uniquely American form of popular literature, was published. This sensational "yellowback," written by Ann S. Stephens, was entitled *Malaeska: The Indian Wife of the White Hunter.* Soon Beadle's New

---

[3]Thomas C. Cochran, "The History of a Business Society," *Journal of American History*, LIV (June, 1967), 9.

[4]The Archives of American Folk Song in the Library of Congress has more than 40,000 pieces of recorded folk music; there are thousands more in state and regional archives, as well as regular commercial issues. In *Folksongs on Records* (1950), Ben Gray Lumpkins lists over 4,000 titles.

[5]"Irving pretended both childishness and antiquity for America, then stood back and saw these things fail before an always triumphant broad daylight which existed to celebrate the absence of childishness and antiquity," writes Terence Martin in "Rip, Ichabod, and the American Imagination," *American Literature, XXI* (May, 1959), 148.

Dime Novels, Frank Starr's American Novels, and the Beadle-Adams combination changed the nation's reading habits. Folkstyle is built on facts and real events, fakestyle on images and pseudo-events. We have seen how fakestyle changed America's heroes.

The 1876 Philadelphia World's Fair gave fakestyle another boost. Exhibits stressed the production of bijouterie—"artistic" bronzes, luxurious furniture, and artificial flowers that had (to quote the French critic Simonin) "the veritable stamp of solidity and good taste." A key statistic involves the sale of jigsaw blades in America, chief source of bric-a-brac and fretwork. About 3,000 a year were sold in 1875—over 500,000 a month in 1878.[6]

"Americans," William Dean Howells complained, "have cast about for the instruction of someone who professed to know better, and who browbeat wholesome commonsense into the self-distrust that ends in sophistication." As if to illustrate his claim, the lead article in *Harper's Bazaar* for July 1, 1876, urged readers to clip items out of periodicals, then paste them "in a pretty scrap album for the library table. Stick on all sorts of little ornaments: monograms, little gilt devices cut from envelope bands, false flowers—anything at all that is pretty."[7]

While ladies were clipping for scrapbooks and Robber Barons were bringing home European art objects by the barrel-load, the era's greatest American writer was still drawing from folk material. Born in a sordid frontier town, schooled in mining camps and riverboat pilothouses, Mark Twain created the last genuinely American folk hero, *Huckleberry Finn*. In presenting Huck, he also showed that a novel could be built on dialogue, not rhetoric. But Huck was overshadowed by a new breed of fakestyle jolly giants—reckless, ruthless, chauvinistic. Horatio Greenough was wrong when he complained that America has "no half-fabulous, legendary wealth, no misty, cloud-enveloped background." A more accurate diagnosis might be that America deliberately rejected these elements of her past in order to create a new interpretation of history.

The Greeks used mythological metaphors as the basis for heroic style, the Romans depended on biographical archetypes; the Middle Ages on hagiography. By stressing a few themes and patterns each epoch greatly increased the focus and intensity of meaning. There is no such cohesive force in American culture—hence no such clarity or intensity. We may get it, for the first time, in the new pop iconography.

Meanwhile, we struggle with the aesthetics and heroics of impermanence. To modern critics an art-object is a temporary center of energy, which motivates for a while, then dies. America went into a furor in 1913 over Marcel Duchamp's

[6]John A. Kouwenhoven, *The Arts in Modern American Civilization* (New York: Norton, 1967), p. 89. Kouwenhoven's analysis of "bric-a-brac" America provides a good introduction to the subject of fakestyle.

[7]Quoted by John Kouwenhoven, *Made in America* (New York: Norton, 1960), p. 89; reprinted as *Arts in Modern American Civilization* (New York: Norton, 1967).

"Nude Descending a Staircase." Half a century later—as Duchamp himself admitted—the Nude was dead; she had become a tombstone to her still-living creator. The same can be said about heroic arts, such as Lindbergh's 1927 solo crossing of the Atlantic. Today impermanence is not only an observable fact, but a stylistic device.[8]

Another key word is *interface*. Originally a chemical term referring to the interaction of substances in a kind of mutual irritation, it has been broadened to deal with the whole culture. In its most natural form interface emerges as random conversation or dialogue—bits and snatches. This is what we see on the avant-garde stage. The interplay of multiple aspects generates insights and discovery. Interface is random contact with the life of forms. One by-product is a new heroic style. The hero becomes a happening. Whatever happens, this style will not be simple or linear. To be contemporary is to give up simple explanations of man and his world, to embrace complexity once and for all, to try both to manage and image it.

Heroic deeds are generally done in mysterious places, where obstacles are as great as imagination unencumbered by fact can make them. This described the Holy Land in the thirteenth century, the brave new world in the seventeenth, the American frontier in the nineteenth. Today, mystery dwells in outer space and on other planets. *What is it like out there?* Will those who go "out there" ever tell us? Perhaps the reign of words will come to an end, along with man's bondage to gravity. Scientists already do things that cannot be made intelligible in words, only in formulae. We may be abolishing speech as the most vital communication between men. This implies that the life of action, the matching of great words with great deeds, might end.

To continue with space-age metaphors, we are all crew members on a single global spaceship, making our way through infinity. The voyage our earth makes is precarious. We depend on a thin layer of soil beneath us, a layer of atmosphere above us, and a hero at the helm—these, and nothing more.

If we are to survive, we must know the other crewmen, even if we don't like them. Entering the final third of the twentieth century, we must invent new systems, symbols, and rituals. They must be born out of processes in which we participate, but over which we may have no conscious control.

Western man lives in a society where most old myths have lost their mana and power. He no longer accepts either the motifs or the materials of Christian mythos, which served him well for centuries. His has been that most terrible of fates—he is demythologized.

When an old mythology disintegrates, a new one originates. To survive is to remythologize. Instead of *discovering* a new mythos, we find ourselves *participating* in it. That is what our pop artists and pop heroes are doing, what our

[8]Harold Rosenberg explores this subject in *The Anxious Object* (New York: Horizon, 1965).

children are seeking with their new tactics, songs, morals, haircuts. They will bury not only us, but our worn-out mythology, too.

When Western demythologizing reached its crest, between the World Wars, a doom boom resulted. Darkness, despair, and doubt spread everywhere. *The Waste Land* that T. S. Eliot described in his 1922 poem was bone-dry:

> He who was living is now dead
> We who were living are now dying
> With a little patience
> Here is no water but only rock
> Rock and no water but only rock.[9]

No place for the hero to thrive here. Other things withered, too—laissez-faire economics, Newtonian physics, stiff-collar diplomacy. The "modern" world, as that term was understood by Locke, Jefferson, Voltaire, and Gladstone, gave way to a post-modern world. Inevitably the heroic style changed radically. The arts pointed the way. Daniel French gave way to Alexander Calder, John Singer Sargent to Jackson Pollock, Stephen Foster to Dizzie Gillespie. We left the world of Descartes and Newton, with closed boxes, for that of Einstein and Wernher von Braun, with infinitely open spaces. The structure of society, the order of ideas, the basic concepts of space and time were up-ended. Where there had been time-honored myth suddenly there was a void. Even the existence of God, that hero of heroes, was questioned. The church found itself in the embarrassing position of having within its affluent confines everything it needed—except God.

One of the brightest popstyle theologians, Harvey Cox, urges his fellow churchmen to seek God not in the sacred cloister, but in the secular city. How, he asks, can man separate sacred and secular, when they are both God's? The sacred always goes bad unless it is working with the secular; the word becomes mere vapor unless it becomes flesh. There is no theology without sociology. No matter how pure and ethereal a religion may be at first, it is always converted into something else.

Realizing this, a group of tough-minded thinkers called existentialists have forced us to think about ultimate problems. Are we free? Have we ever been free? What does it mean to exist now, genuinely?

The golden thread of thought goes back to Plato, who pondered essences, and Aristotle, who stressed existence. That to him was reality. Man is as he does; action justifies life. Existence is action and involvement. In today's idiom—are you swinging?

Pop culture, with all its faddish stunts, asks these same questions in a new idiom. New sounds and stagings penetrate the modern conditions, ridiculing outworn dogmas and platitudes. There are many different ways and levels on

---

[9]Excerpt from "The Waste Land" by T. S. Eliot. Reprinted by permission of the publishers, Harcourt Brace Jovanovich, Inc.

which existential concern can be shown. Our cultural package is all of a piece. Change seems most radical in some areas only because we know more about them, or are more involved with them. The radical common denominator is that we accept change as a normal condition. *Dubito, ergo sum.*

From Descartes through Hegel, Western thought was dominated by rationalism, system-building, and the notion of progress. As in formal theology, housewrecking has been the order of the day. Dominant themes of twentieth-century philosophy are disillusionment, pessimism, the lure of destruction. Paradox prevails; we live at a moment of economic optimism, and political pessimism. Automation, computerization, nuclear fission, and rocketry should have made us free—but have only tyrannized us to a degree unparalleled in history. Our ancestors thought we would, by now, have built the brave new world. Instead, we seem unable to prevent blowing it up. Here is the overwhelming problem for contemporary heroes to face and solve.

They must learn to cross new bridges, touch new godheads. Think how theology could be enriched by encompassing ecology, which studies the interrelationship of organisms and their environment. Until recently, ecology was largely the bailiwick of biologists concentrating on plant environments. Now ecologists say man's total environment includes not only the physical and biotic, but the cultural and conceptual. Material from the traditional humanities, arts, social sciences—and why not theology?—should be gathered. Only interdisciplinary efforts can focus on the holistic man in his total surroundings. Man is moving into an era of *total environment* and radical new styles. Confronted with that movement, theologians would seem to have three alternatives—change the image they now present, adapt to needs of twentieth-century society, or retreat into pedantic triviality.

If only yesterday's heroes and saints are revered, in the capitol and the cathedral, the government and church will emerge as the safe-deposit box where archaic images are stored. To find new heroes, institutions must make adjustments. In rethinking they may see that new ideas and labels apply admirably to old truths. Christianity as revealed through the Gospels is a kind of happening. Why should He have been conceived of a Virgin, rejected by His own people, hung on a cross? Was ever a story more astounding (to the unbeliever, absurd) than this? While oldstyle theologians mourn the death of God, new media let their light shine on all men. The shining light—epiphany! God is dead only for those who seek Him in a square tomb. He's definitely alive for those watching the tube.

To recognize the absence of myth is the first step toward resurrecting it. By 1960, that recognition was widespread in America. The heroic style is being refashioned. Remythologizing is under way.

America has never been an aristocratic society, but it has aped Europe's for generations. If America was (to quote Mark Twain) "fresh out of kings," it produced scores of kings and queens for sports events, agricultural fairs, and every product on the store shelf. In our ambivalent effort to establish democracy, we first concentrated on politics (during our Revolution), then economics (during the New Deal). Perhaps we can now create an environmental democracy, in which we both accept and improve the twentieth-century world. The March of the Poor on Washington in 1968 showed how far we still have to go. We must not be afraid of America, the things in it, the way it operates. Boredom, frustration, repetition, waste, and delay are all built into the model. A new generation no longer thinks of used-car lots, billboards, and flashing neon signs as part of the Wasteland. Instead they are raw material for visual involvement—the stuff out of which pop heroes are made. The entire environment can be seen as a work of art, a teaching machine designed to maximize perception. For the first time artists can be, in the full sense of the word, popular heroes. But it must be on the people's terms, not the élite's.

When most men lived in the country, folkstyle allowed us to mythologize American culture. By deflating rural values, fakestyle demythologized our lives. The job today is to remythologize them.

Certain distinctions between the main heroic styles in the last three centuries emerge not as factual syllogisms, but as suggestions.

Folkstyle	Fakestyle	Popstyle
oral	verbal	multisensory
traditional	nostalgic	experimental
realistic	romantic	psychedelic
earthy	sticky	tart
homespun	factory-spun	polyester
continuity	transition	explosion
improvised	ersatz	electronic
cowboy	Buffalo Bill	Bonanzaland
community sing	folk festival	Disneyland

Stylistic changes are reflected in the work of young writers like Susan Sontag and Tom Wolfe, young campus heroes like David Harris. In *Against Interpretation* Miss Sontag includes an essay "On style," arguing that style is the principle of decision in a work of art, the signature of the artist's will. She puts her own signature on "Notes on Camp," widely regarded as one of the most influential essays of the decade. "Camp" is love of the unnatural—of artifice and exaggeration. She traces camp's origins to eighteenth-century Gothic novels, chinoiserie, and artificial ruins, and sees it responding to "instant character," thus supplementing the new Age of Circuitry. New style-makers are usually not writers, according to Miss Sontag, but artists, film-makers, social planners, TV technicians, neurologists, electronics engineers, and sociologists. Basic texts for this new cultural alignment are found in the writings of Marshall McLuhan, Buckminster Fuller, John Cage, Siegfried Gidieon, Norman O. Brown, and Gyorgy

Kepes. "Sensations, feelings, the abstract forms and styles of sensibility count. It is to these that contemporary art addresses itself."[10] The way of camp is not in terms of beauty, but of stylization. Are we to witness the rise of campstyle in America?

If so, Tom Wolfe must be accounted a Daniel Boone who led us across its frontier. Touring the country to find out about postwar teen-age culture, Wolfe chose the name for his full-length report from the incredibly stylized custom cars California kids design and produce—*Kandy-Kolored Tangerine-Flake Streamline Baby*. In the "Introduction" style is central to his whole thesis:

> Since World War II classes of people whose styles of life had been practically invisible had the money to build monuments to their own styles. This took the form of custom cars, the twist, the jerk, the monkey, the shake, rock music generally, stretch pants, decal eyes. All these things, like Inigo Jones's classicism, have started having an influence on the life of the whole country.

To Wolfe, Baby Jane Holzer, the society girl who went pop, is "the hyperversion of a whole new style of life in America." She is a symbol, just as is Las Vegas—"the Versailles of America, the only architecturally uniform city in the Western World." Gangsters built it in an isolated spot, just as Louis XIV went outside Paris to create his fantastic baroque environment. The Las Vegas hoods celebrated, very early, the new style of life of America—"using the money pumped in by the war to show a prole vision of style."

Wolfe's special hero—"The Last American Hero"—is Junior Johnson, the Carolina country boy who learned to drive by running whisky for his bootlegging father and grew up to be a famous stock-car racing driver. "Junior Johnson is one of the last of those sports stars who is not just an ace at the game itself, but a hero a whole people or class of people can identify with."[11] He "turns on" the white Southerner the way Jack Dempsey stirred up the Irish and Joe Louis the Negroes. Johnson is a modern popstyle hero, involved with car culture and car symbolism; Wolfe is his Boswell.

His images are as hard-edged, clear, objective, precise as pop painting, or as the two-minute summaries by a master popstyle TV journalist like Eric Sevareid. Here is Wolfe's description of the IRT subway station at 50th and Broadway at 8:45 on a Thursday morning:

> All the faces come popping in clots out of the Seventh Avenue local, past the King Size Ice Cream machine, and the turnstiles start whacking away as if the world were breaking up on the reefs. Four steps past the turnstiles everybody is already backed up haunch to paunch for the climb up the ramp and the stairs to the surface, a great funnel of flesh, wool, felt, leather, rubber and

---

[10] Susan Sontag, *Against Interpretation* (New York: Dell, 1967), p. 300.

[11] Tom Wolfe, *The Kandy-Kolored Tangerine-Flake Streamline Baby* (New York: Farrar, Straus, 1965), p. 131 (paperback ed., Pocket Books, 1967).

steaming alumicron, with the blood squeezing through everybody's old scle-rotic arteries in hopped-up spurts from too much coffee and the effort of surfacing from the subway at the rush hour.

The tendency here, and in most pop prose, is not to pontificate, but to probe, to twist the cultural kaleidoscope, to travel without a road map. And that, you may be sure, the Old Boys can never approve. No wonder they have trouble with Barbara Garson's *MacBird*! This gay, gaudy play, most widely heralded political parody in the 1960s, goes its own outrageous way, toward no particular point. MacBird's outcry sums it up: "Unity, Unity, wherefore art thou, Unity?" Lyndon B. Johnson has the distinction of being the first presidential anti-hero in American history. Other presidents (including an earlier Johnson) have been attacked and scorned, but only popstyle could have done it in this manner.

Once the beatnik witches have assured Johnson (alias MacBird) that he can be president if Kennedy (alias John Ken O'Dunc) is assassinated, our shotgun parody is off and popping. The Egg of Head (Adlai Stevenson), the Earl of Warren, the Wayne of Morse, and Lord McNamara get into the act. Everyone does his thing. Riots, sit-ins, foreign interventions, demonstrations, and skullduggery play their part in the creation of a new Pox Americana. In the words of MacBird:

> We mean to be the firemen of peace
> Dousing flames with freedom's forceful flow.

Paradoxically, the mediocrity of the play serves a purpose. The more it puts us on, the clearer becomes the message. What can you do with a parody that parodies straw men and falsehoods rather than real men and foibles? Will the real catharsis please stand up?

MacBird is a minor play pointing to a major tendency—to ridicule not only people, but art-forms. The line between "impure life" and "pure art" is no longer considered valid. Not only Happenings but public events and demonstrations become theater. In a real sense, the various riots, marches, and protests of the 1960s were means for dramatic expression and catharsis in American life. The TV screen became Everyman's theater. Everyone had a box seat.

In this setting no one can *plan* to be a hero, the way a general plans a battle or an architect a building. No one knows when he is "on stage" or "off stage"—which camera is focusing on which person now? (No wonder President Nixon avoided campaign television debates.) Or, if there are six cameras, which button is the studio technician pushing to put one image into 100,000,000 minds, and keep the other five out? If we leave mass media, do we move *into* the action or *away* from it?

Such questions open up the whole area of leisure in popstyle America. Just what we can anticipate is explored in the Spring 1968 issue of *TDR, The Drama Review*. The day of the Fun Palace is upon us, where Gala Days and Nights will be filled with:

Instant Cinema	Juke Box Information
Genius Chat	Adult Toys
Clownery	Star Gazing
Fireworks	Concerts
Battles of Flowers	Rallies
Science Gadgetry	Learning Machines
Kunst Dabbling	Theater

All for your delight! New wealth, mobility, flexibility, and social interdependence demand an awareness of the vast range of influences and experiences open to all at all times. Since the Fun Palace Foundation was registered as a Charitable Trust in 1966, some of these dreams-on-paper may be realities within a few years.[12]

Already the reach is on for new modes of expression; new discoveries are on display. Thus, a single issue of the avantgarde popstyle newspaper *Village Voice*, for April 11, 1968, advertises:

"The Space Music of Sun Ra"—A Freeform Excursion into the Far Reaches of Sound and Sight

"Alive, Through the Glass Lightly"—A Turn on For Kids and Adults Who Never Believed Alice Was 9 Feet High

"Hair—The American Tribal Love-Rock Musical."

"An Electric Easter—A Total Theater, The Art Form, the Gesamtkunstwerk of the Future"

"The Groove-Tubers, Regular TV With Hair"—It Discovers an Example of What Television Could Be; or Could Have Been.

Ads such as these, plus the staccato prose of Stephanie Harrington, Leticia Kent, Don McNeill, Michael McDonald, and Sally Kempton, made the *Village Voice* one of the best barometers of style-change, and proof that sensitive reporting comes in any style, any idiom.

They also suggest that in their newstyle involvement with popular culture, young Americans are discovering new modes of experience, new ways to achieve depth and total involvement. Old walls of snobbery and elitism are tumbling down. The "highbrow" seems more and more ridiculous as he preens his own feathers. In an incredibly varied and altering culture, we find a priceless artistic and stylistic pluralism. If we can separate the real from the phony, the serious from the pseudo, we may move into one of man's most creative epochs. This calls for skillful and interdisciplinary criticism, which will "both confront the implications of the new sensibility and build on the substantial achievements of the mass culture critics."[13] This is indeed a major reponsibility of the new intellectual generation.

[12] Preliminary drawings and a "Non-Program" for a Laboratory of Fun appear in *TDR, The Drama Review*, T XXXIX (Spring, 1968), 127 ff.

[13] John G. Cawelti, "Reviews," *American Quarterly*, XX (September, 1968), 259.

Recent activities within the historian's camp indicate that this confrontation is taking place. The "consensus school" of the 1950s, which held that most of the heated controversies of America's past were hyperbolic, a kind of ritual warfare associated with politics, has been challenged and in some instances discredited.[14] America is not "one nation under God, indivisible." Tension, not consensus, is the dominating theme. A "New Left" school of radical historians will have nothing to do with consensus and the Establishment. Chief among their heroes is Herbert Marcuse, who calls for intolerance against movements from the right and toleration of movements from the left—since the left alone is the agent of history. To avoid the "systematic moronization" of America we must resist goods and services that render us incapable of achieving an existence of our own and make us "one dimensional men." Living in what another able young historian, Michael Harrington, calls *The Accidental Century*, we must move *Toward a Democratic Left*. We must have more democratic debate and more effective popular control over huge government programs if our democracy is to endure, he argues. One hears the echoes of the old Jeffersonian line: "Give the people light and they will find their way."

As the writings of men like Harrington show, the fear of apathy and automation that saturated the 1950s has changed to violence and the fear of revolution in the 1960s. Students, linked together as never before in the Age of Circuitry, are revolting everywhere. No more talk of the "Silent Generation." Obviously young people are turned on—engaged in an intense search for personal commitment. Seeking a prototype, Gina Berriault chose David Harris, 1967 student president at Stanford University.[15] Harris has pale-blue eyes, rimless glasses, a substantial mustache that makes him appear older than twenty-one, and large photos of Charlie Chaplin and Mahatma Gandhi on his wall. The books on his shelf are Nietzsche, Kierkegaard, A. J. Muste, and the *Upanishad*. He talks with a fast mixture of beat jargon, academic terms, and words in common usage. Meeting for the first time with Stanford's President Wallace Sterling, Harris wore a work shirt, Levis, and moccasins. He doesn't dress oldstyle, one presumes, because he doesn't think oldstyle; in the words of Thoreau (a popstyle favorite), he listens to the music of a different drummer.

So do his contemporaries whose student lectures were published under the title *A Student Look at America* (1967). One of them, twenty-five-year-old Louis Cartwright, said that the new hero is one who "knows nobody knows—and isn't afraid of not knowing." The key to the heroic personality is not achievement, but potential, since "we are a potential world of men who require no

---

[14] See John A. Garraty, "A Then for Now," *The New York Times* (May 12, 1967), Section 7, p. 1.

[15] Gina Berriault, "The New Student President, David Harris of Stanford," *Esquire*, September, 1967.

corrals." The New Reality, says twenty-eight-year-old Phil Baumgartner, is "the power of courage to bring the individual so immediately in contact with the here-and-now that all expectation or possibility of death is wiped out."[16]

All around us in the 1960s we see the "failure of success." Studies of alienated youth who will make and be tomorrow's heroes indicate they will not settle for the bag of toys that fascinated devotees of Horatio Alger. Typical of the times was Jan Myrdal's *Confessions of a Disloyal European*. Son of the great Swedish economist whose book *An American Dilemma: The Negro Problem and Modern Democracy* helped shape a whole generation of liberal thinking, Jan sings not a hymn, but a eulogy to revolution. Our civilization is full of promises that are never fulfilled—reeking with bad faith. Prejudice and hatred are wrong, war is madness, massive inequality is intolerable. Suddenly the world seems filled with young people who are neither ideologues nor psychological misfits, but pragmatists who had no recourse but to become radicals. Not only their politics but their programs are radical. There is no vaccination against the "malaise of affluence." Thus Jan Myrdal describes himself lying in a bed he has not made or left for three weeks, practicing yoga breathing with his legs up against the wall.[17] Young people around the world seem on the same wavelength. What does this imply for the hero, American style?

Young men and women who formulate this lifestyle reflect the mood of the 1960s. They also remind us, after our survey of several centuries, that man is the only being who asks questions about being—about power and potential beyond himself. Power plus structure equals a life of being. America is searching for a new ontology. Cultural relocation and heroic transformation are radical interests of a new generation.

Image-makers are engaged in a worldwide scavenger hunt involving African sculpture, Zen fables, Indian music, the camp style of Victoria, the click-clack of computers, the primitive masks of Mali. By telescoping time, tradition, and geography the first universal heroic tradition may emerge. All world history is its past; all the world's its stage. The arts may be one before the church is one. The atelier is more ecumenical than the altar.

Yet it is not in the church but in the laboratory that the germs of this culture will best flourish. Science is the foundation of the new mythos. There are indications that biology may be grasping the lead from physics. The whole psychedelic spectrum, like work with DNA and RNA, points to revolutionary ideas. They will be dramatized in new heroes. We are on the verge of what the

[16] Otto Butz, ed., *To Make a Difference* (New York: Harper & Row, 1967), p. 231.

[17] Jan Myrdal, *Confessions of a Disloyal European* (New York: Pantheon, 1968). See also Kenneth Keniston, *Young Radicals: Notes on Committed Youth* (New York: Harcourt, Brace, Jovanovich, 1968).

twentieth century's greatest poet, William Butler Yeats, called *The Second Coming:*

> The darkness drops again; but now I know
> That twenty centuries of stony sleep
> Were vexed to nightmare by a rocking cradle,
> And what rough beast, its hour come round at last,
> Slouches towards Bethlehem to be born?[18]

[18] From "The Second Coming," *Collected Poems* by William Butler Yeats. Copyright 1924 by The Macmillan Company, renewed 1952 by Bertha Georgie Yeats. Reprinted by permission of The Macmillan Company.

CHAPTER IX

critical
thinking
into
writing

The nature of the essay is expository, a process of "exposing" or unfolding, making ideas clear. Whatever means the writer uses—classification, comparison-contrast, cause-and-effect, inductive, first-to-last, or others, as explained in Chapter IV on "Paragraphs"—the means are all ways of organizing topics, illustrations, facts, judgments. In addition to organizing, writers must be concerned with sound reasoning. *Exposition* and *argumentation*, explaining and supporting an assertion, depend on *critical thinking*, reasoning that does several things:

- *offers explanation*, by defining, describing, outlining, narrating, categorizing, relating, separating, distinguishing
- *tests an idea*, by examining assumptions, alternative ideas, looking to consequences, identifying logical fallacies, distinguishing between facts and inferences, evaluating the relevancy of data, examining the adequacy of the supporting material, noting inconsistencies in reasoning or supporting evidence, appraising the worth of an idea or phenomenon
- *proves an assertion*, by applying known facts and concepts to the asserted notion, drawing correct inferences from the evidence used, arranging the arguments and the evidence effectively, providing adequate supporting illustrations and the like, introducing valid authorities as support
- *creates new outlooks or patterns*, by combining, compiling, integrating, devising, generating, modifying, reconstructing, critiquing, interpreting previously known information in new ways

The writer who understands the processes of critical reasoning can arrange his ideas to defend them against error as well as spot weaknesses in others' assertions.

To be believed, to make one's ideas prevail, the writer must demonstrate three things:

- *that he is objective*—The writer must demonstrate that his assertions are rationally arrived at, not dependent on the prejudices derived from his cultural conditioning.
- *that he has adequate knowledge and understanding*—The writer must demonstrate that he knows his subject—that is, knows common terms, specific facts, basic concepts, appropriate and correct methodology—in its complexity.
- *that his analysis and judgment are plausible*—The writer must show that he has distinguished between fact and opinion, that he has introduced relevant supporting evidence, that his reasoning is not faulty, that he has chosen the wisest view of those available, that his supporting evidence is adequate, that he is logically consistent, and that his judgments are of value.

In his analysis and judgment-making, the writer will be concerned with several critical thinking processes, each of which is explained in one of the following four sections:

Defining
Determining fact, opinion, and preference
Probing for alternatives, assertions, implications, and consequences
Avoiding faulty reasoning

DEFINING

A first step in sound reasoning is to define the principal words or concepts that command the essay direction. When we speak of a subject—a liberal arts education, sex, existentialism, language, or justice, for example—the first problem is to define what we mean by the words. For this reason, introductory paragraphs very often engage the reader with a special definition as a means of laying the necessary groundwork for the argument to follow.

We should, before anything else, define "defining." Briefly, *defining* is a process of assigning a set of characteristics to a word or expression in order to differentiate it from other words or expressions and to locate it among them. Defining is an act that must precede writing above all other considerations, whether the definitions appear in the final draft or not. Not to define terms before writing is to invite fogginess and ill-reasoned ideas. Is man free? The answer depends on one's definition of "free," and, to the surprise of many, "man." Is God dead? The answer hinges on the meaning we assign to "God" and to "dead," though this is only a beginning, for other words that also need defining are likely to occur in the response to such questions.

Those who fail to insist on clear definitions in such serious matters as religion, politics, sex education, or censorship of books or films might justly be called lazy, fearful, or simply uninformed. When choosing words, writers must consider *connotations*—suggested or implied meanings—as they write. Words like "un-American," "black," or "parent" in a particular context can be quite explosive or misleading if speakers or writers do not define them properly.

The "proper" way to define words or expressions is in the formal, dictionary manner. *Each definition has two parts:* (1) *a class or group term and* (2) *differentiating characteristics.* Thus, a "girl" is a female human being (the class or group term) who is young and unmarried (differentiating term). To be even more precise, it might be necessary to define "young." Furthermore, *depending on the context*, a "girl" could also mean a man's or boy's sweetheart, a female servant or employee, or, by connotation, an immature or innocent young woman, as in the statement, "Gladys, I fear, is still a mere girl, even though she is twenty-seven years old." Here are a few examples of formal definitions:

The Word or Expression	Class Term	Differentiation
genocide	the act of deliberate extermination	of a national or ethnic group
hansom	a low-hung, two-wheeled vehicle	which is drawn by one horse for two passengers, the driver being mounted behind and the reins running over the roof
local colorist	a type of realistic fiction writer	who represents the distinctive characteristics or peculiarities of a place or period in novels, stories, or plays

The point of these illustrations is to dramatize the two-part nature of definitions and to point up the need for such systematic thinking while writing, *even though the definition itself does not appear in the essay.* Such careful thinking is simply sound strategy.

In the definition process, it is also wise to remember a few cautions:

First, definitions should not contain any variation of the word being defined. The writer who states that "democracy is a form of government in which the laws are designed to treat people democratically" has written a bit of silliness.

Second, the class term should not be too restrictive to be useful; thus, the definition of respectable as "a respectable person is one who has earned and received his neighbor's admiration" is useless. What if all the neighbors are crooks and hypocrites—yet he is an honest man who always tells the truth?

Third, differentiations may not distinguish adequately between the term and similar closely related terms. Heroism defined as "extraordinary valor under threat of personal injury" is difficult to distinguish from bravery or even stoicism.

Fourth, a definition should not be merely a comment on the term. For instance, the statement that reads "a film is obscene when I can't allow my daughter to see it" is not really a usable definition of obscenity at all, though many people act on such hazy definitions.

Avoiding these definition faults is a way of avoiding misguided human action, for meanings affect the course of human life. A property owner will need to know how much property he must own, for how long, and what kind before the law allows him to vote as a "property owner." Likewise, students who are of voting age need to know whether they qualify as "residents" if they have left their parents' home for college. The definition of "residents" may determine whether students slog through snow to cast their ballots at the local precinct or whether they make the acquaintance of a notary public to countersign their absentee ballots or whether they are prevented from voting altogether. Definitions make a difference.

Writers often abuse their responsibility to define objectively by using an emotional basis for their argument. Highly emotional issues often lead to distorted definitions whereby only unfavorable connotations are attached to the defined word. "Pornography," for instance, when defined as "written or graphic communication used to exploit the bestial desires in a person" distorts the word and deceives the reader through the connotations in the expression "bestial desires." If the definition contained "prurient interest" for "bestial desires" and indicated that pornography could not serve a socially redeeming value, the definition would have been explanatory, not argumentative. Such a word as "pornography" illustrates quite well the importance and the difficulties of defining abstruse concepts, for this word, with the word "obscenity," is in the process of nearly constant refinement by Supreme Court decisions and law-makers at all levels of jurisdiction. The main source of contention and emotional upheaval therefore usually stems from differences in definitions, especially if the law is involved as well. What about "radicals," "police action," "law and order," "traitor," "freedom"—or the differences among "riot," "protest," and "demon-stration"? In the definitions lie the bases for the full range of human action, from legally sanctioned killing to total license of action.

And definitions change with time. In a less dramatic way, such words as "art film," "religious," "heroic," "love," "middle American," "commercial," "mod-est prices," or "successful" play their parts in our lives, changing meanings, chameleonlike, as we age and mature, regress, or become cynical. As our definitions change, we change our ways. Being "heroic" yesterday might have meant volunteering for the draft; today, it could mean refusing to be inducted. Previously, being "religious" might mean being a church congregation member and attending church regularly; at another time, it might mean active involve-ment in solving the problems of humanity, wherever they might be.

While defining is relatively simple at the literal, dictionary level, whole essays or even books might be written to define a word. Words such as "hard," "surrealism," "creativity," "censorship," "segregation," "religious experience," "the unconscious," or "modern" occasion lengthy discussions that may result in new outlooks or even transform the direction of an academic discipline or even an entire society. In such efforts, the writer must, as with all defining, *differenti-ate the word from other words, clarify value judgments, or remove ambiguities.* ("The concert was provocative and enjoyable." In what way "provocative"? What is "enjoyable"?) Such a process often involves the writer in relating abstract terms to people, places, things, and events—or in providing examples or allusions that help the reader understand what is involved for human action in the operation of the term.

This effort absorbed Herbert J. Muller in his statement about the meaning of freedom. While this is only a small piece of a chapter called "The Meanings of Freedom" in his book *Issues of Freedom*, it illustrates the fancy wordsmithing that is necessary to explain an idea of freedom so that most readers can understand its parameters and its operation in life:

In formal terms, *freedom* in this work will mean "the condition of being able to choose and to carry out purposes." This definition has three immediate implications: (1) the primary dictionary meaning—the absence of external constraints; (2) practicable purposes, or an actual ability with available means; and (3) a power of conscious choice, between significant, known alternatives. It accordingly involves the common ideas of freedom *from*, freedom *to*, and freedom *of*, but it leaves open the question of freedom *for* what. In simple words, a man is free in so far as he can do something or choose not to do it, can make up his own mind, can say yes or no to any given question or command, can decide for himself the matter of duty or *for* what.

While Muller proceeds to qualify and amplify this central concept throughout the chapter and, actually, the book, he has handily dealt with a complex term in an orderly and visualizing way. His exploration of the meanings of the word "freedom" is the basis for his three-volume account of freedom throughout history.

No one can regard the religious, technological, educational, or political events of the past or present without relating them to these notions of freedom, once they are fully understood. The process of definition can therefore result in an entirely new outlook on life itself, reexamining the meaning of the past, present, and future for the lives of human beings. That is one possible result of the Muller work, but other examples also abound today, such as the black historians' labeling of most history books as "white history" or others' labeling the process of campus protests as "revolution." The implications of such shifts in meaning or outlook extend to the rim of known history.

DETERMINING FACT, OPINION, AND PREFERENCE

A writer who is thinking critically learns to distinguish among *facts, opinions,* and *preferences.* Writers nearly always have two obligations to meet in their essays: they must first make judgments and, second, enable the reader to judge their judgments. The first involves opinion-making—that is, considered judgment. The second necessitates providing facts. To clarify the difference, imagine this dialogue between Adam and Eve.

Adam: What *is* the distinction between *fact* and *opinion*?

Eve: A *fact* can be verified as true or false—by proving that there is general agreement or by demonstrating that it meets the defined criteria for truth or falseness. It is objective. An *opinion* is an expression of attitudes toward a fact. It is subjective.

Adam: Ok. I get it. But what is the relationship between fact and opinion?

Eve: Opinions—considered ones—are drawn from facts. Opinions when supported by facts are judgments. The more facts that support a judgment, the more firm valid judgment becomes.

Adam: That makes sense. Now, we seem concerned with the *truth* of facts and the *validity* of opinions. What is the difference?

Eve: *Truth* means "in accordance with reality," while *validity* means "well grounded on evidence." Evidence can be facts and will consist of observations, common knowledge (as, we know horses have manes without observing them), firsthand experience, testimony from reliable witnesses, and reports or testimony from professional experts, such as a researcher, a laboratory technician, or a sexologist—provided that they testify in the area of their expertise.

Adam: I see. The validity of a judgment depends, therefore, on the facts that support it. How many facts do you have to have before you accept the validity of a judgment?

Eve: Really, that is a difficult question and has to be answered according to the kinds of factual information you are working with. Knowing how Americans will vote in the election next year is opinion until the election occurs, but, if a sample population is large enough and identical to the characteristics of the total voting population, then a candidate might accept the opinion takers' poll as a "truth"—and act on it. On the other hand, you wouldn't need nearly as many facts to establish that a stream, say, is polluted. One case of hepatitis among persons who drank from the stream could establish the "truth." But, the hepatitis case might establish *suspicion* for many persons, and they would demand that the water be tested for pollution. If the test is made, that one fact would establish the truth.

Let me put the whole thing in a better nutshell. The fewer the judgments and the more facts, the greater validity the judgments have. Does that answer your question?

Adam: It certainly does. But I have one other problem for you. What if you can't really establish an idea as fact or opinion? For instance, what if one of our children says, "The world is a great place," and another says, "The world is a boring, horrible place." Now they have both been living in the same place, known the same people—in short, had access to the same "facts." They state different opinions, however. Could both be right? That is, could both—or neither—be "facts" as you have explained it?

Eve: My, I like an intelligent man. That's my *preference*. I know we'll hit it off all right. *That's my preference, too.*

You've struck a fine point, but an important one. Two persons familiar with the same facts might come up with different opinions toward those facts. Preferences are the most interesting statements of all, for preferences lead to disputes. Many of the world's writers will make their reputations by persuading readers *to their preferences*—and away from others' preferences. As evidence for the validity of these preferences, they use not only data from the senses, reliable witnesses, and experts, but also their experience and judgment of such data. It is a matter of taste, therefore. And the validity of one's taste depends on standards, criteria for judging. By one set of standards, one of our children could establish that the world is "a great place." According to his standards, the truth of his preference is established. Likewise, the child who regards the world as "a boring, horrible place" might use another set of standards. By these standards, his preference can also stand as true. You need to pay careful attention to the standards a person uses. Otherwise, you could be bilked, led astray, hoodwinked.

Adam: You know, the more you say, the more I realize that you are quite an intelligent woman! What I can't understand is how you got us in such a mess of trouble back at the first place we lived in.

Eve: Well, perhaps my appetite overruled my reason. That's my *opinion* about the *facts* of that episode. But this making it on our own—that's my *preference*.

Adam: I'm glad. That's my *opinion*, too—and my *preference*!

Adam and Eve illustrate the differences between these three concepts that infiltrate every known essay. Keeping them straight should help the writer to provide the kinds of facts or standards that should convince the reader of the soundness of his judgments.

Distinctions like these are not always the easiest to master. To feel the strength of your mastery of the differences, consider the following assertions. Do two things: First, identify which is fact, opinion, or preference. Second, what kind of support does each assertion need in order to establish truth or validity? Supply some sample evidence yourself for each one as a kind of imagination-stretching feat. Notice the range of different tests of adequacy, of truth or falsity, that you must supply.

- Nature is hostile to man.
- Anyone who ever saw a film knows that Humphrey Bogart was one of our greatest actors.
- Hemingway's writing is far superior to that of William Faulkner.
- Salt helps people perspire more easily.
- Chocolate tastes better than peppermint.
- The early bird gets the worm.
- Tragic heroes are not possible in contemporary America.
- If you eat many carrots, your eyesight will improve.
- No life exists on the moon.
- Democracy is the fairest type of government for the individual man.
- Women are most feminine when they are soft, pliant, passive, accepting, and generally submissive.
- Work hard, save your money, and you will succeed.
- A football field is one hundred yards long.
- A picture of a nude female is obscene.
- In ten years, nearly everyone will have a five-foot-square color TV screen in his home.

You have discovered, if you have tried these statements, that several require some form of validity test; others defy such tests. Some require a great deal of supporting evidence; others require very little. Some seem provable; others appear beyond proof. The trick is to use the same tests of supplying appropriate and adequate verification as you make your own assertions.

PROBING FOR ALTERNATIVES, ASSUMPTIONS, IMPLICATIONS, AND CONSEQUENCES

Probing Questions

Writers are by nature question raisers. Everything in their sight, their hearing, their experience is a fit subject for the inquiring mind. They want to know what this or that means, what pattern lies hidden in the chaos of events, what truth hides behind the illusion, what is valuable and what is not. When well aimed, their questions reveal problems or issues that their readers might not have discovered or thought about before. Writers, when they serve these functions ably, are the sensitive interpreters of our experience, of the ideas that affect us—in order for us to live with more awareness than we otherwise would. Not all writers use exactly the same pointed questions as those mentioned here, but these are perhaps the dominant forms of the questions that test the strength and weakness of any assertion. These are the questions that lead persons to their own judgments about the subject of some assertion, and these questions assist the writer in evaluating the strength of his own ideas—before he directs them at his readers.

Who is Making the Assertion?

Sometimes people have special interests for making assertions. While not every person harbors an ulterior motive for stating an idea, or trying to persuade someone else to another way of thinking, the alert reader or listener should nevertheless consider the possibility that assertions sometimes arise from private interests. For instance, if you are buying a car or a dress or a dining room table and a salesman tells you, "This product is the best on the market," he will obviously gain from selling you the product—though he could be telling you the truth. The best action is to ask him quickly what makes him think so. In this way, you charge to the basis of the statement and then review the acceptability of his criteria for your own needs. If you read that the Republicans will win the next state election, you should immediately notice who made the assertion and consider what his motives might be—*as well as* the evidence he advances to verify his statement.

On still another level, if you read that "legally, the adolescent in our society has almost no basic rights at all," you should still ask whether the speaker is a sociologist who is using his collected data to demonstrate this idea objectively— or whether a teenager is trying to persuade you to grant more freedoms to him or his peers. Not to ask this first basic question is to be naive—the "sucker that is born every minute," as P. T. Barnum put it.

What Are Some Alternative Ways of Looking at the Same Subject?

That is, what other ways can you devise to consider the subject of the statement? Once you discern alternative views toward the same subject, you then need to consider *the basis* for the superiority or inadequacy of these alternative notions. In recent years, many writers have said a great deal about the necessity to lobby for restrictions on gun ownership in this country. They seem to base their assertion on the dire consequences of easy availability of firearms in a civilization where people live so close together. Reasonable as this might sound, the careful reader should be able to consider alternative ways of avoiding such "dire consequences."

A more careful public education about the use of firearms might be one alternative; restricting use of certain kinds of guns which cause the most difficulty is another, placing restrictions on selling guns through the mails is another, and still another is requiring permits to own guns, whereby the unfit or the known criminal would be denied a permit. Each alternative has its strengths and weaknesses. The critical writer—and reader—anticipates these objections quite often and cites reasons why his assertion is the wisest and why the others are not feasible or desirable.

Written or spoken arguments are often so beguiling that we lower our defenses and accept them without struggling with the possibility that better alternative approaches to the same subject exist. Inquiring toughly into our own beliefs is quite often the most difficult task we ever face during any given day. Try, therefore, to discover as many alternative approaches to these assertions:

- The best way to change the bureaucratic system of an institution is to hold mass protests and, if necessary, interrupt the work of those who must keep it going.
- John must be a communist. He thinks communists should be able to hold seats in Congress and any state or local government.
- To suppress the insect population in the cities and towns, we simply have to spray insecticides often enough and hard enough to do the job. I know that kills the birds frequently, but there's really no other way to do the job effectively.

Now, if these were easy enough, write down three or four of your own beliefs and probe them until you find at least two alternatives for each idea as a means of achieving some purpose that you can identify. If you can accomplish this, you are well on the way to mastering a basic skill of self-criticism that the sensitive writer needs.

What Are the Assumptions (Implied Assertions) on Which the Statement Is Based?

In other words, what unstated idea provides the basis for the statements? Usually, assumptions are implied notions that we take for granted. Quite often, writers or speakers simply assume that other people think the way they do—and so they assert an idea without naming what they are also assuming. Sometimes, however, when the writer thinks that some readers might doubt his notion, he might identify the assumption openly: "Assuming that great art must resemble the subject it is supposed to depict, modern abstract art cannot be great." By making his key assumption obvious, he is quite fair—and also identifies the ground on which his central idea can be questioned. If the reader can demonstrate that such an assumption about art is not valid, then we can call the assumption an *unwarranted assumption*. The ground is thus removed from the assertion, and the assertion must then be abandoned until some other assumption takes its place.

Identifying assumptions is a bit tricky. Try, therefore, to identify the assumptions—the notion taken for granted—in each of the following statements:

- Young people would not revolt against society if they were successful in it. (Only unsuccessful people revolt? Revolutionaries are always unsuccessful people?)
- Roy must be a communist. He is, after all, in favor of water fluoridation. (Water fluoridation is a danger to our political system? Only communists favor water fluoridation?)
- If you study efficiently two hours outside of class for every hour in class, you should succeed in the course. (You are studying the right subject? You listen carefully in class? Basic formula for success in the course?)
- Spectator sports cannot be educational, since only activities that exercise one's mental skills or increase one's knowledge are educational. (Spectator sports do not increase one's knowledge or exercise one's mental skills?)
- What we need is a President who speaks intelligently, relates to the people he meets very effectively, and takes a strong stand against increasing income taxes. Then we'll have a President who can lead this country to great things. (Unless the President speaks intelligently, he cannot lead the country to great things? Our current President does not speak intelligently? What other assumptions are present here?)

Once you find the assumptions, you may not be so willing to accept these statements—assuming that you might have otherwise. As a way of increasing your ability to identify assumptions rather quickly, pick up the nearest magazine and scan it to find statements containing unstated assumptions. Inspect a recent piece of your own writing to identify some assumptions that you have not made clear. Listen to the instructor of your next hour's class; how many statements does he make that contain unstated assumptions? Remember that just because they are unstated does not mean that the stated idea is not valid or that you are being gulled of your belief. Probing for assumptions is simply an insurance that you are not persuaded to an idea that contains an objectionable, unstated basis.

What Are the Implications of the Assertion?

In short, what else is involved in the proposition? If you accept the writer's idea as true, what else are you also agreeing with at the same time? Ideas, in other words, have consequences in other ideas which are closely tied to the original assertions. Notice that both assumptions and implications constitute a gap between what is said or done and what is meant. If you suddenly slight someone with whom you have usually been friendly, you imply by your action that you disapprove of him or his actions. Your nonverbal communication contains implications.

Implications in writing, however, are often more difficult to discern. If a person writes, "The aim of a college education is to teach people to think logically and critically as well as help them to accumulate knowledge to make a living after graduation," one implication of this statement is that the development of socially constructive attitudes is not a responsibility of a college education. Another implication is that neither artistic expression nor development of emotional potential is a fit aim of a college. Still another is that religious or spiritual development is not an appropriate task for the college to undertake.

If we take the implications one step further, it is obvious that the college program of courses, out-of-class activities, and in-class instruction would necessarily need to be designed to meet the original aim only. Such an implication might lead to drastic changes in budget, the type of faculty members hired and retained, the materials used in classes, and the buildings on campus. Colleges would be quite different places indeed, though some persons have seriously subscribed to the notion that critical and logical thinking and the accumulation of knowledge and information are appropriate tasks of the college.

Implication-finding is probably a somewhat more common search than that of probing for assumptions or alternatives. It is, after all, a bit easier. In fact, we often infer ideas where they do not exist. A person who asserts that he does not believe literally in the Bible might be interpreted as having implied that he does not "believe in the Bible" or that he is not a member of a religious faith. Another person might see an insidious implication in the fact that he saw one of his neighbors talking with a known drug addict. Still another might regard the writer of the statement that "Prostitutes are necessary to the mental health of a society" as a sex criminal or an enemy of the law. None of these inferences need be true at all, but they are ones that surface in writing and conversation, nevertheless. The dangers of overreading implications are surely as great as not noticing them at all.

Try your hand at inferring appropriate implications from these assertions:

- I like Don when he is at home or at the office. (But I do not like him elsewhere?)
- Political activities have increased on college campuses. We should notice the unprecedented attention they receive and their part in setting the pattern for the future. (Political activities get too much attention? Political activities now will mean more political activities in the future?)
- Our increasing leisure time will surely force us to evaluate the importance of work and worker productivity as an indication of goodness in our culture. (Work index equals goodness? Productivity means culture is good? Leisure time is bad? Leisure time needs to be thought of as good?)
- Americans seem to have no past. Their cities change faster than the inhabitant's lifetimes. (Change allows no ties with the past? Change is good? Past is good?)
- People do not generate the high energy level of creativity that they did in the past. "Getting along" and being agreeable, both ideals in our culture, probably contribute a great deal to dampening real creativity and differentiation in life styles that goes with the creative urge. (Creativity is at a new low in our culture? Little differentiation in life styles now? "Getting along" and being agreeable are not good ideas? Creativity is good?)

The gaps between what we say and what we also mean abound in writing and speaking. As you read your next assignment or a magazine for pleasure (do we imply that assignments are not "pleasure"?), identify three or four statements that contain implications. See whether you can write them down. Then, inspect them to see if your inferences are warranted.

What Are the Consequences or the Significance of the Idea?

Usually, in essay writing, the conclusion (if it is not simply a summary) consists of an exploration of the implications and significance of the main ideas and the evidence used to support those ideas. This conclusion, after all, is the end product of the essay inquiry; it contains the considered judgments about the value, the uses, the consequences in the lives of human beings of the ideas about the subject of the essay. Consequences, moreover, though closely allied to the matter of significance, are still somewhat separate in meaning. You can identify the consequences of an idea by asking, "If I think or act like the proposition states—or if other people do—then what will happen? How will lives be affected? How will property be affected? Are the possible effects desirable or undesirable?"

Obviously, to have valid answers, the reader needs to ask, "On what basis do I know these things will happen or that they are desirable or undesirable?" Significance, on the other hand, derives from these consequences. On the matter of significance, we might ask, "What does the idea amount to in the long run? How will it affect people's lives and property (matters of significance)? Is the idea a significant advance or decline in attitudes or belief?" All this is to say that we generally judge significance by the extent or the intensity of the consequent effects on human lives, property, or values.

If you accept the idea that premarital sex is wrong and that people should feel guilty about it, then what are the possible consequences? Psychologists and mental health experts generally testify that the consequences are significant indeed; but so do clergymen. These significant consequences can form the main part of the concluding judgments of an essay on premarital sex.

Another common notion is that magazines like *Playboy* and nudist magazines should not be available in drugstores—and, many would say, anywhere. What are the possible significant consequences of acting on such a notion? A first step would be to identify the positive and the negative consequences of the easy availability of such magazines. Depending on one's standards, a writer might see positive values in frank and open communication of such materials to persons who otherwise might draw the conclusion that a picture of the human body— and thus the human body itself—is a mystery, a kind of shamefulness that one can learn about only in sanctioned times and places. Such an argument ultimately leads to the decision that such magazines are healthy and ought to be available. By contrast, possible negative consequences might be a generation of young people who treat sex lightly and who overlook more enduring values of character and personality. Both judgments need to be based on cited instances and perhaps research studies to be convincing.

The important task is to follow a subject to its potential significance and consequences so that some justifiable judgment grows out of the evidence. Here are some ideas that contain potential consequences of some significance. Find as many as you can in each one:

- A nation-wide peace demonstration might hasten our departure from a war in which our country is engaged.
- Our automobiles are really too big for the available roads. The federal government should pass a law restricting the size of cars to something the size of a Corvette or a Mustang.
- So much fat goes into hamburgers that the fat additives should be outlawed and chicken should be used instead.
- "The Pill" should be dispensed freely through college infirmaries, through doctors' offices, and by prescription through drugstores.
- Industries should not be allowed to build their plants along bodies of water in order to prevent massive water pollution.

Now, to try your skills, provide alternative notions to the above ideas. And try to identify assumptions and implications in those ideas. Finally, find a few beliefs that your friends have extolled on occasion and trace the possible consequences. Are they significant consequences or not? On what basis do you make your judgment?

The probing for alternatives, assumptions, implications, and consequences are not the only important questions you can ask, but they are the main ones. Practicing them until they become a constant part of your thinking habits should result in your strengthening the depth and quality of your ideas in both listening and writing. That, at least, is the object.

AVOIDING FAULTY REASONING: FALLACIES

While the preceding section treats the process of inquiring critically into the strengths and weaknesses of any assertion, it is also important to attend to the numerous faulty paths to forming judgments. Those who use them, consciously or not, pass them off as valid, legitimate means of drawing conclusions. The shame of this is that no one is served well by such faulty thinking; false arguments affect the lives of human beings, so it is most important to identify false reasoning while reading and to avoid it while writing. The fallacies named here are the more common false arguments.

Overgeneralization

Perhaps it is human nature to draw the quick conclusion on too little evidence. At least, generalizing from a very few instances is the easiest way to draw a simple conclusion. But people have been known to advocate the drafting of all able-bodied young college men in time of war because they saw three or four such students doing nothing but reading a book and getting a sun tan on a nice spring day while a war was going on. Likewise, after opening a chemistry book and looking at the diagrams and equations, some students hastily assert that chemistry is a hard subject and not very enjoyable either.

Opinion based on a few instances often arrives in writing as though it is some universal law. After reading two novels and a short story by Ernest Hemingway, the enthusiastic reader might write that "Hemingway is among the greatest writers of American literature." This might or might not be true, after all, but basing the judgment on such bikini-sized evidence certainly does Hemingway no justice, particularly if the reader's acquaintance with American literature is not extensive.

How can you spot an overgeneralization when you meet one in your own writing? If you find yourself using words like "absolutely," "always," "never," "truly," or similar superlatives, then you should review very carefully the accuracy of such wording before committing yourself. Ask yourself, "Have I provided enough evidence to include this word in the statement?" If, after a three-week trip to Paris, you write your friends that "The French are quite open about sex," you might consider a similarly-derived statement by a Frenchman who visits the United States for three weeks and stays in your home. What if he said, when he returns to France, "The Americans are simple-minded"? You might consider this unjust. Why? Because what you and the Frenchman are saying is that, from the point of view of a person with your tastes and limited experience, this *appears* to be true. Such qualifications provide the necessary halter to runaway generalizations—and your writing is more believeable, most likely, as a result.

Arguing Against the Man

This false reasoning strategy is a kind of irrelevance. A writer or speaker, perhaps out of frustration, directs his arguments against the man who presents the argument rather than the argument itself. Some persons do not play the usual Mendelssohn "Wedding March" at their weddings because Mendelssohn developed a reputation as cad, carouser, and philanderer. The work thereby becomes intertwined with the man, and reasonableness disappears.

If you are more interested in crushing the person who advances an unwelcome argument, then abuse, unsavory details about him, sarcasm, half-truths, and recriminations are your weapons. If someone asks such tough questions as "Is law necessary?" or "Can the Democrats actually accomplish something worthwhile?" you might reply, "Only a subversive would ask such a question." Thus, honest inquiry into the subjects themselves is lost. On the other hand, if the point of arguing against the man is to discredit a dishonest or badly informed man on the subject, then this is a legitimate use of such a strategy. Otherwise not.

Sampling Fallacies

Statistical information is a sturdy type of support for our conclusions, and writers use such data quite often; the problem is that statistics can mislead a reader a great deal. For example, seven out of ten doctors might recommend Lisp as the best quality mouthwash on the market—but what kind of doctors were they? On what criteria did they base their judgment? How many were in the total sample? Whom did they work for? (For the Lisp Mouthwash Company?) On what basis were they chosen? When did they render their opinion? How many other mouthwashes did the doctors consider?

Such a seemingly harmless statistical statement, if swallowed without questioning, is actually a distortion of a valid statistically based argument. Statistically supported arguments should always include statements about the sample size, the method of obtaining it, the variables, and the limitations of the data. In this way, assertions based on such data have a chance to succeed as true statements.

Consider the fraternity man who dates two coeds from Sunseed College and then reports as a kind of authority on the Sunseed women and their habits. His sample hardly justifies his making any assertions about Sunseed women, or indeed about the nature of the two women he dated if he has known them only a short while. It is not likely that the two he dated were "typical."

Television networks have similar problems when they try to discover how many people are watching a given program. In order to discover the audience size, they cannot poll each TV set for every one of their programs through the week. And it would be just as false to poll the sets in one city. Instead, they make studies of television owners and then try to replicate the characteristics of the total population in a much smaller group of 2,000 or so families who own sets. If they have correctly determined the variables of the total group and successfully selected a similar small group, they should obtain the *same* proportion of persons in the small group watching programs as a similar proportion of the total population watch.

If the smaller group were selected on the basis of their owning a telephone, however, then the surveyors might commit the same sampling error as the *Literary Digest* did in the 1936 election when its editors asserted that Alf Landon would win. He did win—with the population that owned telephones— but he lost with the larger population that, as a group, did not own as many telephones as the *Literary Digest* poll group did.

The questions to ask for statistical sampling evidence as a basis for an assertion include: *Are there enough respondents to justify the assertion? Are the statistical instances representative of the total involved population? Were the circumstances for the gathering of the information roughly the same for everyone polled?* Affirmative answers to these questions should produce less quibbling over the accuracy of the assertion growing out of the sampling evidence.

The False Analogy

An argument by analogy, extended comparisons, states that two situations are similar in some respects and that *therefore* they are similar in *other* respects, too. Analogies are useful in clarifying an explanation or in describing, as comparing human beings to machines. Human beings are not like machines, nor are groups of men like body parts. The universe is not a clock, and what was true in 1925 may not be true today.

Running a national government is not like running a local school or a business. The monarch is often called the head of state, and some say that when the head is cut off, the other parts cannot live. Governments and populations are not comparable in any literal sense. "Life is like a mountain railroad," one writer said. "Keep your hand upon the throttle and your eye upon the rail." If you take that statement too literally, you will run off the track of clear reasoning. *Clarification* by analogy is one thing; argument by comparison is another. Here are some further examples of false analogy:

- Kennedy forced the Russians to back down in the Cuban crisis; Nixon should force the Vietnamese to back down. (Here are the hidden assertions: two crises are the same in all aspects; Russians and Vietnamese are the same in all aspects; Kennedy's and Nixon's behavior should be the same in all aspects.)
- If the state requires a driver's license test, it should also require a bicycle test. (Hidden asertions: Bicycles and cars are alike in all respects; drivers and bike-riders are alike in all respects; driving and bike-riding are alike in all respects.)

- Marijuana smoking is no more harmful than alcohol drinking; alcohol is legal; marijuana should also be legalized. (Hidden assertions: smoking marijuana produces same effects as drinking alcohol; marijuana and alcohol are alike in all respects; people smoke pot for the same reason they drink alcohol.)

The Either-Or Fallacy (or The False Dilemma)

This false strategy is an "either . . . or" error. In short, if you are not for me, you must be against me. The assumption here is that no middle ground exists. How many times have you heard the assertion, "I certainly am not going to knock myself out studying. There's a lot more to life than reading a book. I say live." The false dilemma is the implied assertion that the student has only two choices: either he studies and dies a bookworm, or he parties and "lives." The middle ground of "study enough, play enough" is ignored as a possibility. Or, a worker might consider that he will lose his soul if he does not attend church and do good works; on the other hand, he worries that his business will fail and that his family will be impoverished if he does not spend all his time working. The worrier sees two choices: either he will lose his soul, or he and his family will end in ruin. He is blind to the third possibility; that is, attending to the interests of both soul and family.

Here are some other fallacious "either-or" statements:

- If we do not poison all the coyotes now, sheepmen will suffer devastating losses to their sheep herds. (Hidden assertions: coyotes have no natural enemies to control them; they invariably attack sheep herds; extermination of coyotes has no ecological effect on total balance of nature.)
- Either you vote for Shad Roe Fisheye or you see this country become totally socialistic. (Hidden assertions: only Shad Roe Fisheye can be effective against socialism; all other politicians want this country to be totally socialistic.)
- Spare the rod and spoil the child. (Hidden assertion: either parents physically punish children or children become incurably spoiled.)
- We must have strong laws forbidding pornography, or our nation will become corrupted. (Pornography always corrupts nations; laws forbidding pornography will always keep nations pure and uncorrupted.)

"Either-or" fallacies are sometimes called "black-and-white" fallacies. (Something is either all black or it is all white; no greys are possible.) The false reasoning is easy to detect if you state the hidden assertions.

The False Cause

Sometimes, people argue that, because one event precedes another, the first event caused the second to occur. This false cause relationship is called a *post hoc* fallacy. A football player might be unusually fortunate in a game; he manages to score three times, block his opponents successfully, and win the crowd's applause. He might wonder at the cause of his success. In the locker room after the game, he discovers that he forgot to take off the pink undershirt his girl friend gave him on Valentine's Day. From now on, he vows, he will wear his pink undershirt at all football games. He falsely concludes that his luck is related to his wearing of the magical shirt.

A more serious kind of false cause assertion occurs, however, when a writer argues that because two events are happening simultaneously, the one causes the other. For instance, he might discover that Nebraskans live longer on the average than citizens of any other state; he also notices that Nebraskans consume more beef and dairy products per capita than the citizens of any other state. Aha, he decides. If you have a large diet of beef and dairy products, you will tend to live longer.

Certainly, a relationship can exist between two events without that relationship being a *causal* one. In the human world of events, causes are complex, multiple. A single cause is immediately suspect of faulty reasoning. Here are a few statements guilty of false cause:

- Because welfare payments are so easy to get, people don't work; all they do is sit back and collect relief checks. (Hidden assertion: the only cause of people's unemployment is the easy availability of welfare payments.)
- Jane Sutherland Brown crashed her motorcycle after a quarrel with her lover. (Hidden assertion: the quarrel was the only cause of the accident.)
- The crime rate will go down if we encourage tough-minded and tough-acting police. (Hidden assertion: crime rate increase is caused by wishy-washy and weak police forces.)
- Of course he's become a liberal; he has gone to college! (College education causes students to become liberal.)

Ferreting out false cause reasoning is easy; simply ask, "Are there other possible causes? Is there really only *one* cause?"

Emotional Fallacies

Fallacies dependent upon or appealing to emotions are called *arguments ad hominem* and *ad populum.* Because personal, financial, and cultural interests are deep within human nature, arguments too often appeal to emotion by arousing fear, appealing to pride, attacking the character of an opponent (see earlier section), making moral judgments, all appeals that do not directly concern the truth or value of a particular measure. For instance, is a man an inadequate senator because he paid no income tax? Or because he once was a mediocre actor? Or because he has a prominent nose? One corporation, as an example, attempted to discredit the character of Ralph Nader in order to protect their own interests.

In addition to the obvious ploys, emotional fallacies frequently touch our unconscious needs and fears to provoke emotional reactions. Three of the more common ones are these:

- *Moral Judgments*
- *Figurative Language*
- *Abstract Language*

Moral judgments are those attitudes which come from cultural conditioning. They are fallacies when they preclude analysis of a particular issue, when they come before and thus stop understanding. And they are usually "automatic" reactions, since most people have never actively questioned the truth or accuracy of the judgments. Whenever you label something, either directly or implicitly, as good or bad, right or wrong, you are making moral judgments. The trouble is that such judgments lead to "either-or" thinking (interracial marriage is wrong; white Protestant marrying white Protestant is good) and blanket approval or disapproval. Here are some examples:

- Our school is the best in town. (Best in what way? Size of building? Athletic teams? Teachers' salaries? Or what?)
- Love is never having to say you're sorry. (Never saying "you're sorry" is good. Always?)
- He's not normal; he wears long hair and flowered pants. (Normality is "good"; long hair and flowered pants are "bad." But what is normal? For whom? When? Where?)
- Good literature is always an inspiration. ("Good" in what sense? Subject matter? Style? Language?)

Moral judgments need to be made *after* careful analysis and objective reasoning, not before.

Figurative language too can lead to faulty reasoning because it is descriptive, not analytical. Thus, it is similar to false analogy, and it frequently leads to moral judgments. Here are a few phrases:

- rampaging exploitation of our waterways
- menacing cloud of creeping libertinism
- coddling decisions of the Supreme Court
- striding with the vigor of untamed manhood

Phrases of this sort move us emotionally, not rationally; they do not lead to objective analysis.

Abstract language fails to be concrete and usually implies a moral judgment. Be on the alert for terms that are considered good ("patriotic," "law and order," "democracy," "duty," "individuality") and those considered bad ("conformity," "godless," "heathen," "dirty," "corrupt"). The able writer will use particularized language.

Other False Strategies

Quite a number of other false means of forming judgments remain. For instance, there is "arguing off the point"—*ignoratio elenchi*. Asserting that democracy is the best form of government and then telling how good America was to your father as "evidence" is arguing off the point.

Another false strategy is "the statement that does not follow"—the *non sequitur*. It occurs when a person writes, for example, "When I was young, I greatly abhorred the daily experience of seeing my brother confined to a wheel chair. I therefore think we must prevent cruelty to animals if we are humane at all." Obviously, the statement about cruelty to animals does not follow the one about the brother's wheel chair confinement.

When a writer *quotes out of context*, he distorts the true meaning of the total passage by selecting portions of it that support his own views on the subject in question. For instance, a writer might quote his source as saying, "Drugs are harmless . . . and stimulating," when the source actually states, "Drugs are harmless as cancer virus and stimulating to such an extent that they eventually destroy certain vital portions of the brain mechanism." The writer with integrity is careful not to quote out of context.

Stereotypes are another way of distorting the true, complex picture of individuals by simply ascribing overgeneralized group characteristics to them. Thus, you might read that elementary education majors are simple-minded, that Midwesterners are naive and unsophisticated, Negroes lazy and slow, Jews tight-fisted, city people cold and unfriendly, or young women all looking for a marriage partner who can give their children freedom from making a living. The best advice for avoiding this common false reasoning is to judge people as individuals first, and members of a group last, if at all.

In general, you can learn to avoid fallacies, and to spot them when others use them, by probing for the hidden assertions and implications. Remember to:

- look for the implied assumption
- state it as an assertion
- consider exceptions to assertions
- determine if assertion is fact, opinion, or preference

LEARNING AIDS

Consider each of the following assertions that various student writers have made in their essays. Identify the false reasoning and how it needs to be altered for accuracy or what additional facts might sustain it as true:

1. Government spending causes inflation.
2. Women, because of their femininity, cannot be great novelists, except in some rare instances like Jane Austen and Emily Brontë.
3. I consistently have maintained that a person should do body exercises each morning and night and eat certain health foods regularly, like yogurt, wheat germ, and tiger's milk. Here I am at sixty, still fertile, having children.
4. Teachers' salaries have risen an average of 6 percent per year for the last six

years. Anyone can see that the economic position of teachers has improved a great deal.

5. Every high school graduate should join the armed forces. It did my two brothers a world of good.

6. The fads and frills of modern high school education have turned the schools into playgrounds. The kids are ripe for plucking by outside agitators and commie sympathizers, not to mention the dope pushers. If we would just teach them some good Americanism and get rid of the tom-foolery, they could buckle down to business and learn something that they could use. (Note that you can also draw upon the defining section of this chapter.)

7. Men are more nervous than women.

8. If students were given more freedom, universities would benefit, because any university profits when its students have more freedom. (Define "freedom" first.)

9. My son is like our neighbor's rooster. He crows when he wakes up in the morning, and he struts around in front of the women all day.

10. Neighbors are nosy.

11. Those strident sons of surfeit and seashore holidays have strayed too often from their task of obtaining the education that the rest of society has made possible for them.

12. Violence in the cause of freedom and brotherhood of man is justifiable.

13. Lucius Brown is an atheist. He washes his car during church time, curses on occasion, has long hair, doesn't think children should pray in school, thinks Billy Graham is wasting his time, and likes science.

the
research
process

A student justifies his status as a student only when he presses beyond dutifully attending classes and routinely fulfilling assignments. Intellectual life, the life of the individual mind, begins when you chafe with the urge to know—to find out for yourself, because your test, your instructor, and the class discussions lay only the premises for ideas. This impulse to find out on your own is the research impulse. Through research, scientists, space technologists, physicists, and biologists have rendered a virtual ocean of knowledge about ourselves and the world. Our moon shots, for instance, depend upon hundreds of research discoveries, some old, some recent. The research linking cigarette smoking to organic diseases, the revolutionary discovery of the structure of the DNA molecule (the fundamental genetic material), the unearthing of archeological findings in Africa or Mexico—all of these exciting and valuable advances stemmed from someone's urge to know and the energy and skill to conduct research.

When you need to learn the address of a friend, when you write to your congressman asking for his opinion on lowering the voting age, when you investigate the historical background of Williamsburg, Virginia, or Geneva, Switzerland, when you inquire around or check the university yearbook for information about a blind date, when you assess the literary status of the American muckrakers, you are doing research. Research is, therefore, the systematic method of uncovering information to answer questions, solve problems, or sustain or reject hunches.

Is there, for instance, an age past which a woman is more likely to bear a mongoloid child? Answer: Yes. Past forty. This phenomenon is known as the Downs' syndrome, named after the researcher who discovered it. You need luggage to go to Europe. What is the best buy for the money? If you read airline regulations, study consumer reports, compare prices, and finally decide what pieces you need, you have conducted research to answer the question. How does one breed and train a horse? How can one qualify for the Olympics? What is the nature of the social criticism in Hogarth's engravings? What are the stages of pregnancy? Although our intellectual interests and abilities reflect the depth and significance of our questions, each of us conducts research for the promise of discoveries in the next trunkful of collected information.

Reportorial or Original Research

Research can be of various kinds. Students and scholars in the humanities and social sciences, for instance, most often create either *reportorial* or *original* research papers. The differences are important to understand, although the purposes are similar—*to discover and interpret new facts and to revise older conclusions, theories, or laws in light of new facts and judgments.*

Reportorial research is the kind of research most undergraduates conduct; they need to know something that others have first discovered or reasoned out in original research. *The reportorial research process is, therefore, one of search-*

*ing through library resources, discovering and compiling findings and judgments
of others, and then drawing conclusions from the collected information.* Sometimes, as in the case of Vance Packard, who collected the findings of numerous
research articles from the social sciences in his book *The Status Seekers*, the
conclusions are original and the contribution thus quite substantial. In the hands
of the less energetic, reportorial research can be simply a useful (if thorough)
compendium of findings about a subject.

By contrast, original research is the first of its kind—the first to interpret a
subject in a certain way, the first to draw conclusions that have not been stated
before, the first to record certain information like statistics or historical documentation, or the first to construct a model of a molecule whose structure was
previously unknown. *Surveys, interviews, laboratory tests, fresh interpretations
of a work of literature or a historical event, statistical analysis, or the unearthing
and systematic study of unknown or unexamined documents, artifacts, archeological sites, or materials of any kind—all these constitute original research.*
Undergraduates are quite as capable of doing original research as the more
common reportorial kind; learning to overcome technical problems and to judge
the significance of the findings of original research, while demanding and
time-consuming, pays rich dividends later.

Illustrations should clarify the differences between these two research modes.
The following are lists of various reportorial and original research topics. Keep in
mind, however, that the skillful researcher could sharpen reportorial topics to
original observations about a subject. The topics are identified by possible titles
of a research paper:

Reportorial	Original
German Attitudes Toward War: Pre-World War I to World War II	Adolescent Aggression: A Classroom Experiment
Ten Attitude Studies of College Students: An Overview	A Survey of College Student Attitudes Toward Drug Use
The Critical Reception of Anne Sexton's Poetry 1962-1972	Anne Sexton's Family Poems: The Feminine Mystique Confessed
Historians' Accounts of Three Civil War Battles	How The South Won The Civil War: A New Look

It should be obvious that the gathering of information from many sources
provides an overview that one or two works cannot provide. An original work
contributes one more set of findings to the information that man needs in order
to improve his lot or to expand his understanding of the human condition. The
distinction between reportorial and original research should be clear to the
college writer, but more important, he must be able to conduct both kinds of
research—sometimes within the same project. The best kind of research always
contains some original contribution, no matter what the subject is.

Pure and Applied Research

Researchers generally distinguish as well between *pure* research and *applied* research. Scientists conduct pure research for its own sake, out of *a desire to know*, helping mankind in generally unforeseen ways; they conduct applied research, *using the findings of pure research*, to solve specific problems of mankind. Pure research is usually the early stage of a useful concept that later researchers apply to various human purposes. Franklin conducted pure research when he discovered electricity; for all he knew, it was useless—but it was there, and he wanted to discover its nature. It was up to people like Maxwell, Bell, Steinmetz, and Edison to apply the energy called electricity to human problems by inventing the telephone, the phonograph, the telegraph, or the dynamo.

The Curies conducted pure research to isolate and identify a previously noticed but unknown chemical element. As a result, they discovered radium, and modern-day scientists applied the Curies' findings to develop atomic-powered submarines, rockets, and to trace chemicals in medicine and agriculture. Although the distinctions between these two kinds of research are important to understand, it is also important to understand the need for both in our culture. Without both, we would all be cavemen and hunters once again. Inquiry and experimentation—curiosity—express man's innate urge to understand the human condition; the educated person not only strives to comprehend his own nature and environment but also tries to improve it.

Types of research do vary. But whether the researcher does reportorial or original research, pure or applied, the value of whatever he does depends upon his itch to know, upon the quality of his research, upon the clarity of the resulting research paper, and upon the careful consideration of the significance and consequences of his findings.

AN OVERVIEW AND THE EARLY STAGES OF RESEARCH

The research process is in truth only slightly divergent from the process you have already explored in Chapter II and in writing other kinds of essays. These are the basic steps:

Preliminary Study
Set up the problem:
- name the subject
- check out for value, interest
- sample periodicals
- assess issues and discover background information
- scan possibilities for obtaining information by survey or by interviews

State tentative
hypothesis:

- state thesis assertion on basis of thinking thus far
- hold this as a "working thesis," subject to change as you discover more about the subject
- make sure this hypothesis can be tested and is not a statement of fact

Investigation
Select sources and
collect notes:

- select sources and take notes from readings and/or the survey or conduct interviews (however you have decided to collect your information)
- use both primary and secondary sources; evaluate statements of your sources as you proceed
- keep an eye on spotting weaknesses in your tentative hypothesis—so you can alter it as you proceed
- at the end of this phase, *revise or affirm the tentative hypothesis*

Writing
Compose rough draft:

- write in formal style
- incorporate quotations and paraphrases
- order essential footnoting
- sort out nonessential footnotes
- avoid plagiarism

Compose final draft:

- revise draft and *rewrite as many times as necessary*
- proofread footnotes and bibliography for correct form AND accurate information

Preliminary Study—Set Up the Problem

Unless you come to experience the delight of discovery, the research effort will soon seem a dull, tedious event—something that happened *to* you and not *for* you. A subject can sometimes make a surprise appearance if you are alert to sense it: What did you dream last night? What were you daydreaming about a moment ago? Why do people dream? What is daydreaming? The creative impulse lies dormant unless we can persist long enough at ferreting out a worthwhile problem from our interests or everyday experiences. We can take things for granted—or we can push them around, angling for a new vision, discovering an unusual analogy, seeing a puzzling difficulty. Above all, let the subject touch you. Let it grow out of your experience and into a source of curiosity. Choose something that relates to you in some way:

Your major field of study: history, science, literature, sociology, art, political science, dance, music, education, retailing, religion, psychology, forestry, urbanology, American studies.

Subjects that have appealed to you through the years: tribal cultures, The Bozeman Trail, paintings, Chartres Cathedral, Schoenberg's music, Beat poetry, existentialism, The DNA molecule, popular advertising, the theologian Bonhoeffer, Hitler, child labor laws, dreaming, homosexuality, or Mayan society.

Contemporary problems: race relations, ghetto conditions, famine, drugs, pollution of natural resources, urban problems, the Supreme Court, changing morality, police brutality, cybernetics, poverty, labor unions, school bussing, middle-class unemployment.

Pet interests: ceramics, op art, men and women in love, jazz, favorite author, exploring natural caves, fox hunting, eighteenth-century dress fashions, medical illustration, techniques of sculpting, black humor fiction, modern architects, sailing problems, city planning, parachuting, organic foods.

Any of these subjects could be trivial or significant, depending upon what you do with it. For example, you could simply explore the history of fox hunting. Or you could demand, on the basis of verifiable information, that fox hunting should be abolished because it is an extravagant waste of aristocratic wealth and leisure. You could explore the significance or interpretation of dreams in order to understand better your friends' or your own dreams. You could simply analyze the cult of rock-and-roll—or you could demonstrate that the lyrics and rhythms reflect youth's disaffection with adult values. You could simply define and describe black humor—or you could show its link with Pop Art in that both expose a society that thrives on exaggeration and materialism. Whatever subject you choose, move it *from facts to ideas*—relevant, imaginative, provocative ideas. Every old idea needs new judgment. Is Macbeth pertinent to the lust for power by some present-day politicians? Is Hamlet a prototype of our rebellious students?

The availability of sources obviously influences your choice of subjects. Some subjects are beyond the resources on campus or in the available libraries. For example, a topic in medicine (intra-uterine transfusion, PKU tests, or the newest drugs in anesthesiology) is hard to research in depth if you do not have access to a medical library. So also, issues in law, engineering subjects, veterinary medicine, or industrial trades, such as lithography or metallurgy, might have to be eliminated, unfortunately.

Types of Investigation   Investigating techniques are not limited solely to library research. You can conduct a survey of your dormmates' attitudes; you can sample opinion among the faculty; you can interview the downtown merchants on the prevalence of shoplifting. *Surveys, samples,* and *interviews* are thus possibilities for research material. *Laboratory research* is another. Your choice of topic obviously can determine the method—or methods—of investigating. Perhaps the idea of taking a survey appeals to you more than spending hours in the library—thus, the method of investigating influences your choice of subject.

Try combining methods: research the library for articles on college student opinions—and see if your fellow students substantiate and validate those articles. Use common sense, though. Trying to poll the local police on their attitudes toward police brutality is obviously a way of beating your head against a stone wall. Try the American Civil Liberties Union files instead. But you might combine what you find to be true about local police attitudes with other studies—about recent Supreme Court decisions on protecting the rights of the accused, for instance. If you want to conduct surveys and sample opinions, consult a survey-research method text in the library for helpful suggestions on writing questions and obtaining a representative sample. Because most research papers derive from library resources, however, we will assume from here on that the research will be in library materials.

Whatever absorbing subject you finally decide upon, you will need to know the history and background of your subject. Preliminary reading also uncovers the names of key writers on the subject, isolates the issues and the questions, and helps to narrow the subject field. Further, you quickly learn about the availability of sources, so that you can modify or adjust the subject if necessary. This early reading is therefore essential to deciding wisely on a topic.

Preliminary Study—State Tentative Hypothesis

Preliminary reading allows you to set up a working or tentative hypothesis—or hypotheses—some belief, attitude, or idea you hope to prove or disprove. The idea has to be tentative because you cannot make a final decision until all the evidence is in, until you have read pros and cons and reassessed your own contributions. Make the tentative thesis one of ideas: of meaning, of value, of policy.

Meanings: "Although some authorities say that the major pattern of imagery in *Antony and Cleopatra* concerns cosmic greatness or magnitude, the major pattern that controls the theme and Shakespeare's intent concerns play-acting, pretending."
Or: "Ghetto children do not do well in the first grade because of the disadvantaged nature of their early pre-school experiences."
Values: "Of the two *bildungsromans, Demian* by Hesse is not as carefully developed as Joyce's *Portrait of the Artist as a Young Man.*"
Policy: "Since the United States Post Office clearly needs professional, competent management, Congress should release its exclusive control over its operations."

Your problem may also be a question, such as "Was Oswald alone or one of a group of conspirators in the assassination of John F. Kennedy?" But then you might rewrite that question into a tentative thesis, such as "Despite the plethora of findings collected by speculators who believe that Oswald was one of a group of conspirators, the Warren Commission's report maintaining that Oswald was acting alone in the assassination of John F. Kennedy is the most rational and objective analysis."

Investigation—Select Sources

You need to evaluate your authorities and your sources. Informed judgments about status and competence make the process of selecting sources much easier. If your source is a book, a magazine, or an encyclopedia, evaluate the audience for that source. How reliable and thorough is an article in *Reader's Digest? Seventeen? Today's Health? Journal of Clinical Psychology? Ramparts?* Is the encyclopedia written for children or adults? How detailed is an article in the Sunday magazine section of the local paper? Furthermore, you need to consider the credentials of your authority. How many other books refer to this authority? What is his background? Check the *Directory of American Scholars* or *Who's Who in America* for his professional training. What do other critics in the field think of his work? A quick check of bibliographies in various books and indexes will help establish his competence and reputation. For instance, James Q. Wilson is an acknowledged authority on the role of the police in society; you will find his name and his works referred to in many articles, reports, or studies you read on that subject. You would want to scan or read his works, then, for you should not depend on simply quoting what others have drawn from his writing.

Furthermore, you need to consider the source in which you located your authority. Are you using a pamphlet by him or a full report? Are you consulting a summary in the *Reader's Digest* or the *American Political Science Review*? Finally, is he writing on his specialty? Noam Chomsky, an original and important thinker in linguistics, has written also on political problems, on the Vietnam war, on the Johnson administration, and on the role of the intellectual. Since he is not a recognized authority in political science, you must therefore evaluate his writings in other ways: How well documented are his articles? How does he marshal his evidence? How much of what he says is opinion? How much fact? You may very well conclude that he is an authority in the articles he has written, even though his professional training lies elsewhere.

Primary and Secondary Sources, Fact and Opinion   Since you are learning the manners of scholarship, you need two other quick tips: (1) distinguish between primary and secondary sources, and (2) distinguish between fact and opinion.

Primary sources are those writings by someone who had a touch-relationship with the period, the person, or the subject under consideration. *Secondary sources* are those writings which are removed from firsthand experience; usually *they are derived* from primary material, from other secondary sources, or both, and are also later in date. For example, if you are writing about Jane Austen's self-imposed limitations on her novels, those novels, her prefaces to them, and her letters to people about her novels are primary materials. An article explaining and interpreting the effects of these limitations is secondary. Or, if you research John F. Kennedy's attitudes toward the Bay of Pigs invasion, primary materials are his speeches, his letters, his documents. So also are observations and comments by staff members who worked firsthand with Kennedy during that crisis. But later evaluation by a biographer or a historian constitutes secondary material.

The value of using primary sources exclusively is that they lead you to your own independent conclusions. You could investigate the influences of paganism in Thomas Hardy's *Tess of the D'Urbervilles* by relying only on the novel itself. You could also use secondary sources to substantiate and corroborate your own conclusions, but be sure to document those sources, of course.

Isolate facts from opinions, too. What President Kennedy said, recorded verbatim in a press conference, is fact. What some staff member believed Kennedy was thinking about is obviously opinion. Likewise, in Hardy's *Tess,* Joan Derbyfield's refusing to allow *The Compleat Book of Magic* in her cottage overnight is fact, indicating Joan's paganism. But the critic who only states that Joan is paganistic without supporting that contention by quoting or paraphrasing that passage, along with others, is merely asserting an opinion—and he thus contributes to a credibility gap.

Thus, you need to distinguish between fact and opinion in your sources *as well as in your own writing*. To argue, for instance, that military conscription is arbitrarily cruel is only opinion until you have cited factual instance after instance after instance to prove that contention. Likewise, asserting that women *and* men need liberating requires similar multiple factual instances to obtain readers' concurrence.

Investigation—Collect Notes

Take your notes on any kind of paper that appeals—cardboard, slates, 4" x 6" cards, whatever. The important thing is to make sure that you can shuffle them or move them around to organize them swiftly into categories when you are preparing to write the paper. Also, it is wise not to create such lengthy notes that they become running summaries of your sources.

Bibliography Cards Be sure to have cards or pages for bibliographies only: that is, record all the publishing information (last and first name of author, title of book, publishing company, place of publication, and date) in one place, on one card or on one page reserved only for that information. Why waste energy racing back to the library to look up publishing information you forgot to include the first time? Write the information in exactly the same order you will use for your entry on the bibliography page, *where all items must be listed in alphabetical order.* (See page 239 for an example.)

Sample Bibliography Cards:

Example for a book:

```
Willcox, Donald. Wood Design. New York:
    Watson-Guptill Publications, 1968.
```

Example for a magazine article:

```
McCormick, John. "The Sound of Hooves."
    Sports Illustrated, July 7,1969, pp. 61-71.
```

Note Cards Try to sort ideas and information into groups and patterns. Test every note you take against the purpose of your paper, against your working thesis, tentative hypothesis, or research question. Some general outline in your head or on scratch paper helps enormously.

As you take notes, ask yourself how this material will fit your purpose, whether it supports or argues against your thesis, where in the tentative outline it might be used. Then label your cards with these outline headings. Almost any topic has stock subtopics, such as background, definition of terms, key personalities, recent advances, or effects—physical, social, psychological. You can certainly label your cards with such subheadings. Or you can specify more completely with titles such as these: types of leukemia research, research grants, most promising avenues, and the like.

Every note card signals its information:

1. author's name and shortened title, plus page number
2. heading to fit into working outline
3. information

Information will be of four kinds—*quotations, paraphrases and summaries, factual statements, and your original ideas that the readings provoke.* Every direct quotation, every copied phrase, every striking sentence you should mark with Gargantuan quotation marks. Everything else will either be paraphrased or summarized. A tip: want to avoid unintentional plagiarism absolutely? *Bracket* all summaries and paraphrases! Later on, in the writing of the paper, you will need to footnote the bracketed material. When you take notes, it is surely wise to record your thoughts below the borrowed quotation or paraphrase so you might easily recall them later—or perhaps move on to even better ones.

As you search, the frame of your outline shifts, enlarges, narrows, widens, in order to revise and refine. The outline headings shuffle around both in your head and on paper—the process is a never-ending one until you reach final draft stage.

Thus, take notes only on what you will be able to use; keep the outline before you as you work. A pile of cards that eventually proves totally irrelevant is a dismaying waste of time—and probably ruins your morale, too.

Sample Note Card:

```
on
Existential Freedom          Berdyaev, Dostoevsky

"The world is full of wickedness and misery
precisely because it is based on freedom--yet
that freedom constitutes the whole dignity of man
and of his world." (pp. 85-86)

(Force world to be good? Result? Loss of freedom.)
```

In short, keep your tentative thesis always in mind as you research the library; match the information you find against your controlling purpose. Does this information fit into the puzzle somewhere? Or is it extraneous? It is wise to remember, however, that the information you find may well sway you into adjusting your thesis to a new angle.

ASSEMBLING THE PAPER
AND AVOIDING PLAGIARISM

Researching the library is time-consuming, exhausting, but intriguing labor. Perhaps you even thought you would turn into a dusty bookworm before you had investigated all the possible sources. Your note-card piles, carefully sorted by outline headings, might appear mountainous at this point. Writing the paper is the final step in the research process.

Writing—Compose Rough Draft

Clear your desk of impedimenta and sort your cards again, reading through them to fix the material in your mind. Revise and refine the outline further, if necessary, paralleling or logically arranging the major ideas. And you should juggle the thesis statement, rewording and recasting as necessary until it expresses your intent exactly. For example, if you were researching the Jim Crow system in the South, you might compose a tentative hypothesis and outline such as this:

Tentative Thesis   The Jim Crow system was devised during the years from 1890 to 1910 to salve the wounds of the southern whites who were bitter over losing the Civil War.

    I. Background—reconstruction position of Negro
   II. Disenfranchisement of the Negro

   III. Rampant racism—the Jim Crow system
   IV. Social and psychological effects
    V. Negro migration to northern cities
   VI. The healing of the wounds

However, in your investigation you learned that the subject was too large and the outline too wide-ranging. As a result, you might well rewrite the thesis and reorder the outline this way:

Thesis Although the Jim Crow system came about between 1890 and 1910 as a result of the white southerners' need to establish political control, the effect was the large-scale Negro migration to the northern cities.

    I. Reconstruction attempts to gain political control in the South
   II. Disenfranchisement accompanied by race-hatred campaigns
  III. Jim Crow laws to bolster disenfranchisement
   IV. Effect—Negro migration to northern cities

After the outline is to your liking, tack or tape it to the wall in front of you. Then begin writing—anywhere. If you do not think of a good way to introduce the subject, write the introductory section later. You might find, as many others have, that the research paper is easier to write than other papers because you have lived with the subject and made your discoveries part of your life.

    The style of the research paper is nearly always formal; most instructors ask that personal pronouns, such as "I" and "you," be omitted. The reason is that the paper should be fairly objective; thus, to write such expressions as "I intend to . . . " or to highlight personal opinion by saying, "I feel . . . " or "I think . . . ," you compromise an objective tone. Your opinion and your evaluation are there, of course, and are clearly evident throughout the paper by your selecting, your ordering, and your compiling of material.

    In effect, you write several mini-essays by developing and expanding each main topic of your outline. Try for the best expression as you go along, revising and rewriting, recasting sentences, changing words, including transitional signals. Add footnotes as you go, inserting them between lines of text, aiding final typing. Why not mark them with red ink or type some symbol to identify them as footnotes?

Incorporating Quotations and Paraphrases A patchwork quilt may win a blue ribbon at a state fair; a patchwork research paper wins nothing. Beginning writers often seem to rely heavily on many quotations, and the papers are thus too heavily documented. One kind of guide is to include no more than three quoted passages on a page, and not more than 20 percent of the total number of words should be quoted material. Finally, you should seldom end a paragraph with a quotation. The end sentence should indicate why the quotation is important or relevant, or it should interpret the information or idea in the quotation.

    Furthermore, you will need to introduce the quotation, explaining or implying its purpose: to substantiate a fact, to reinforce an idea, or to illustrate a point. Thus, you indicate *within the text of the paper* the name of the authority you are going to quote or paraphrase, and then footnote the passage or the summary statement. And you link that quotation or paraphrase to the matter at hand. Finally, if the quotation is four or more typed lines in length, set it off from the rest of the paper by indenting four spaces and single-spacing the quotation. For example, you might want to quote from E. M. Forster's "What I Believe." Here is a reduced, typewritten page to illustrate this principle:

E. M. Forster amplifies this point when he writes:

    One must be fond of people and trust them if one is
    not to make a mess of life, and it is therefore es-
    sential that they should not let one down. They often
    do. The moral of which is that I must, myself, be as
    reliable as possible, and this I try to be.[1]

Reliability, as Forster points out, is an essential part

of personal relations, though these are "bourgeois luxur-

ies" today, in his words.

Notice that the footnote number appears at the *end* of the quotation. Furthermore, as the Forster paragraph illustrates, indented quotations are *not* enclosed in quotation marks.

Variety in introducing reference material is no harder to come by than variety in diction or sentence structure. Try these verbs to replace "so-and-so says" when they are appropriate:

insists	reports	admits
points out	writes	claims
demonstrates	suggests	states
explains	verifies	reminds
asserts	acknowledges	argues
avows	maintains	amplifies

And recast the introductory phrases:

E. M. Forster observes that . . .

In his essay "What I Believe," Forster states . . .

Forster, in "What I Believe," implies . . .

Fishwick interprets the situation in this way:
Substantiating his first point, Fishwick further demonstrates that . . .

In short, vary the phrasing to your purpose and cement the quotation within the paragraph.

Essential Footnotes   Writers provide footnotes for two reasons: (1) to satisfy the highly critical reader (the skeptic demands proof for everything you say); and (2) to acknowledge his debt to an authority. Thus, *you must footnote every direct quotation and all important statements of fact or opinion which you have learned from other sources but written in your own style.*

Nonessential Footnotes   Granted, your reader is skeptical—but he also wants to make the best use of his time. He will think he is watching a film that has slipped off the projector's track if his eyes have to jump from text to footnote to text to footnote. Such ricochet reading is unnerving—and induces motion sickness. Thus, you spare him the necessity of looking at footnotes for some statements. Footnotes are *not needed for obvious truths* (The population explosion has created unprecedented demands upon our world food supplies); *for facts of general knowledge* (Humphrey lost the 1968 presidential race to Nixon); or *for your own opinions or observations* (Our scientific prowess must be quickly marshaled in order to farm the seas).

Likewise, if you must include a dictionary, simply write: "*Webster's Third International* defines 'dogmatics' as. . . ." And if you quote from the Bible, try to weave the name of the book, chapter, and verse into the text, as in "Paul, in Romans 2:10, admonished the early Christians against. . . ."

Finally, try to distinguish between *general* information about your subject and *specialized*, authoritative information. General information will be those

---

[1]This general information about the history and people of the Dead Sea Scrolls occurs in a variety of sources, including the following: Mowry, The Dead Sea Scrolls and the Early Church; Van der Ploeg, The Excavations at Qumran; Potter, The Lost Years of Jesus Revealed; "A Reporter at Large," The New Yorker; and "The Untold Story of the Dead Sea Scrolls," Harper's. All of the general information included in the rest of this paper appears in these sources, and scholars familiar with the Scrolls consider it common knowledge.

facts that occur again and again in almost every source you read. For instance, the common social patterns of American Indian tribal culture will be described in every thorough reference book or journal you use. Thus, to save your reader's time as well as your own, you might very well list those sources containing the same background information in one *explanatory footnote* early in the paper. And write, in that same footnote, that all other *general* information in your paper can be located in any of those works you have listed. (For an example of an explanatory footnote, see the preceding page.)

Therefore, be sure to summarize, to write in your own words, that general information. When you quote or insert or refer to specialized information or judgments (found in only one of your sources), you must document as usual. If in doubt, footnote—and ask questions later.

Another style of explanatory footnote provides facts or observations that are supplementary to the textual content itself. Such use of the explanatory footnote is a kind of authorial aside. Here is an example from Marshall Fishwick's *The Hero, American Style*:

```
        10Booker T. Washington was an ardent admirer of
Harris's work and Uncle Remus's philosophy.  He wrote
Harris to express "appreciation of your enlightened at-
titude toward my race."
```

The reader is thus informed of a significant explanation without burdening the main text with extraneous information.

Literary Text Citations   In a literary paper, writers often follow the convention of documenting fully their first reference to a novel, a book of poetry, or a collection of short stories by writing a formal footnote. Thereafter, however, quotations from that literary work need only be identified (if the writer works with *one* novel, or book, or collection) by inserting the page number in parentheses immediately after the quotation and before the end punctuation. (See the sample research paper on pages 234-238 for examples of this convention.) If the writer discusses two or more works by the same author, then he needs to include the brief title of the work as well as the page number or numbers in the parentheses.

Avoiding Plagiarism

Plagiarism is academic dishonesty—using, borrowing, stealing another writer's words, phrases, sentences, ideas, even organization without giving credit to that person. The temptation is great sometimes; you might not have time to write the paper yourself and your roommate or suitemate writes so easily. Or, the last magazine you looked at contained an article expressing what you think you think, but expressing it better than you think you could. And you are up to the collarbone with so-so grades. Everyone needs help—all he can get, in fact. You *can* use others' writings—*as long as you give credit to your sources.* Trying to pass off another's words as your own is a bit like the emperor and his new clothes: unfortunately, the attempt only reveals your nakedness too clearly.

Even so, many instances of plagiarism occur because students misunderstand exactly what the offense is. The following list describes writing that constitutes plagiarism:

1. *Using another's phrase, sentence, or paragraph without quotation marks.* Be sure to use quotation marks and to indicate the source within the text and/or in a footnote. (See example on page 224.)
2. *Using another's ideas or his structure without properly crediting the author.* (Example: an author categorizes types of violence into four groups. If you want to adopt those categories, give credit to that author for his structure.)
3. *Paraphrasing without introducing or documenting.* Merely arranging or rearranging phrases is *not* paraphrasing, and thus also constitutes plagiarism. (See example on page 224.)
4. *Using another student's work and submitting it as your own.*

Use your sources honestly and advantageously in these ways:

1. In your text, introduce the quotation or paraphrase with the author's name. Such an introduction helps, especially when the cited authority offers his critical evaluation.
2. Place quotation marks around all *exactly* quoted material, including single words and phrases. (All inserted words should be enclosed in brackets. See pages 98-99 for use of brackets.)
3. Paraphrase with your own words and your own style, making sure that you are not simply juggling the author's sentence patterns or phrases.
4. Document properly: footnote each quotation and paraphrase, and create a bibliography entry for each footnoted book, journal, magazine, newspaper, lecture, tape, or other borrowed material.

Examples of Plagiarism and of Honest, Effective Use of Source Material Study carefully the following examples to learn the differences between honest and dishonest uses of source materials. The following is a statement you might borrow for your research paper from Friedenberg's "The Modern High School: A Profile" (See the "Exemplary Essays" section at the end of Chapter VIII for the full essay.):

First of all, they learn to assume that the state has the right to compel adolescents to spend six or seven hours a day, five days a week, thirty-six or so weeks a year, in a specific place, in the charge of a particular group of persons in whose selection they have no voice, performing tasks about which they have no choice, without remuneration and subject to specialized regulations and sanctions that are applicable to no one else in the community nor to them except in this place.

Here are versions by writers who want to use Friedenberg's statement:

Version I

```
Students assume that the state has the right to compel

adolescents to spend seven hours a day for thirty-six

weeks in a specific place.  They are in the charge of a

group in whose selection they have no voice.  And they

perform tasks without renumeration.
```

Here the student is obviously guilty of plagiarism. Not only has he failed to give credit, but also he has merely rearranged the sentence parts.

Version II

> Students believe in the state's right to compel adoles-
> cents; to force them to spend seven hours daily in a
> specific place; to insist they submit to the charge of
> a group in whose selection they have no voice; to make
> them perform tasks without renumeration.[1]

---

[1]Edgar Z. Friedenberg, "The Modern High School: A
Profile," in <u>Crisis: A Contemporary Reader</u>, ed. by
Peter Collier (New York: Harcourt, Brace & World,
Inc., 1969), p. 135.

This version is also plagiarism, even though the student carefully included a footnote. He has not really paraphrased, since he has retained the author's words and phrases rather than developed his own style and vocabulary.

Version III

> Friedenberg maintains that schools treat teenagers as
> though they were draftees or prisoners in a concentra-
> tion camp. He insists that students "learn to assume
> that the state has the right to compel adolescents to
> spend six . . . hours a day . . . in a specific place
> . . . performing tasks without remuneration." Further,
> he argues that those persons to whose authority stu-
> dents must submit are not elected by those students.[1]

¹Edgar Z. Friedenberg, "The Modern High School: A
Profile," in Crisis: A Contemporary Reader, ed. by
Peter Collier (New York: Harcourt, Brace & World,
Inc., 1969), p. 135.

This version is an example of satisfactory handling of the original source material. The student has identified and acknowledged the author in the text; quoted phrases are enclosed in quotation marks, with ellipses to indicate skipped phrases. In addition, the substance of the material is well expressed in the student's own words. And he has included a footnote—an effective and honest use of authority. (See the next section for commonly used footnote and bibliography forms.)

Writing—Compose Final Draft

You have rested, indulged in a hot fudge sundae, praised yourself for such arduous but satisfying work. A few days' interim helps considerably when you revise. You will need to rewrite many of the still-awkward sentences, recasting, inserting transitions, changing words, expanding and cutting. You may even have to make a trip back to the library for additional information or to check on the accuracy of a quotation. If all of these tips seem obvious, it is this revising process that frequently marks the distinction between a barely acceptable paper and an above-average one. Now that you are ready for the final typing, *use your style manual constantly* (see page 226 for list) as a guide for form:

- check the title page
- check every footnote
- check every bibliography entry

Every student can write a properly documented and correctly typed paper if he reads the directions in his manual and follows them exactly, watching the placement of every comma, every period, every parenthesis.

Further, check to see that all paragraphs are well-organized, that each one is linked to the previous one, that all are linked to the thesis. (Read Chapter XII, "Evaluating Your Own Essay," for further help. *See especially page 267 for a checklist "Evaluating Your Research Paper."*) Proofread each introductory phrase, each linking phrase, each concluding sentence following the quotations and paraphrases. And remember to footnote all statements that need documentation. Advertise the names of those worthy authorities who support and contribute to your search for truth.

Finally, you should hold in your respectful hands the product of those long, long hours. You have learned the precision of scholarship.

FOOTNOTE AND BIBLIOGRAPHY ILLUSTRATIONS: MOST USED ONES

Most colleges and universities endorse one of these widely used style manuals: William G. Campbell's *Form and Style of Thesis Writing*, or the revised *MLA Style Sheet*, or Kate L. Turabian's *A Manual for Writers of Term Papers, Theses, and Dissertations*. Each explains and illustrates the conventions of documentation. The conventions allow for an orderly, properly referenced presentation. Inconsistent footnotes and bibliography entries only confuse you and your reader. Your copy of a style manual is an indispensable tool, as integral as your dictionary and thesaurus. Here are some sample footnote and bibliography entries to assist you in early papers and to allow for quick appraisal of mechanics, such as spacing, periods, commas, parentheses, and underlining.

- **Footnote for a book by one author:**

> [1]David Howard Dickason, William Williams: Novelist and Painter of Colonial America (Bloomington: Indiana University Press, 1970), p. 78.

    Corresponding bibliography entry:

> Dickason, David Howard. William Williams: Novelist and Painter of Colonial America. Bloomington: Indiana University Press, 1970.

Notice that the footnote contains four essential facts, offering the information the reader would need if he were locating the book himself: *author's name, the book's title, place and date of publication, and the specific page*. Also, the first line is indented *four to eight spaces*, but the second is not. Look carefully again at the punctuation: the comma after Dickason separates the author's name from the title; the parentheses separate the publishing information from the title; the second comma separates the page number from the publishing information and the title. Every footnote ends with a period. Finally, *titles of books and periodicals must be underlined*.

   The bibliography entry is arranged somewhat differently. The bibliography lists all the sources that you document in your footnotes *in alphabetical order*, by author's last name, or, if the author is unknown, by the first significant word of the title. And since you have not read *all* the works on your subject, the title of the page is "Selected Bibliography" or "Works Cited." Thus, each bibliography entry begins with the author's last name, with the line beginning at the margin. The second line is indented *four to eight spaces*; each entry is single-spaced. Periods instead of commas are used, and parentheses are omitted since the facts of publication are primary here. Page numbers for books, but not for other works, are omitted.

   Footnotes occurring later in the paper but referring to the same book use a quick, short form, if you are using only one book by that author, as in:

[4]Dickason, 166.

The Latin abbreviations of *ibid., op. cit.,* and *loc. cit.* are no longer universally necessary to indicate repeated sources in new style footnotes. If, however, you use two or more sources by one author, you need simply to use the last name and an abbreviation of the titles to distinguish among them for the reader.

   Several exemplary models of frequently used footnote and bibliography entries follow. For other kinds of references, such as a public speech on tape, an original manuscript, a letter, an interview, or tables and figures, you will need to consult a complete guide to form and style in the research paper.

- **Footnote for a book by two authors:**

[2]Paul Rotha and Richard Griffith, The Film Till Now (London: Spring Books, 1967), p. 467.

   Corresponding bibliography entry:

Rotha, Paul, and Griffith, Richard. The Film Till Now.
      London: Spring Books, 1967.

- **Footnote referring to the introduction of a book:**

[3]Dwight Macdonald, "Introduction," Acid Test, by John Simon (New York: Stein and Day, 1963), p. 11.

Corresponding bibliography entry:

Macdonald, Dwight. "Introduction," <u>Acid</u> <u>Test</u>, by John Simon.
        New York: Stein and Day, 1963.

● **Footnote for a book by an editor or editors:**

⁴Stuart Levine and Nancy Oestrich Lurie, eds., <u>The</u>
<u>American</u> <u>Indian</u> <u>Today</u> (Deland, Fla.: Everett/Edwards, Inc.,
1968), p. 188.

Corresponding bibliography entry:

Levine, Stuart, and Lurie, Nancy Oestrich, eds. <u>The</u> <u>Ameri-</u>
        <u>can</u> <u>Indian</u> <u>Today</u>. Deland, Fla.: Everett/Edwards,
        Inc., 1968.

● **Footnote citing an author's component part within a book by an editor:**

⁵P. Albert Duhamel, "The Novelist as Prophet," in
<u>The</u> <u>Added</u> <u>Dimension</u>: <u>The</u> <u>Art</u> <u>and</u> <u>Mind</u> <u>of</u> <u>Flannery</u> <u>O'Connor</u>,
ed. by Melvin J. Friedman and Lewis A. Lawson (New York:
Fordham University Press, 1966), p. 102.

Corresponding bibliography entry:

Duhamel, P. Albert. "The Novelist as Prophet." <u>The</u> <u>Added</u>
        <u>Dimension</u>: <u>The</u> <u>Art</u> <u>and</u> <u>Mind</u> <u>of</u> <u>Flannery</u> <u>O'Connor</u>.
        Edited by Melvin J. Friedman and Lewis A. Lawson.
        New York: Fordham University Press, 1966.

- **Footnote for a quotation by one author in a book written by another:**

⁶Batho and Dobrée, <u>Victorians</u> <u>and</u> <u>After</u>, quoted in
<u>The</u> <u>Image</u> <u>of</u> <u>Childhood</u>, by Peter Coveney (Baltimore: Pen-
guin Books, Inc.), p. 111.

Corresponding bibliography entry:

Batho and Dobrée. <u>Victorians</u> <u>and</u> <u>After</u>. Quoted in <u>The</u>
        <u>Image</u> <u>of</u> <u>Childhood</u>, by Peter Coveney. Baltimore:
        Penguin Books, Inc., 1967.

- **Footnote for a book in a paperback series:**

⁷Theodore Roszak, <u>The</u> <u>Making</u> <u>of</u> <u>a</u> <u>Counter</u> <u>Culture</u>,
Anchor Books (Garden City, N.Y.:   Doubleday & Company, Inc.,
1969), p. 64.

Corresponding bibliography entry:

Roszak, Theodore. <u>The</u> <u>Making</u> <u>of</u> <u>a</u> <u>Counter</u> <u>Culture</u>. Anchor
        Books. Garden City, N.Y.:   Doubleday & Company,
        Inc., 1969.

- **Footnote referring to an article in a popular magazine:**

⁸Grahame J. C. Smith, "The Ecologist at Bay," <u>Satur</u>-
<u>day</u> <u>Review</u>, January 2, 1971, p. 69.

Corresponding bibliography entry:

Smith, Grahame J. C. "The Ecologist at Bay." <u>Saturday</u> <u>Re</u>-
        <u>view</u>, January 2, 1971, pp. 68-69.

- **Footnote referring to an editorial in a newspaper with numbered sections:**

⁹Editorial, The New York Times, Jan. 25, 1970, Sec. 4, p. 14.

Corresponding bibliography entry:

Editorial. The New York Times, Jan. 25, 1970, Sec. 4, p. 14.

- **Footnote referring to an article without a by-line in a newspaper with lettered sections:**

¹⁰"Land Cost is Cited in Housing Crisis," St. Louis Post-Dispatch, Feb. 1, 1970, p. 1D.

Corresponding bibliography entry:

"Land Cost is Cited in Housing Crisis." St. Louis Post-Dispatch, Feb. 1, 1970, p. 1D.

Note that the city is part of the title in the first two newspaper examples. Parenthetically insert the city for clarity if it is not part of the title, as the next entry illustrates.

- **Footnote referring to a newspaper article with a by-line; city is not part of title:**

¹¹Michael Baily, "Bright Year for British Shipping," The Times (London), Jan. 30, 1970, p. 20.

Corresponding bibliography entry:

Baily, Michael. "Bright Year for British Shipping." The Times (London), Jan. 30, 1970, p. 20.

Note that the following entries do not use "p" for page numbers, because these sources are identified by their volume numbers.

- **Footnote referring to an article in a journal:**

  ¹²Elizabeth L. Cleff, "A Modest Proposal for the Educating of Women," The American Scholar, XXXVIII (Autumn, 1969), 620.

  Corresponding bibliography entry:

  Cleff, Elizabeth L. "A Modest Proposal for the Educating of Women." The American Scholar, XXXVIII (Autumn, 1969), 618-627.

- **Footnote referring to a signed encyclopedia article:**

  ¹³Edward R. Hermann, "Water Pollution," Encyclopaedia Britannica, 1969, XVIII, 182.

  Corresponding bibliography entry:

  Hermann, Edward R. "Water Pollution." Encyclopaedia Britannica. 1969. Vol. XVIII.

- **Footnote referring to an unsigned encyclopedia article:**

  ¹⁴"Adobe," Encyclopedia Americana, 1968, I, 174.

  Corresponding bibliography entry:

  "Adobe." Encyclopedia Americana, 1968. Vol. I.

In general, each subsequent footnote referring to a work that has been fully documented earlier should be a shortened form for the reader's convenience. Number all footnotes consecutively throughout a short paper.

Successful and accurate manuscript preparation requires slavish devotion to instructions in the style manual. Although no one likes being a slave, the resulting copy resembles the work of a master and will be more easily readable to those who recognize and expect the conventions that master writers use.

A SAMPLE STUDENT PAPER

A student wrote the following paper for a literature class. Not all of the paper is included, but the introduction, early development, and conclusion display an effective use of primary source materials: a few of Updike's short stories. The student shapes the quoted material to her purpose and substantiates her ideas by references to authority. She provides the paper with significance by relating the stories to contemporary life—to man's religious turmoil and search for values. Further, the title page and bibliography page, as well as the documentation techniques, are respectable samples.

Note the literary text citations in parentheses *before* the end punctuation. The first reference to the collection of short stories, of course, is properly documented by a complete footnote. Also, because student researchers usually do not, and need not, consult all available sources on a specific subject, the heading "Selected Bibliography" is appropriate for the bibliography page.

THE CONCEPT OF CHRISTIANITY

IN SELECTED STORIES BY JOHN UPDIKE

by

Wendy Pannier

Course title

Professor's name

Date

THE CONCEPT OF CHRISTIANITY

IN SELECTED STORIES BY JOHN UPDIKE

One theme pervades several of John Updike's short
stories in his Pigeon Feathers collection. Little plot
occurs in most of these stories; instead, the author uses
meticulously mirrored images of his readers so they can see
life and possibly themselves more accurately. "Pigeon
Feathers," "The Astronomer," "Lifeguard," and "Packed Dirt,
Churchgoing, A Dying Cat, A Traded Car," are all distinct,
although each short story has the same focus, the struggle
to find or keep religious faith. Although "Pigeon
Feathers" ends rather conclusively, the other three stories
remain unresolved (as do many problems in life), leaving
any resolution to the reader's imagination. In these four
stories, Updike wrestles with the problems of belief and
nonbelief. He does not sermonize or moralize, but he
handles the conflicts with great subtlety.

"Pigeon Feathers" suggests a sense of confusion from
the first line, when Updike states that "things were upset,
displaced, rearranged."[1] In the same paragraph, the author
writes that David, the fourteen-year-old protagonist, is in
a state of "disorientation" (84). The reason for this
state is that atheism, in the form of H. G. Wells's account
of Jesus as "an obscure political agitator, a kind of hobo,
in a minor colony of the Roman Empire" (85), clashes with
David's blind, childlike faith. His first response to this

_____

    [1]John Updike, Pigeon Feathers and Other Stories, Crest
Book (Greenwich, Conn.: Fawcett Publications, Inc., 1959),
p. 84. Subsequent numbers will indicate pages from the
same book.

interpretation is that the account is a fantastic false-
hood; his second is that it is a vain attempt to contradict
the blasphemous statements; the third is mental confusion
when he is beset with worries of death and immortality.
Reviewing his past life, his prayers, and his teachings
only serves to reinforce Wells's point that "hope bases vast
premises on foolish accidents and reads a word where in
fact only a scribble exists" (87).

David finds no solution from his parents or pastor.
His father's comment that human individuals have souls
"because the Bible tells us so" (87) is reminiscent of the
child's hymn "Jesus Loves Me" and seems a gross over-
simplification as he scrutinizes the problem of Christian
dogma. Reverend Bobson is also unable to give satisfactory
answers to David's questions. His only answer is that
Heaven is "like Abraham Lincoln's goodness living after
him" (96), which further disillusions the boy who feels
this amounts to saying that heaven does not exist at all.
His mother's simple, illogical comments only compound his
despair. David feels betrayed because the doctrines of
Christianity seem beyond explanation, and, because no one
can understand his quandary, he feels disoriented and alone.

David's fear of death continues unabated; his sense of
hopelessness increases. Resolution of his intense mental
turmoil comes rather unexpectedly when he notices the wide
variety of patterns, colors, and shades of pigeon feathers,
each carefully designed, and unique. David decides that a
God who lavished such craft on worthless birds who were
often exterminated as pests would surely permit man to have
immortality and would not destroy his whole Creation--but
would let David live forever.

While David's conclusion might seem like a resumption of childlike, blind faith, Updike seems to be using David's youthful sensibilities to resolve the problem aesthetically. The important factor is that the main character questions and reevaluates his beliefs before coming to a conclusion about his faith. Updike implies that it is the struggle between belief and nonbelief that is a major problem today for young, inquiring individuals.

David reappears in the last story, "Packed Dirt, Churchgoing, a Dying Cat, A Traded Car," to continue his pilgrimage of faith. This time he is a married man with four children who suddenly loses his faith. After he feels lust for a woman he meets at a party, David rejects God because He has permitted him to sin in his heart. He felt that "the God who permitted me this fear was unworthy of existence" (177). This is ironic because it is his personal religious faith and reinforced Sunday School morality that causes his torment, not God per se.

David is then called to the bedside of his dying father, who, he learns, has also rejected life-long religious convictions. Despite the two characters' loss of faith, Updike subtly indicates its continuing importance in their lives. David still attends church, and his father still has the power to "shed faith on others" (187), such as with the girl from the Lutheran Home Missions. While Updike presents no direct evidence that David rediscovers or reaccepts his faith, David's final comment is that "we in America need ceremonies" (188). While not openly religious, Updike might have meant ceremonies on one level to signify religious ceremonies and the rituals of faith.

The two David stories study the pressures that secular
society exerts against widely-held sacred concepts of life.
When these pressures and individual disorientation
coincide, religious faith collapses, at least temporarily.
However, life without faith is a fearful vacuum from which
both Davids eventually emerge. . . .

Updike seems to imply that Christianity is not possible
for the Twentieth Century man in America. However, nothing
could be further from the truth. Updike insists
on the value and necessity of some kind of spiritual faith
without which his characters would remain disoriented.
His work suggests that religion today at least deserves
recognition. Such an idea might not be merely empty
idealism. At the present time, Americans are facing religious turmoil, from the "God is dead" concept to dissent
within individual churches. Updike seems to understand the
very real difficulties of being a Christian today, but he
still subtly encourages the possibilities for faith.

In America, man has always been concerned with ethics,
namely, how he should act and what he should value. American ethics have obviously changed through the centuries
from Puritan times, when it was acceptable and even expected
for an upright person to spend much of Sunday in church or
at least following religious pursuits, to the present when,
as the narrator in "Packed Dirt, Churchgoing, A Dying Cat,
A Traded Car" depicts, people hurry out of church "to
assume the disguise--sweaters and suntans--of the nonchurch-
goer" (171). Moreover, some of Updike's characters suffer
from an almost Calvinistic guilt. In "Packed Dirt," David

8

renounces God because he feels guilty about his lustful thoughts. In "The Astronomer," Bela's atheistic views sway Walter, and he feels guilty; his faith is too weak to resist their attraction. The author suggests that Americans have thrown off the shackles of traditional religion as our ancestors knew it and have arrived at an adaptation of Wordsworth's natural piety.[2]

Updike is saying that man must have something to live for, something to direct his life. Individuals in society today often feel fragmented, disoriented from nature and one another. The former ceremony of church services is all but left behind, and yet Updike keeps saying that people still need some form of ritual, even if in a revised version. Demands of relevancy echo through college campuses across the nation today, for students demand relevancy in education while, in a sense, they are actually seeking relevance in life. John Updike comments on the human condition as he sees it by examining and questioning the problem of religious relevancy. His conclusion is that man needs something to grasp, and, in his view, a reinterpreted Christianity is the most effective voice on issues that actually matter today.

------

[2]Alice and Kenneth Hamilton, John Updike: A Critical Essay (Grand Rapids, Mich.: William B. Eerdmans Publishing Co., 1967), p. 30.

SELECTED BIBLIOGRAPHY

Doyle, Paul A. "Updike's Fiction: Motifs and Techniques."
    The Catholic World, September, 1964, pp. 356-362.

Hamilton, Alice, and Hamilton, Kenneth. John Updike: A
    Critical Essay. Grand Rapids, Mich.: William B.
    Eerdmans Publishing Co., 1967.

Moore, Harry T. "John Updike," Amplified Telephone Tape No.
    47. Stephens College, May 14, 1964.

Updike, John. The Music School. Crest Book. Greenwich,
    Conn.: Fawcett Publications, Inc., 1966.

    . Pigeon Feathers and Other Stories. Crest Book.
    Greenwich, Conn.: Fawcett Publications, Inc.,
    1962

    . "Rabbit Run," Amplified Telephone Tape No. 48.
    Stephens College, May 18, 1964.

    . The Same Door. Crest Book. Greenwich, Conn.:
    Fawcett Publications, Inc., 1959.

library
investigation

The tentative thesis is the starting point for your research paper; the final thesis is the conclusion of your research—the end-product of your inquiry into the available information and authoritative opinion on a topic. The significance of your thesis depends upon the quality of the research preceding it. That research should be informed, systematic, thorough, selective, and, ultimately, directive. In other words, you should know your topic well enough to survey and locate all possibly relevant types and forms of materials; you should be able to evaluate and select the best from the sources you have found; and finally, you should be able to adapt, refine, and direct your tentative thesis to a statement adequately supported by your research.

Assume that you are assigned a research project in which you are to use no more than five references on any valuable subject interesting to you. Your curiosity has been piqued by the subject, dream interpretation. Consulting first the card catalog and then the library 'shelves, you find grouped together five books, all indicating clearly by their titles that they deal with your topic. Resist the temptation to grab all five and begin reading, limiting your research to only those five references. Even if these sources make it clear that two authorities, Freud and Jung, developed different theories of dream analysis, they might not explain that the two psychoanalysts basically disagreed about the definition of the term "unconscious." You could become confused by contradictory statements, or worse yet, unintentionally put such statements into your paper. Moreover, these five books may not be current enough to include results from recent studies (probably reported in journals) on the physiology of sleep, studies which have added to our understanding of dream content.

In short, the grab-five approach to library research is limiting. You might achieve an excellent paper beginning this way; you probably will not, however. A better approach is the five-step procedure outlined below. Not only is it comprehensive, allowing you to adjust your hypothesis—or hunch—to your findings, but it is also systematic. The five steps are:

1. Getting basic information
2. Analyzing your subject
3. Searching for references
4. Evaluating references
5. Adjusting your research idea

STEP ONE: GETTING BASIC INFORMATION

A library is more than a storehouse of books; it is a varied collection of informative and imaginative materials—books, magazines, journals, pamphlets, newspapers, records, tapes, and prints—organized for use. *Using it properly depends on knowing what to look for and how to look, on a basic understanding both of your topic and of library organization.*

Begin, then, by checking the vocabulary and identifying information for your subject. If you are investigating "pep pills," what are their technical names? If you are exploring the thought of Martin Buber, how is he classified as a philosopher? Who are the principal authorities on his ideas? If your subject is suicide, what studies have been made on this behavior? If you are looking for critical comment on a story by Flannery O'Connor, when and where did this author write? What place does she hold in the development of literature?

For answers to questions like these, your best source is *the reference section of a library*. Reference books are special, noncirculating books, essentially answer books that you refer to for information or guidance. The guide books are called indexes—or pointers—to the various forms of library material and will be discussed later. The information books are usually encyclopedias, dictionaries, outlines, directories, and compendia of facts. Under *dreams*, any good general encyclopedia, such as the *Britannica*, or the *Americana*, will distinguish between the theories of Freud and Jung; current yearbooks for the encyclopedias will report recent research. *Webster's Seventh International Dictionary, Unabridged* explains that "pep pills" are usually amphetamines.

Specialized reference books in philosophy, religion, social science, language, science and technology, art, literature, history, and biography extend what you learn from the general volumes. According to the *Merek Index of Chemicals and Drugs*, amphetamines include Allodrene, Benzedrine, Dexadrine, and other commercial drugs, prescribed medically to alleviate depression, obesity, and narcolepsy (among other things); overdose leads to hallucinations, delirium, peripheral vascular collapse, and death. These details could help you in three ways: by explaining technical and commercial terms you encounter later in your reading; by suggesting subject headings—*drugs, medication*—to lead you to further sources; and, perhaps, by suggesting to you a more unusual topic. Narcolepsy, paroxysmal sleep, is a mysterious affliction—one from which college students sometimes seem to suffer.

The Encyclopedia of Philosophy identifies Martin Buber as a Jewish religious existentialist, distinguished for his differentiation between I-It and I-Thou relationships, and interested, during his later years, in psychotherapy. It also lists works in English by (primary sources) and about (secondary sources) Buber. Thus, if he is your topic, you are prepared to seek fuller treatment of his ideas, not only in works that deal exclusively with him but also in others you can find on contemporary Jewish thought, existential theology, and existential psychology. Furthermore, you will recognize that a book on existential psychology containing a chapter on I-Thou relationships concerns your subject, even though the book's title does not mention Buber.

The *suicide* article in the *Encyclopedia of the Social Sciences* is so organized that it reviews for you various parts of the subject and thus points to ways it can be narrowed. You could write on either its social or psychological significance. Choosing social, you could compare western with oriental attitudes toward self-destruction, or 19th with 20th century western attitudes. Choosing psychological, you could restrict yourself to methods of suicide prevention. Listed in the lengthy bibliography which concludes the article are enough studies of suicide notes to make the notes alone an adequate focus for a research paper.

As you can see, initiating your research with the answer books of the reference department informs you about the vocabulary, scope, and bibliography of your subject of interest so that you may search further more intelligently. In later phases of your work, reference books are also useful in explaining terms in your reading—What *is* libido? Or, in helping you evaluate your findings on a literary subject—What is Leslie Fiedler's reputation as a literary critic? (See "Main Library References To Consult," pages 253-261, for detailed information about reference works.)

STEP TWO: ANALYZING YOUR SUBJECT

Now you should pause to survey the importance of what you have learned and relate it to your subsequent searching. Knowing what you are looking for, how ought you to approach the search? As we observed before, libraries contain a variety of forms of materials, organized for use. Newspapers and journal articles, chapters of books, individual pamphlets, audiotapes, even records may pertain to your topic. To make all such items accessible to you, libraries employ numerous schemes of classification and subdivision, and supply various guidelines directing you to them.

The card catalog and the indexes are your guides; the author, title, and subject entries, along with subject, form, and time subdivisions are your guidelines. In effect, a library anticipates what you already know about your topic and what you need to know. You, in turn, must anticipate the library system. For a book dealing directly and obviously with your topic, this is simple. For more general, or more obliquely related books, or for other forms of material, investigate the various categories of learning that overlap your field.

After determining, for example, from *The Oxford Companion to American Literature*, that Flannery O'Connor (1925-1964) was a southern woman author of grotesque novels and short stories, you have the following clues for locating further information about her and her work. In addition to her name as an entry for works by and about her, you may look under subject headings covering 20th century literature, short stories, novels, southern writers, women writers, 20th century American writers, and special literary techniques. Each of the formal subject headings below will be helpful:

American literature
American literature—20th century
American literature—20th century—History and Criticism
American literature—History and Criticism
American literature—Southern States
American literature—Southern States—History and Criticism

Fiction—20th century—History and Criticism
Novelists, American
Short Stories, American
Women as Novelists
The Grotesque in Literature
Symbolism in Literature

Although some of these headings pertain more directly to your subject than others, all may be useful. Commentaries on her novels may mention her short stories; general works on her period or genre may refer to her style. The indexes in the general books and descriptive subtitles of general magazine and journal articles will indicate criticism of her works. Within each index, and in the card catalog, are subsidiary guidelines, called "see" and "see also" references, to aid you in recognizing other appropriate headings.

The more personal your inquiry, the more imaginative you must be in devising a useful range of headings to consult. Here is a set of terms one student used for study of contemporary young men's attitudes toward conscription:

Selective Service
Draft—Military
Conscription
Induction
Conscientious Objectors
U. S. Armament—Military Draft
Military Service, Compulsory
World War—Civilian reaction
World War—Psychological aspects
Colleges and Universities—Demonstrations
Students—College and University
College Students—Political activities
        —Viet Nam
        —Draft
        —Peace movements
Patriotism

Because such subject headings often overlap and because they vary from index to index, the more headings you think of as potentially applicable to your topic, the better you can take advantage of the guidelines provided.

STEP THREE: SEARCHING FOR REFERENCES

After informing yourself and analyzing your topic, you are ready to make a thorough and systematic search for material relevant to your topic. Only when you have checked *all* possible resources can you be sure of finding the best references available. Even such peripheral materials as tapes and records may be valuable: T. S. Eliot's own reading of an obscure line from a poem could help you explicate it; taped interviews with Ralph Ellison might reveal more about the structure of *Invisible Man* than any critical article; the most recent information on the aftereffects of LSD could be in a government document in the pamphlet file.

Take the time, therefore, to make a thorough search, checking all of your potential author and subject entries in each index. Keep a record of the subject headings you have used; others might arise naturally as you move along. Take full information on the references you find: author, title, form of publication, date, and pages. This collection of references becomes your working bibliography. When you have compiled it, such bibliographic information will help you decide where to begin reading. Here is a suggested route for your search (it is diagrammed on page 247) with clues for making the best use of each guide.

First Stop: The Card Catalog   Literally the core, the heart of the library, listing not only circulating materials but other indexes and reference books as well, the card catalog is the nexus of the network of invisible lines leading to the largest portion of library offerings. Works are entered by author, subject, and title, interfiled in one alphabet. "See" and "see also" references indicate other related entries. Here are some clues to effective use of the card catalog:

The call number in the upper left corner of the catalog card gives location and subject information. The number is a subject classification, and related material occurs under the same number. Special notations indicate special locations: R=reference book; q=oversized material, shelved separately at the end of each major subject division.

Subject "tracings" at the bottom of each catalog card indicate the subjects treated in the book. Looking under those additional headings in the card catalog will lead you to related information.

Some important exceptions to the usual author, title, subject, alphabetical arrangement of the card catalog are:

1. Subdivisions for historical periods are chronological.
2. Works *about* an author are filed after works by the author, but works about a specific title (for example, Faulkner's *The Sound and the Fury*) are filed directly behind that title.
3. Common titles, such as *A Guide to United States History*, or *The Handbook of Music*, often have no title entry and are filed according to subject and author (or editor) only.

Second Stop: The Index Tables   While the card catalog indexes only the material in a given library, the major bibliographic indexes located on the reference tables list generally available material. If you learn from one of these indexes that an item is in print, you must check to see whether the library has it. The almost algebraic details of decoding bibliographic entries and checking locations often keep students from taking full advantage of index books;

actually, two minutes spent with the key in the front of any volume of an index will teach you to interpret its entries, and location can always be double-checked by a trip back to the card catalog. Other means for determining location are noted in the discussion below.

You are probably familiar with the *Readers' Guide to Periodical Literature*. Remember, however, that this guide directs you primarily to articles in *popular* magazines, that these articles are usually written by journalists rather than specialists, and that popular magazine articles frequently omit any indication of how information within them can be checked for accuracy. Remember, too, that the *Readers' Guide*, as well as other indexes listed below, are issued chronologically and that you will probably want to consult several volumes as well as paperbound supplements, for each set. Most libraries will have many of the magazines listed in this index. The *Kardex* guide to a library's holdings will give you exact locations.

Social Sciences and Humanities Index, formerly called the *International Index,* is a guide to journal articles written by specialists in the subjects covered by the title. Again, the *Kardex* is your location guide. Ordinarily, the articles you locate through this guide will be well developed, carefully documented arguments written by recognized authorities. One such article on teen-age suicide might be worth a dozen of that what-is-wrong-with-today's-youth variety you find through the *Readers' Guide.*

The same quality of specialized, authoritative article is found in the *Public Affairs Information Service Index.* This index lists journal and magazine articles, books, parts of books, and pamphlets about government and community affairs. Headings in this index may be both more technical and more specific than those in the *Readers' Guide* (thus "military administration" in *RG* is "U. S.–Military policy" in *PAIS*), because *PAIS* headings are more carefully analytical. Magazine and journal references cited in this index can be checked for location in the Kardex; books and pamphlets in the card catalog and pamphlet file, respectively.

Particularly useful in a small library is the *Essay and General Literature Index,* because it provides author, title, and subject entries for individual chapters from general works. Both essay collections and single works are analyzed. Here is a sample entry:

Agee, James

      About

    Behar, J. On Rod Serling, James Agee and popular culture.

    In Hazard, P.D. ed. "TV as Art" Some essays in criticism p35-63

When you have found that a chapter of a general book deals specifically with your topic, check the book's author and title (Hazard, *TV as Art*) in the listing at the back of the volume you are using. Some librarians enter call numbers next to those references which are available in their library.

Another especially valuable research tool is *The New York Times Index.* Because *The New York Times* newspaper, which it indexes, is so thorough,

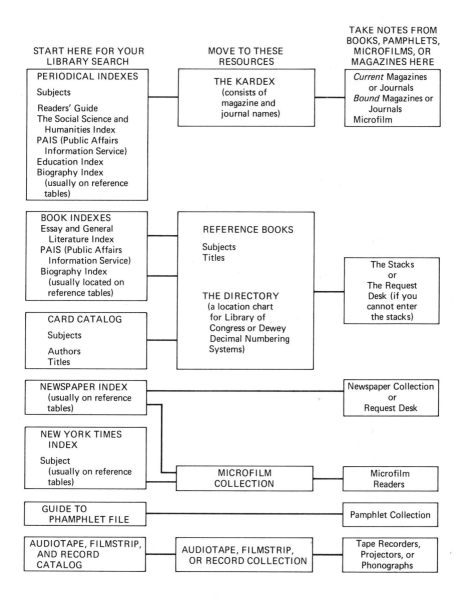

START HERE FOR YOUR
LIBRARY SEARCH

MOVE TO THESE
RESOURCES

TAKE NOTES FROM
BOOKS, PAMPHLETS,
MICROFILMS, OR
MAGAZINES HERE

PERIODICAL INDEXES

Subjects

Readers' Guide
The Social Science and
   Humanities Index
PAIS (Public Affairs
   Information Service)
Education Index
Biography Index
   (usually on reference
   tables)

THE KARDEX
(consists of
magazine and
journal names)

Current Magazines
   or Journals
Bound Magazines or
   Journals
Microfilm

BOOK INDEXES
Essay and General
   Literature Index
PAIS (Public Affairs
   Information Service)
Biography Index
   (usually located on
   reference tables)

REFERENCE BOOKS

Subjects
Titles

THE DIRECTORY
(a location chart
for Library of
Congress or Dewey
Decimal Numbering
Systems)

The Stacks
or
The Request
Desk (if you
cannot enter
the stacks)

CARD CATALOG

Subjects

Authors
Titles

NEWSPAPER INDEX
(usually on reference
tables)

Newspaper Collection
or
Request Desk

NEW YORK TIMES
INDEX

Subject
(usually on reference
tables)

MICROFILM
COLLECTION

Microfilm
Readers

GUIDE TO
   PHAMPHLET FILE

Pamphlet Collection

AUDIOTAPE, FILMSTRIP,
AND RECORD
CATALOG

AUDIOTAPE, FILMSTRIP,
OR RECORD COLLECTION

Tape Recorders,
Projectors, or
Phonographs

247

inclusive, and responsible, the index to that paper leads you to valuable information, not only about current events, but also about such subjects as art, scientific discovery, education, fashion, and many others. Notice that the *Index* gives column, page, section, and date information for each subject entry. Notice also that the entries are quite specific and different in form from those in the preceding indexes; the subject headings are like headlines, giving a capsule notion of the news story's content. "See also" references precede rather than follow direct entries, as they do in the card catalog and other indexes. *The New York Times Index* is by far the most complicated of all library indexes, and its complication is compounded for the researcher by the necessity of reading the actual news stories on microfilm; nevertheless, the newspaper itself is such an excellent resource that *it is worth your time to study the directions for using the Index and to learn how to use microfilm readers.*

Consulting all five of these indexes is advisable even if you are unsure about whether they will list your particular topic. Other indexes of special usefulness for some research paper topics are *The Biography Index, The Education Index, Twentieth Century Short Story Explications,* and *Poetry Explication.* (See "Main Library References to Consult," pages 253-261, for further explanation.)

Third Stop: The Kardex The *Kardex* is a special location guide for magazines and journals. You save time by checking locations for all your magazine and journal citations at once. Back issues of magazines and journals are either bound or kept on microfilm. Current issues of magazines and journals and their immediate back issues are usually stacked on the shelves. A typical Kardex entry reads like this:

Drama Review Current issues: Main Floor-Center
Bound: v7, Fall 1962-V14, Summer, 1970
at bindery: v. 11 1966-67.

The message: all issues of this journal since the issue for Summer, 1970, are shelved on the main floor; issues from Fall, 1962, to Summer, 1970, are bound and shelved; the issues in volume eleven, 1966-1967, are unavailable because these issues are being bound together.

Fourth Stop: The Pamphlet File A reference folder will list the subject headings for the pamphlet file. You cannot finally determine whether a library has a pamphlet useful to you without consulting the file directly, but you can check here to find out whether the pamphlet headings include your topic. Particularly important pamphlets are sometimes bound by the library and catalogued as books. If you are led by *PAIS* or *The Education Index* to seek an especially important pamphlet, it is, therefore, worth looking for it in both the pamphlet file and the card catalog.

Fifth Stop: The Record Catalog This catalog lists the library's holdings of phonograph records by composer, title, performer, and subject. Consulting a special heading, such as "Readings in Literature," is a short cut to a complete listing of renditions of poetry, drama, and prose.

STEP FOUR: EVALUATING YOUR REFERENCES

If you have made the named stops, by now you should have listed numerous references to books, parts of books, magazine and journal articles, newspaper stories, and possibly records and pamphlets. Survey your entire list. You can begin to sort out and read those whose titles suggest they are directly relevant to your topic. What other criteria can you use to be sure you select the best from what is available to you?

Two external tests are *currency* and *authority*. First, be conscious of the dates of publication for your sources. For a paper on recent urban renewal, a book published in 1936 will not be helpful. A research paper that mixes data from 1936 and 1964 defeats the writer's argument. On the other hand, if your topic is witchcraft, a reference two or three centuries old could be a treasure. Set the time limits that best fit your topic. Second, be conscious of the reputation of the author of your source. Is he a specialist in his field? Either the source itself or information you find in the reference collection may tell you. Reference books, such as *Who's Who in America, American Men of Science,* and articles located through *The Biography Index,* can give you a sense of the reputation of an author.

A good way to find out a book's reputation is to survey the reviewers' reactions to it at the time it was published. *The Book Review Digest*, on the reference shelves, will give you samplings from such reviews as well as citations of the reviews themselves. *The Library of Literary Criticism*, and several similar reference books, focus particularly on review digests for imaginative literature. Of course, numerous renowned authorities have said hopelessly stupid things, some as recently as yesterday; nevertheless, consideration of currency and authority can help you select the potentially preferable reference from a large group.

More significant are the *internal tests of validity*. Base *your* research report on works by those authors who most precisely document their facts and who most systematically argue their conclusions. Real research—yours or theirs—permits another thinker to consider the same problem in the same way and reach his own conclusion. Unverifiable statistics—"three out of four American college students have tried LSD"—and unprovable assertions—"Prehistoric man first communicated by grunts and groans"—are irresponsible; do not compound such irresponsibilities by incorporating them into your paper. You cannot, of course, be responsible for the ultimate truth of every assertion in each reference you use for your paper, but you can and should be selective.

STEP FIVE: ADJUSTING YOUR RESEARCH IDEA

A certain danger is inherent in hyperselectivity. It can lead to what might be called the last minute lament. Beginning with a general interest in education in the ghetto, you have followed all the steps listed above. You have found out from reference books general information about ghetto life and ghetto education and names of authorities in the study of ghetto problems; you have analyzed your topic and decided that headings such as "urban problems," "socially handicapped children—education," "New York City—education," and numerous others will be useful to you. You have found in the card catalog, EGL, PAIS, SSHI, *Education Index*, and *The New York Times Index*, as well as in *Readers' Guide* literally hundreds of relevant items.

In the process of surveying these items, you have narrowed your topic to an aspect that intrigues you: the problem of measuring IQ for ghetto school children. You have discovered from some preliminary reading that two research teams disagree about the significance of such measurement and that several specialists in education and intelligence measurement have compared and evaluated their findings. Thus, you have selected the time limits of your study, decided which sources you need, and developed a preliminary judgment about the authority of your sources. From reading some *New York Times* articles and perhaps two journal articles, you might find the names of two books and three journal articles that should provide the basis for your paper.

You look for the books and both are missing from the shelf; you look for the journal articles and discover that your college library does not subscribe to one, the second is at the bindery, and the third—surprise—is on the shelf. But what do you do now? Weep? Not necessarily. First, double-check. Ask at the circulation desk about the books. Perhaps one is on reserve. If one is checked out, ask when it is due. If the book is already overdue, the library will call it in for you; if it is not but is truly central to your paper, the faculty member or student who has it may be willing to share it.

Perhaps now, after following these steps, you would prefer to escape. Or— more constructively—adjust your thesis. As a general rule-of-thumb, you can assume that your topic is too broad if you have more than twelve equally useful references; too narrow if you have only two or three. If you are really unable to find the material you need for a topic you know to be well selected, properly narrowed, and significant, try varying it. For instance, if you cannot focus satisfactorily on the problems of measuring IQ, what about measuring learning? You can combine what you already have, which undoubtedly touches on the measurement of learning, with other material. If you can find only one reference on Basque dance, what about contrasting it with folk dances of Spain and France? Just as you have narrowed to a topic, you can also broaden it.

Assuredly, a good research paper depends on patience, imagination, research skill, and flexibility—a rare but winning combination.

LEARNING AIDS

1. Design a research plan on the cultural role of women. Limit the topic by historical period, by specific roles. Indicate all the resources in the library you would investigate.

2. Design a research plan for investigating Victorian morality. What limits could you set? What resources would you use?

3. The following paragraph is from a book entitled *Dialogue on Women*, published by the Bobbs-Merrill Company, Indianapolis, 1967. The article in which this paragraph appears is entitled "Wanted: A New Self-Image for Women," by David C. McClelland.

> But let us consider further what some younger college women have been calling "femininism"—a kind of militant femininity which glories in the differences between the sexes and insists that to be a woman more or less as defined by the characteristics reported above is a wonderful thing. In fact, according to their point of view, to adopt the male pattern is to "sell out"—to admit that the masculine approach to life is better. The difficulty with this feminine protest movement has been that it has lacked a very clear idea of the distinction between the male and female images. Thus, it often is little more than the emotional feeling that "we don't want to be men," combined with a kind of shame-faced admission that "we're not sure what that means except that we are probably admitting we won't amount to much. . . . "

   a. Using your own vocabulary, phrasing, and sentence structure, write a summary of McClelland's paragraph.

   b. If you use the summary in your paper, do you need quotation marks? A footnote?

   c. Choose a sentence you would like to quote in your paper. Write an introductory phrase for it. Then write a phrase linking the quotation to some idea of yours. Then write a concluding sentence in which you comment on McClelland's sentence.

   d. Write a sentence in which you incorporate some phrases or clauses from the paragraph. Do you use quotation marks? A footnote?

   e. Using the facts of publication given above, write a footnote for the quotation. Write a corresponding bibliography entry.

4. Here is a statement by Arnold Kettle, in *An Introduction to the English Novel*, Vol. 1 (New York: Harper and Brothers, 1960), p. 95:

> Emma is the heroine of this novel only in the sense that she is its principal character and that it is through her consciousness that the situations are revealed; she is no heroine in the conventional sense. She is not merely spoilt and selfish, she is snobbish and proud, and her snobbery leads her to inflict suffering that might ruin happiness.

Here are versions of student use of Professor Kettle's statement:

Version I

> Emma, the heroine of this novel, is not a heroine in the conventional sense. But she is its principal character; through her consciousness the situations are revealed. She is spoilt and selfish, snobbish and proud.

Version II

Emma, although she is the novel's principal character, is no conventional heroine. She is a snob, leading her to cause suffering, ruining others' happiness.[1]

Version III

Kettle insists that Emma is "no heroine in the conventional sense." He notes that she is "not merely spoilt and selfish, she is snobbish and proud." Further, he argues that her class consciousness causes her to offend the sensibilities of other characters.[1]

Which of the three versions are examples of plagiarism and why?

---

[1] Arnold Kettle, An *Introduction to the English Novel*, Vol. I (New York: Harper and Brothers, 1960), p. 95.

MAIN LIBRARY REFERENCES TO CONSULT

The library reference section should speed your investigation of specific subjects of interest to you. If you seek materials about a geographical location, a rare art object, or a contemporary musician, many time-saving sources await your use. Below are seven categories of sources:

Periodical indexes
Encyclopedias
Dictionaries
Genre indexes
Biographical references
Literary criticism references
Bibliographical references

Under each of these seven headings are the titles and descriptions of their contents of frequently consulted sources throughout college and university libraries.

Periodical Indexes

Art Index   This is a cumulative guide to articles published in fine arts periodicals and museum bulletins, such as *Metropolitan Museum of Art* (Bulletin), *Musées de France*, and *Landscape Architecture*. Look under subject, such as lithography, or artist, such as Hans Arp, or city, such as Lausanne, Switzerland. Arrangement is alphabetical.

Book Review Digest   This almost-monthly index contains current reviews of nonfiction and fiction published or distributed in the United States. In the first section of each volume, look under the author's name or the important person named in a title to find excerpts from reviews of, say, an anthology of essays by Kenneth Rexroth or a book of Modigliani's drawings. The editors identify the reviewer, issue date, volume and page numbers of the periodical, and even the number of words in the review. In the second section is a subject and title index.

Book Review Index   Since 1965, the monthly issues of this index have served as an up-to-date guide to recent reviews of newly published books. Under the author's name, such as John Cheever, and the book title is a list of magazines, critics, volumes, issue dates, and page numbers on which the reviews begin.

The Education Index   Arranged according to subjects, such as bookbinding, thermochemistry, and youth hostels, this index lists articles from such educational periodicals as *College English* and *American Annals of the Deaf*, from such yearbooks as *Association for Student Teaching* and *Claremont Reading Conference*, and from such educational proceedings as *Middle States Association of Colleges and Secondary Schools*.

The New York Times Index   This index offers a condensed summary of day-to-day news which the editors classify according to subject, such as economic conditions, or names, such as Gamal Abdel Nasser, or geographic headings which they subdivide. Then, under these alphabetical entries, the editors present items chronologically. The precise column number follows the date of each entry, and cross-references are frequent aids.

Public Affairs Information Service (P.A.I.S.) This index lists various types of material you can find in the library focusing on economic and public matters. Government documents, such as *Social Security Bulletin*, pamphlets, such as *Federal Probation: A Journal of Correctional Philosophy and Practice*, monthly bulletins, such as the *Canadian External Affairs*, and journals, such as the *Forensic Quarterly*, as well as current periodicals and books are included. Listed also are directories for medical laboratories, public works, textile industries, and many other organizations. Publications from all English-speaking countries qualify as entries as long as their focus is on statistical and factual information.

Readers' Guide to Periodical Literature This guide lists articles in popular magazines, such as *House Beautiful, Newsweek,* and *Ebony*, as well as more specialized magazines, such as *Poetry, The Negro History Bulletin,* and *Mental Hygiene*. Articles referred to tend to be written in a journalistic style appealing to general audiences. You may look under general subject or a specific author or title to locate an article.

International Index to Periodicals (1907-March, 1965) *or* **Social Sciences and Humanities Index (new title beginning April, 1965)** This is an index to major periodicals concerning humanities and social sciences throughout the world. Alphabetically arranged are subjects from aesthetics to spectrophotometry to Zuni Indians and authors from Henry Adams to Angus Wilson. Although periodicals presented in this index are published chiefly in the United States, Canada, England, Scotland, and Holland, they encompass world-wide interests. A few examples are: *Asian Survey; Books Abroad: an International Literary Quarterly; The Ecumenical Review; International Labour Review; Journal of Near Eastern Studies; Modern Language Quarterly;* and *Slavic Review: American Quarterly of Soviet and East European Studies.*

Encyclopedias

The Columbia Encyclopedia A large work in one volume, widely-inclusive subjects from Navajo Indians, to such terms as rococo and post-impressionism, to large cities, as Rome and to any American town boasting over 1000 population, to biographical sketches of Nobel prize winners, such as Sinclair Lewis, and to descriptions of mythological tales, such as Pyramus and Thisbe, are all succinctly presented. This new encyclopedia is designed for speedy reference.

Encyclopedia Americana Composed of 29 volumes plus an Index, this reference work is arranged by subject alphabetically. Contributors are listed in the first volume, but many articles remain unsigned. Even though you will find information on the usual, wide-ranging subjects, the editors have emphasized American music, art, county seats, and people. Writer Saul Bellow, his works, and his photograph, for instance, are a separate entry, whereas the *Encyclopaedia Britannica* simply mentions him under "American Authors." Likewise, American towns of all sizes are described, such as Hastings, Nebraska.

Encyclopaedia Britannica Within 23 volumes is extended information about such places as Luxembourg, such dramatists as Ibsen, such languages as Arabic, and innumerable other alphabetically arranged subjects. Contributors' initials follow the articles, and these intials are decoded at the end of the Index. The Index also contains a glossary of foreign geographical terms and an Atlas with its own index.

The Encyclopedia of Philosophy In eight volumes are signed articles on ancient, medieval, and modern philosophical concepts and theories of not only leaders in religion and ethics but of physical and social scientists and mathematicians. The contributors explore the philosophical significance and implications of the ESP phenomena, aesthetics, Gnosticism, modern logic, mysticism, psychology, reasons and causes, the relativity theory, semantics, and vagueness, as examples. They even offer a three-column article on "Nothing." And throughout this encyclopedia are biographies emphasizing the contributions to philosophy of such men as Aristotle, Francis Bacon, Hans Reichenbach, Arthur Schopenhauer, and Henry David Thoreau.

Encyclopedia of Religion and Ethics This is a 12-volume work of reference to every major system and movement of ethics, such as Puritanism, and to each of the world's religions, such as Muhammadanism. Articles are devoted to the many gods worshipped by man, such as Aiyanar, dress symbolism, locks and keys in magical rites, feet-washing, and topics of this nature not easily attainable in other sources. The editors have elaborated on terms, such as "soul" and "metempsychosis," and on philosophers, such as Descartes. Cross-references to the many phrases of philosophy and theology and related areas of sociology, anthropology, and economics are frequent.

Encyclopedia of World Art This work is an all-encompassing 15-volume collection of both written information about and photographs of any prehistoric to modern forms which attract aesthetic judgment. The divisions of articles include *historical focus*, tracing art civilizations and their cycles, as well as their overlapping of styles, and *geographical focus* on specific areas, such as France or Pakistan. These two divisions invite frequent cross-references. A third type of article, the *conceptual and systematic*, explains attitudes recurring in and theories about art, such as eclecticism, and explains techniques, such as cinematography. Alphabetically arranged according to subject, such as arms and armor, or to artists or architects, such as the Saarinens, the articles are in the front section of each volume, and the plates presenting architecture (close-up and aerial views), ceramics, paintings, jewelry, furniture, tapestry, portraits, pottery, sculpture, and frescos are in the second section.

McGraw-Hill Encyclopedia of Science and Technology Air filters, amino acids, marine microbiology, Ictidosauria, rocks, the geochemistry of lithosphere, lung disorders, stereophonic sound, tetracycline, and tobacco are among the numerous subjects the editors have included in 14 volumes, index, and yearbooks. A bibliography usually follows the signed articles.

New Catholic Encyclopedia These fifteen reference volumes, published in 1967, contain signed articles not only of the history of the Catholic Church and its doctrine but all religions, scientific advancements, and people who have influenced the Catholic Church. The topics are wide ranging including

American art, the Apostles, Arabian philosophy, Carmelite Nuns, German literature, God, the human soul, Moslem medicine, secularism, and symbolism. Color plates, drawings, and photographs of church architecture, the catacombs, and men such as Paul Claudel and Rabindranath Tagore are frequent. This reference work is *not* a revision of *The Catholic Encyclopedia* (15 volumes), published in 1907-1914. The researcher might wish to consult both works to see what changes have occurred in the Catholic views of such topics as saints and celibacy.

The Oxford Companion to the Theatre   This is a one-volume encyclopedia of world theatre covering all theatrical topics, from the National Theatre building of Iceland, to extensive biographical information about playwrights, such as Bertolt Brecht, from listing their plays, to background sketches of actors, to descriptions of the stage door, the trap, stage lighting, and flying effects, to explanations of dramatic genre, such as burlesque. Throughout this alphabetically arranged reference work are lengthy articles about the historical development of drama in many countries, such as Switzerland and England.

You may wish to consult the following Oxford Companion encyclopedias which employ the same format and are as thorough as the one discussed above: **The Oxford Companion to American History, The Oxford Companion to Canadian History and Literature, The Oxford Companion to American Literature, The Oxford Companion to Classical Literature, The Oxford Companion to English Literature, The Oxford Companion to French Literature,** and **The Oxford Companion to Music.** Other important encyclopedias include: **Harper's Encyclopedia of Art; Jewish Encyclopedia; Encyclopedia of Banking and Finance;** and **Encyclopedia of Social Sciences** (see page 242).

Dictionaries

Bryan's Dictionary of Painters and Engravers   In five volumes, this work offers biographical information on centuries of artists from the obscure, such as engraver C. Albrecht, to the renowned, such as Rembrandt and Titian. Photographs of great works, such as Michelangelo's "The Creation of Man," often follow the description of the artist and his work. Another reference source in this area is **Cyclopedia of Painters and Painting**.

Dictionary of American Biography   Within 20 volumes are lengthy signed articles about Americans, no longer living, such as university president James B. Angell, ornithologist John J. Audubon, actor Maurice Barrymore, composer George Gershwin, Abolitionist Abigail gibbons, U.S. President Thomas Jefferson, Puritan scholar Cotton Mather, merchant Richard Sears, and jeweler Charles Tiffany. The index has six individual indexes containing names of persons included in the biographies; their birthplaces; the educational institutions they attended; their occupations; topics discussed in various articles, such as Continental Congress; and the contributors, with a list of persons they have written about.

Dictionary of American History   In succinct articles, the editors have described the Allegheny River, the Anti-Horse Thief Association, the Blount Conspiracy, political cartoons, the Casket Girls, tomahawk claims, and the National Woman's Party, as examples. Also within these alphabetically arranged five volumes plus supplement are some longer articles with cross-references about such subjects as ocean shipping, the Civil War, South Carolina, education, Negro in America, Panama Canal, religion, and the Supreme Court.

Other worthy reference books about history are: **The Cambridge Ancient History** (12 volumes from before 1500 B.C. to A.D. 324, plus four books of plates); **The Cambridge Medieval History** (eight volumes from Constantine to the Renaissance in Europe); **The New Cambridge Modern History** (14 volumes in chronological order from 1493 to the present, plus an atlas); **An Encyclopedia of World History** (single volume, chronologically arranged from ancient to medieval to modern); and **Larousse Encyclopedia of Modern History** (single volume from A.D. 1500 to the present).

Grove's Dictionary of Music and Musicians   In nine volumes plus a supplementary volume updating information to 1961, this reference work reaches back to 1450 for all areas related to music. The editors' style and organization as they explain musical terminology, such as "fugue," is understandable to both amateurs and accomplished musicians. Both lengthy biographical articles about composers, such as Franz Liszt and Wolfgang Amadeus Mozart, and brief sketches of others, such as Baldi, are included. To illustrate the rhythm of the bolero or to explain "arpeggio," for instance, the arrangement of musical notes appear within the article. Pictures often follow. Also, the editors describe important musical civilizations, such as Salzburg, Paris, Vienna, and Milan, and they list operas. Although universal in scope and encompassing all styles of music, whether it is Chinese, Moorish, or folk, this resource emphasizes the English musicians.

Harper's Dictionary of Classical Literature and Antiquities   In one volume, the writers explain terms and names linked with the antiquities whether it is the Greek measure, Phoenix, the Byzantium Imperium, an Athenian orator, a river, a kitchen utensil, or a mythological goddess. Diagrams of temples and coins, drawings, and photographs of architecture aid the reader. Greek and Latin spellings follow the English spellings whenever applicable.

The New Century Classical Handbook   Similar in format to *Harper's Dictionary*, this single volume concentrates on classical Greece and Rome. It also offers maps of these early empires. Pronunciation keys follow terms or names, such as Phocylides. Then, another single volume which is similar in format to the two mentioned above is **The Oxford Classical Dictionary**. It, however, has no visual aids.

Other dictionaries you may wish to consult include: **Dictionary of National Biography, Funk and Wagnall's Standard Dictionary of Folklore, The Interpreter's Bible Dictionary, Dictionary of the Bible, Dictionary of Philosophy and Psychology, Oxford English Dictionary**, plus the dictionaries mentioned on pages 103, 110-11.

Genre Indexes

Essay and General Literature Index   In dictionary arrangement, this is a composite list of essays in almost every field. This index arranges entries according to author, subject matter, and some titles. Simply look up an author's name, such as James Baldwin, to find his works, books about him and his works, and critiques of his individual works.

Granger's Index to Poetry   Each of the five editions and the 1960-1965 supplement is divided into a title and first line index, author inde.., and subject index. Therefore, you would use the first section if you wanted to know the author of "My Heart Leaps Up," the second section if you were interested in finding a poem by Wordsworth, and the third if you were selecting poetry about the heart. Because the later editions add new selections, they delete some of the selections in the earlier editions.

Play Index   Each volume of this reference guide covers several years of plays, such as 1961-1967. Within each volume are four parts. The first section alphabetically offers plays according to *subject matter*, such as animals or Christmas; *form*, such as plays in verse or one-acts; *playwright*, such as August Strindberg; or *title*, such as *Hairy Ape*. The second section lists the collections of plays indexed in Part I. *Best American Plays* is an example. The third section is valuable to directors casting a play, because it categorizes plays according to the number of actors as well as designates which plays have all male, all female, or mixed casts. It also lists puppet plays. The final section is a directory of publishers.

Short Story Index   The first edition lists and categorizes 60,000 stories according to subject matter, title, and/or author. If the reader wanted to select a story about astrologers, for instance, he would find ten stories under that entry. Each story of an author, such as Anton Chekhov, is listed under his name, along with all the anthologies or works in which the story was printed. The 1959-1963 supplement includes 9,068 more stories.

Collections of memorable quotations from essays, novels, poetry, plays, or short stories are available in such reference sources as Bartlett's *Familiar Quotations* and Stevenson's *Home Book of Quotations*.

Biographical References

American Men of Science   This alphabetically arranged biographical directory has two divisions: *Physical and Biological Sciences* (six volumes plus supplements) and *The Social and Behavioral Sciences* (two volumes). Under a scientist's name, such as Dr. Leonard Stutman, a specialist in hematology and cardiology, is personal, educational, and career data, and a description of his chief scientific investigations. Then, his most recent address follows at the end. Throughout the larger *Physical and Biological Sciences* division, references appear advising where to locate information about the social scientists and men who are in earlier editions only.

Biography Index   This is a cumulative guide to articles in popular magazines, professional journals, and books relating to biographical information. This includes genealogies, diaries, fiction, belles lettres, autobiographies, as well as strictly biographies. Alphabetical in arrangement, the Index devotes most of its information to individual names, such as Anna Pavlova, but a smaller second section indexes professions and occupations, such as magicians and geneticists.

Contemporary American Authors This reference work contains a critical survey and 219 bio-bibliographies of authors recognized before 1940, such as Stephen Vincent Benet, Robinson Jeffers, John Dewey, H. L. Mencken, and Upton Sinclair.

Contemporary Authors This reference collection is published semiannually and has over thirty volumes in which you will find information about the personal life, career, avocational interests, and list of writings, including works in progress, of published writers, such as academician Lewis B. Mayhew, or novelist Joyce Carol Oates. Use the index to find in which volumes the editors have presented a writer.

Current Biography Yearbook In this annual reference work, you can find brief biographical sketches and often photographs of civil rights leader Coretta King, gastronomist Craig Claiborne, actress Lynn Redgrave, labor union organizer Cesar Chavez, film director François Truffaut, economist George P. Shultz, singer Buffy Sainte-Marie, comedian Dan Rowan, and philanthropist C. S. Mott, for examples, and any other important living person.

Living Authors This work contains biographical sketches and photographs of Thomas Mann, Dorothy Parker, Conrad Aiken, and other authors prominent before 1935 (the title, unfortunately, is no longer accurate).

Twentieth Century Authors This large volume contains biographical articles and photographs on innumerable writers of biography, such as Mari Sandoz; of criticism, such as Herbert J. Muller; of drama, such as Eugene O'Neill; of short stories, such as Sherwood Anderson; of Danish travel, such as Isak Dinesen; of history, such as Gerald Brenan; of scenarios, such as Frederick Hugh Herbert; of poetry, such as Miguel de Unamuno; of social science, such as David Riesman; of philosophy, such as Jean-Paul Sartre; of humor, such as James Thurber; and some whom the editors decline to classify specifically, such as Gertrude Stein. In addition to biographical information, each author's books and works about his books are listed. The first supplement to this biographical dictionary updates information to 1955.

American Authors: 1600-1900 Concentrating on three centuries of writers and organizing this one-volume reference book similar to the above volume, the editors included both major contributors to our literature, such as Edgar Allan Poe and John Fiske, as well as those of lesser significance, such as Amelia Ball Welby, and Nathaniel Ward. Because so much of the written matter of the 1600's came from diarists, jurists, and clergymen, the editors have included them. Sarah Wister, Peter Oliver, and Alexander Whitaker, respectively, are examples. See also: **European Authors: 1000-1900**.

British Authors Before 1800 Having the same format as **Twentieth Century Authors**, this large volume offers biographical articles on James Boswell, Oliver Goldsmith, Richard Brinsley Sheridan, and their contemporaries.

British Authors of the Nineteenth Century With a similar format to the previous volume, this work concentrates on Lewis Carroll, Sir Walter Scott, Lord Byron, and others writing during their time.

The most current biographical reference volumes, published every two years with new entries, are: **Who's Who in America** (about prominent living people in the United States); and **Who's Who** (chiefly about leading British men and women). If your topic concerns American art, college administration, education, or politics, Latin America, show business, the Gospels, industry, Indian writers, the theatre, women of Canada and the United States, or aviation, you will find a special **Who's Who** volume for each of these and other subjects.

Literary Criticism References

Moulton's Library of Literary Criticism of English and American Authors
These four reference volumes contain critical analyses of the significant works from the Old English epic poem, *Beowulf,* through the Edwardian play *The Importance of Being Earnest.* Often, the editors offer both early commentary, written at the time of publication of the literary piece, and modern commentary as they present authors alphabetically within each period of writing, such as "Early Seventeenth Century." Usually, you will find biographical information about an author, such as Ben Jonson, a list of his works, personal letters or notes concerning him, and critiques of several of his individual works.

A Library of Literary Criticism: Modern British Literature   These three volumes continue where Moulton's work ended except that they offer British authors only. The editors present authors alphabetically, and critiques of their works within each article chronologically; this arrangement enables the reader to see the sustained or changed attitudes of critics toward a writer, such as Graham Greene, through the years. Complete bibliographies of the author's works are at the *end* of each volume. See also **A Library of Literary Criticism: Modern American Literature;** and **A Library of Literary Criticism: Modern Romance Literature.**

Short Fiction Criticism: A Checklist of Interpretation Since 1925 of Stories and Novelettes (American, British, Continental) 1800-1958   This single volume lists 33 years of critical analyses of short stories and novelettes whose length does not exceed 150 pages. Under Thomas Wolfe, for instance, are ten short story entries. Then under each entry, such as Wolfe's "The Lost Boy," the critics, titles of the critical articles or books, and page numbers are listed.

Twentieth Century Short Story Explication: Interpretations of Short Fiction Since 1800   The format of this reference work is similar to **Short Fiction Criticism.** The first edition concentrates on critical commentary on short stories published from 1900 to 1960. The first supplement covers three more years and the second supplement extends the listings through 1964.

Bibliography Indexes

Bibliography of American Literature   Covering the last 150 or so years, this several-volumed work presents, alphabetically by authors, a chronological bibliography of American authors' works with notations of numbers of volumes and types of binding.

The Cambridge Bibliography of English Literature (600-1900)   In three volumes plus index and supplement are bibliographies of books about the life of and the works of and critiques of writers, such as Geoffrey Chaucer and William Shakespeare.

The Concise Cambridge Bibliography of English Literature (600-1950) Although this is similar to the above work, the editors have limited material to only comprehensive essays and books in this field.

If you have selected a general subject or wish to find information about works of a specific author, consult the many books devoted solely to bibliographies, such as **The Negro in America: A Bibliography; The Literature of Political Science; A Faulkner Glossary; Jack London: A Bibliography; Steinbeck: Bibliography.**

Other Sources of Interest to Today's Researchers

The American Negro Reference Book Many lengthy articles and tables of statistics about the American Negro from Colonial times to today are in this book.

International Library of Negro Life and History This work is divided into three parts: the 14th through 18th century; the 19th century; and the 20th century. Large drawings and photographs of prominent Negroes, such as William E. B. Du Bois, an early leader of Civil Rights Movement, and Abolitionist Frederick A. Douglass, accompany most of the biographical material.

Men of Space In each of eight volumes, the writer portrays ten of the world's leading space explorers, researchers, or developers, from James Van Allen to Virgil I. Grissom, as well as the organizations related to space, such as NASA and ESRO.

The Negro Almanac In one large volume, you will find not only sketches of Negro personalities, such as Sidney Poitier, Marcus Garvey, and Willie Mays, in films, education, sports, religion, and politics, but articles about the legal status, family size, "soul" food, employment, earnings, and voting attempts of the Negro. The editors begin with a historical review and then discuss landmarks, documents, and organizations influencing the history of the Negro, mainly in America. Tables, charts, paintings, and photographs are many.

Reference Encyclopedia of the American Indian For a listing of the associations involved in and the government agencies of Indian Affairs, of the museums with Indian exhibits, of the reservations and communities, tribal councils, and schools, as well as a Who's Who section listing prominent American Indians, such as baseball player Stephen Cosgrove, consult this large reference book. You will also find a thorough bibliography of the 2,000 books relating to North American Indians, as well as a list of periodicals devoted to some phase of Indian culture.

evaluating your own essay

After a good writer has roughed out the first draft of his essay, he will revise and rewrite as many times as necessary (and possible) to clarify, to reorder, to amplify, to prune, to heighten the artistry of his prose. Tolstoy, for instance, laboriously dipping his pen after every few words, writing every page of his lengthy novels by hand, still revised and recast sentences until he finally was satisfied with each paragraph. Frequently, libraries display pages of rough manuscript that have been reworked by authors, and viewers are almost invariably impressed with the large number of scratched-out lines and scratched-in corrections. Displays of rough manuscript pages by Wright Morris, a contemporary novelist, reveal his craftsmanship: nearly every sentence and paragraph on a page has been revised—words are changed, sentences recast, dialogue shortened, paragraphs expanded.

Beginning writers owe to themselves the chance to improve their prose by careful revision: what may seem to be a below-average essay in the beginning can frequently become an above-average one if the student is willing to revise deliberately and extensively. Here two quick suggestions might help: Allow a day or more to elapse before rewriting; you will then be able to judge your rough draft more objectively, and revision is likely to be more creative. Also, ask a friend to read, to comment upon your essay; you can then evaluate the effectiveness of your subject and style. The remaining suggestions in this chapter should highlight the strengths and expose the weaknesses in your papers.

A CHECKLIST FOR CLOSE INSPECTION

After you have revised the rough draft, use the following checklist to see if you have considered all possible corrections and improvements:

Words   Have I been deliberate in my word choice?

- Vague, abstract words changed to particular words?
- Wordy passages cut to economical expressions?
- No trite phrases, awkward colloquialisms, or slang?
- No jargon or unnecessarily technical language?
- Same tone throughout?
- Some allusions, some polysyllabic words, many colorful but precise words?
- A few metaphors, images, analogies?
- Some rhythm, balance, parallelism in phrases and sentences?

Sentences   Have I constructed sentences and revised them thoughtfully?

- All unintentional sentence fragments eliminated?
- Changed commas to semicolons between independent clauses *not* linked with *and, but, or, nor, for, yet,* or *still?*
- All "There is" and "There are" phrases eliminated and sentences recast?
- No passive voice except where obviously effective?

- Short, choppy sentences recast into more mature and complex sentences?
- Sentence structures varied, some with participles and appositives, some with subordinate clauses, and one or two short but effective sentences?
- Modifiers close to nouns and verbs they affect?

Grammar and Usage   Have I eliminated all grammar errors that seem to have slipped in?

- No "The-reason-is-because" phrases?
- Verb tense consistent and clear?
- Each pronoun clearly linked to its antecedent?
- Each pronoun agreeing in number (singular or plural) with its antecedent?
- Each verb agreeing in number (singular or plural) with its subject?

Punctuation   Have I placed all marks correctly? Have I chosen marks for effect as well as clarity?

- Comma separating independent clauses linked with conjunction?
- Commas separating all elements in a series?
- Parenthetical or nonrestrictive elements (interrupters) set off with a pair of commas?
- Long introductory elements and afterthoughts set off with commas?
- All end quotation marks *outside* all periods and commas?
- Semicolons, colons, and dashes used as well as commas and periods?
- Apostrophes in the precise places?

Spelling   Have I eliminated all spelling errors?

- All typographical errors corrected?
- All dubious spellings checked in the dictionary?

TESTING THE ORGANIZATION

Before typing the final copy of your essay, you will want to review the organization of the whole essay and of each paragraph. Use the following checklist to test the organization:

- Thesis sentence well constructed?
- Thesis sentence either directly stated or implied within the first paragraph?
- Thesis summarized or developed at end of paper?
- Topic sentence in every paragraph clearly related to thesis by repetition of a key word or phrase?
- Each paragraph linked to previous paragraph by transition or key word?
- Each paragraph on one subject only?
- Each paragraph well developed with five or six sentences?
- Each sentence logically related to previous one so that the paragraph has momentum and coherence?

- No needlessly repetitive sentences?
- No vague or cloudy sentences?
- Nothing left unsupported by evidence?
- Nothing left unexplained?
- Detail, evidence, examples abundant and apt?

AVERAGE, BELOW-AVERAGE, OR ABOVE-AVERAGE?

Surely, you think, there is nothing more to be done! You have scrupulously checked every mark of punctuation, every possible spelling and grammar problem; you have revised most of the sentences; you have strengthened the organization by adding transitions and repeating key words. But something more can be done—you can don your reader's hat and step into his shoes: you can assume your reader's attitudes and his standards. Certainly, professors in various college subjects will apply different standards for different assignments. However, most professors who teach essay writing do evaluate student papers according to the same general criteria. Although the following standards are not necessarily the only ones (nor are they rigid or dictatorial), they seem to be common enough to warrant attention.

The Average Essay

Thesis: Idea obvious, generalized, ordinary. Probably mentioned in class.

Development: Also obvious; little or no fresh divisions of thought. Related to thesis but only generally. Nothing particularly emphasized. Transitions between paragraphs are present but weak or monotonous.

Details: Some, but not very many, not enough to make development meaningful. Generalizations weakly supported, not well explained. Gaps in thought, lacking adequate connections or transitions between thoughts. Writer expects reader to read his mind to supply all that the writer is thinking about but doesn't take the time or effort to write down.

Mechanics: *Sentences* correct. No comma splices, no fragments. Structure primarily simple or coordinate; few or no subordinating clauses or phrases. *Punctuation* adequate, but usually a few, often repeated, errors. *Diction.* Vocabulary clear, accurate, not slangy, ordinary, general, vague, or abstract. Lacks freshness, vividness. Some misspellings.

Evaluation: An acceptable college paper, but reader is unable to respond to content because of the generally ineffective development and because of the obviousness of the content. Most markings then concern organization and development; hence, markings are likely to be few in number.

The Below-Average Essay

Thesis: Inadequate, too obvious, vague, confused, not sufficiently limited, so generalized as to be lacking in meaning.

Development: No clear divisions of thought; subjects seem to be written

266 Evaluating Your Own Essay

down randomly, lacking progression. Topic sentences unrelated to thesis, or related too vaguely.

Details: Inconsistent, not related to topic sentences, meandering from one instance to another, subjects varied. Details drawn from class lectures or discussions. Usually only one or two supplied per paragraph. Paragraphs nearly always choppy. Incoherent relation between sentences.

Mechanics: Bad. *Sentence structure* awkward, childish, or both. Comma splices and sentence fragments intrude.
Diction, generally vague, dull. Sometimes imprecise, or slangy, or childish. Many misspellings, punctuation neither accurate nor adequate.

Evaluation: This kind of paper a chore to read. Writer obviously unconcerned about communicating anything. Writer does not seem to care about what he wrote or how he wrote it. Or writer has finished paper so quickly he has had no time to rewrite it. Reader so enslaved by writer's many problems that if there is a jewel of a thought somewhere, it is so encrusted with superficial dirt that reader is unable to see it.

The Above-Average Essay

Thesis: Significant, clearly defined, some freshness, some originality, well limited; thesis sentence well constructed. Writer has obviously done some thinking on his own.

Development: Each topic sentence in each paragraph clearly related to thesis and to each other topic sentence. Transitions good. Reader follows writer's logical processes. Each paragraph designed for a purpose, and design is obvious to reader. Each paragraph shows fresh evidence of writer's original thinking, adding his own thought to material covered in class. Emphasis clear, proportion consistent with emphasis, material fresh.

Details: Rich in details. Generalizations *explained and supported.* No gaps in thought; reader does not have to read writer's mind; instead, reader is led to new awareness, or new insights, or stimulated to further thinking. Examples are not solely nor primarily those mentioned in class. Arrangement or design of details is apparent (reader can visualize writer's outline). Transitions clear, logic orderly.

Mechanics: *Sentences* interesting, effective, correct. Generally sentence structure is complex, with effective, interesting, logical use of subordinate clauses and participial phrases. Coordinate sentences are not only strung together with "and's" and "but's"; rather, writer also uses semicolons (correctly, of course) and logical coordinates (such as "nevertheless," "furthermore," "finally," "in addition," and the like).
Diction. Vocabulary is precise, somewhat sophisticated, interesting, vivid, fresh, but unusual words not inserted so obtrusively that they call attention to themselves. No misspellings, no flagrant punctuation errors.

Evaluation: This kind of paper a delight to read. Reader is aware of writer's careful attention to development and organization, as well as writer's care in saying precisely what he means. Reader knows writer was concerned about what he wrote and how well he wrote it. Reader is, as a result, liberated by writer's care so that the content engages reader's attention. Thus, markings concern content primarily.

The superior paper reveals the same characteristics as the above-average paper but with increased articulate cogency and significance.

EVALUATING YOUR RESEARCH PAPER

In evaluating the final draft of your research paper, you need to consider the quality and quantity of your research process. Here are some points to locate possible weaknesses:

- Focus of subject properly limited?
- Parts of paper proportioned according to intent? (Background material too lengthy? Explanatory section too brief? Conclusion too sketchy?)
- Organization of the whole paper logical and orderly?
- Subheadings used? (For longer papers, to communicate organization throughout paper)
- Research project valuable to me or to class? (Or has it been researched many times before in precisely the same manner?)
- Research project original in some way, not merely reportorial?
- Personal response to subject included in some way?
- Sources diversified? (Am I relying on only three or four books and/or magazines?) All possible sources checked?
- Sources authoritative, scholarly, original?
- Authorities introduced? And in a variety of ways?
- Quotations effectively chosen? (Do they illustrate exactly what I want them to illustrate?)
- Paraphrasing accurate but *in my own words*? (Am I sure I am not using author's words and phrases?)
- All quotations and paraphrases fit my intent? (Have I indicated why and how quotations and paraphrases are important to my paper?)
- All footnotes properly written? Quotations and paraphrases properly documented?
- Bibliography properly written?

INDEX OF AUTHORS

INDEX OF SUBJECTS